THE MAN WHO
WAS NEVER
KNOCKED DOWN

THE MAN WHO WAS NEVER KNOCKED DOWN

THE LIFE OF BOXER SEÁN MANNION

Rónán Mac Con Iomaire

ROWMAN & LITTLEFIELD
Lanham • Boulder • New York • London

Published by Rowman & Littlefield
An imprint of The Rowman & Littlefield Publishing Group, Inc.
4501 Forbes Boulevard, Suite 200, Lanham, Maryland 20706
www.rowman.com

Unit A, Whitacre Mews, 26-34 Stannary Street, London SE11 4AB

British Library Cataloguing in Publication Information Available

Library of Congress Cataloging-in-Publication Data

Names: Mac Con Iomaire, Rónán, author.
Title: The man who was never knocked down : the life of boxer Seán Mannion / Rónán Mac Con Iomaire.
Description: Lanham, Maryland : ROWMAN & LITTLEFIELD, [2018] | Includes bibliographical references and index.
Identifiers: LCCN 2017052385 (print) | LCCN 2017053942 (ebook) | ISBN 9781538110614 (electronic) | ISBN 9781538110607 (cloth : alk. paper)
Subjects: LCSH: Mannion, Seán, 1956- | Boxers (Sports)—Ireland—Biography. | Boxing—History.
Classification: LCC GV1132.M24 (ebook) | LCC GV1132.M24 M334 2018 (print) | DDC 796.83092 [B]—dc23
LC record available at https://lccn.loc.gov/2017052385

♾™ The paper used in this publication meets the minimum requirements of American National Standard for Information Sciences—Permanence of Paper for Printed Library Materials, ANSI/NISO Z39.48-1992.

Printed in the United States of America

To Máirín
Grá mo shaol

CONTENTS

CONTENTS

PREFACE

Upstairs in the Twelve Bens bar in Dorchester, Boston, Seán Mannion sits among a tangle of precariously stacked tables and chairs. To the left, an empty bar awaits the next function. To the right, a painted mural of Connemara reminds Seán of home. Downstairs, it's getting busy, the well-worn clothes of honest labor gathering around the bar after another day on the sites. Bottles of Bud, pints of Guinness.

We're interviewing Seán for a movie documentary on his life. He's been brought back here for obvious reasons. Drink. Seán used to be an enthusiastic customer of the Twelve Bens. His picture, in full-on boxing pose, still hangs on the wall downstairs. A brutally handsome creature, the good looks that robbed so many hearts before drink caught up with him and exacted a revenge of sorts.

Today, however, he's dry. He looks back on his drinking past with a melancholy tinged with a denial of sorts. Off the drink and moving back to Ireland within the next few days. Back to his beloved Ireland. Ros Muc. Back for another shot at the good life.

Fast forward nine months later. It's New Year's Eve. The phone rings. I look at the screen—Seán Mannion.

"Hey, Seán, cén chaoi a bhfuil tú [how are you]?"

Seán's back in Boston. He's back drinking. His family haven't been able to get in touch with him for over a week and are worried he's missing. He's not missing. He's drinking.

"I'm going to drink tonight," he says, "but I'm off it from tomorrow."

~

It had only been two years previously when I first visited Seán Mannion in Boston. At that time, he was dry. Proper dry. Working, coaching, focused.

Driving down East Broadway through the center of South Boston, Seán was giving me a guided tour of where his pro boxing career began. The gyms in which he sparred with some of the most dangerous criminals in U.S. history, Whitey Bulger's gang.

Suddenly, the car in front of us comes to a stop. In front of it is a large white SUV, which has come to a halt in the middle of the road for no apparent reason. When the driver in front of us starts sounding the horn, the door of the SUV opens. Out gets a well-built, angry-looking man.

"Shut the fuck up, you asshole."

The SUV driver is standing in the middle of the road, both arms raised, both middle fingers extended toward the driver in front of us.

"Fuck you, asshole."

Sitting beside me, Seán laughs.

"That's Joey DeGrandis. He fought three times for the world title. I used to spar with him years ago. If the guy in front of us knew who he was beeping at, he'd stop pretty quick. I wouldn't go pissing Joey DeGrandis off."

We pull out of the traffic, leaving DeGrandis and the other guy behind us as we drive to the gym in which Seán spent much of the 1980s. Jimmy Connolly's gym, on the fourth floor of 383 Dorchester Avenue, is long closed. Instead, we head into Welch's Gym next door. The place is wedged. In the middle of the room stands a boxing ring full of young kids, sparring with the full-on fury of youth. By the walls, punchbags hang off steel girders, sweat flicking from the brows of those attacking them. Seán would be back later that evening to train a young boxer from Donegal by the name of Michael McLaughlin, another Irishman drawn to America by the dream of pro boxing.

"Hey, are you Seán Mannion?"

A man walks over, accompanied by a young girl.

"This is my daughter, she really wanted to meet you, she sees your photos on the walls around here."

Seán shakes the man's hand, he pats the girl on her head.

There are framed posters hung everywhere, publicizing great bouts of years gone by. Marvin Hagler. Rocky Marciano. Seán Mannion.

"Mannion!"

The roar comes from the back of the room. Sitting down on one of the benches is a giant of a man with a smile on his face and a woolen cap pulled down over his forehead.

"Seán Mannion, how the fuck are you?"

He gets up. They shake hands.

"Hello, Kevin, long time no see."

Kevin McBride, former U.S. and Irish heavyweight champion, infamous for knocking down and beating Mike Tyson in 2005. Tyson quit boxing after that fight.

Seán introduces us and tells him what I'm doing in Boston.

"They should put up a statue of Seán in Galway," said McBride, "and you can put that in your book.

"This man is a fucking legend."

ACKNOWLEDGMENTS

I was nine years old when I first met Seán Mannion, a child in awe at meeting his hero after Seán's return to Ireland following his World Boxing Association (WBA) world title fight against Mike McCallum in 1984. It would be almost 30 years later before I would meet Seán a second time, approaching him with the idea of a biography on a life that had taken many turns in those intervening years.

I'm not sure what I expected when I met him again, but given his chosen career, it wasn't soft-spoken humility. But that was Seán, a contradiction of underplaying his achievements while rueing the lack of recognition for the same achievements. We agreed from the start that any telling of his story would have to be bedded in truth and honesty, however uncomfortable that may be, and it was uncomfortable at times. Seán has always railed against certain stories about him that he insists are untrue, but accepts that a history of drinking and fighting will always leave question marks around his career and personal life.

This project started with Seán's story, published in Irish, in a biography called *Rocky Ros Muc* (Seán was insistent that the first telling of his life would be in his native language) published by Cló Iar-Chonnacht in 2013. An award-winning feature documentary movie, also called *Rocky Ros Muc*, followed. Now, with the publication of *The Man Who Was Never Knocked Down*, I am extremely grateful to Seán for his candor and openness, not to mention his friendship, as we have gotten to know each other over the recent years.

Many people contributed to this book in many ways, providing interviews, scrapbooks, photographs, and contacts. I would particularly like to thank Seán's family in Ireland and in the United States: Paddy and Nellie in Ros Muc for their time, their memories, and their amazingly valuable collection of newspaper clippings; Seán's sisters in Boston, Bab, Nan, and Eileen, who sadly passed away in 2014; and Josie, Nóirín, and Briocán in Connemara. Thanks also to Patrick, Áine, Carina, and Ava in Dorchester for their help.

A special thanks to Mike McCallum in Nevada for the memories of his own amazing career and of his world title fight against Seán; Tony Cardinale, Seán's former lawyer and confidante, in Boston; Rick Mandris in Miami, who worked with Angelo Dundee and coached Seán; Patrick Nee for his unique insight over breakfast into life in South Boston in the late seventies and early eighties; the legendary Micky Ward for his memories and understanding of Seán's training and fighting; John "Red" Shea for an unflinching account of life in the Whitey Bulger mob; Kevin Cullen of the *Boston Globe*, for providing such rich context regarding the Connemara Irish in Boston; and Michael Patrick McDonald, author of the truly incredible *All Souls: A Family Story from Southie*.

Thanks also to Danny Long, Danny Cronin, and all of Seán's former sparring partners who gathered for interview sessions in the Twelve Bens pub in Dorchester and the Goalpost in Quincy. Thanks also to Seán's friends and relatives who gathered in those two pubs to recount their tales and memories: Joe Finnerty, Pádraic Tom Bán Breathnach, Michael Reaney, Joe Mulkerrins, Colm Mhary Mannion, Tommy óg Mellett, Máirtín Khate Conroy, and Paddy Mac Craith.

I'm grateful to Colm Ó Súilleabháin and his wife, Nóirín, who welcomed me into their home and gave me a valuable insight into the founding of the Piarsaigh Boxing Club. Thanks also to Colman Ó Flatharta, Coilmín Ó Mainnín, and Josie Ó Giobúin for their insights into Mike Flaherty and the setting up of the boxing club.

Thanks to James, Erin, Méabh, Aoife, and Éamon for their help and hospitality in Pembroke, Massachusetts, along with Bríd and all of the Maye family in nearby Marshfield.

Thanks to Michael McLaughlin, who let me sit in on his training sessions as he embarked on the same path as the man from Ros Muc, shouting instructions from the corner.

A special thanks to the mayor of Boston, Martin J. Walsh, who made space in a very busy diary to accommodate both the book and movie in an interview recalling his own youth in Ros Muc and his memories of Seán.

Thanks to the archivists in RTÉ Raidió na Gaeltachta, who provided valuable recordings, along with Nuacht TG4, who provided a copy of Róisín Ní Eadhra's 1999 documentary, *Aisling Ghéar*. Thanks also to Seán Bán Breathnach for an interview on his coverage of the two Mannion fights broadcast live on RTÉ Raidió na Gaeltachta.

Thanks to the library staff in An Cheathrú Rua for access to their excellent collection of local magazines and journals, and a thank you to Máire and Breandán Feirtéir for the access to their own personal library that helped so much during research.

I'm very grateful to Lochlainn, Micheál, Deirdre, and all the staff at Cló Iar-Chonnacht, who originally commissioned *Rocky Ros Muc*, for all their help and support. I'm also hugely grateful to Michael, Máire, and all at Below the Radar, who produced the documentary film arising from the book, and for their generous provision of material gathered during that process.

I would like to thank Nick Walters of David Luxton Associates for his valuable direction and input into shaping this book.

Of course, this book would not be possible if it wasn't for Rowman & Littlefield committing to publishing it. Working with my editor, Christen Karniski, has been a pleasure, and her input has always been insightful and informed, easily overcoming the small matter of a 3,000-mile-distant working relationship!

Finally, I would like to thank the four who gave me live feedback on each chapter as I wrote it, who advised me and who let me know (gently!) what worked and what didn't. They are my wife, Máirín, my old friend, Breandán, and my mother and father, Mairéad and Tomás.

I'm particularly grateful to Máirín, who gave me the time, support, and encouragement to write this book, who was always available to dispense her particularly insightful advice, and who managed to distract Marcas, Cóil, and Róisín long enough to a create a mental writing space in our home!

Go raibh maith agaibh uilig.

1

BIRTH, DEATH

Teresa Mannion was not a violent woman. Yet violence stalked her like a shadow from the moment she was born.

Seán Mannion's mother was born in the South Dock area of inner-city Dublin on Holy Thursday, 1916. Four days later, Patrick Pearse stood on the steps of the nearby General Post Office and read out the Proclamation of Independence. His words proclaimed an uprising in the city that ultimately laid the foundation for the creation of the Irish Republic, but it was an uprising uncompromisingly crushed by the British army. Within six days the Easter Rising was over, 450 people killed, 2614 injured, and nine missing.

Meanwhile, in 4 Brady's Court, Mary McGrath lay in bed after an extremely arduous birth, her newborn daughter, Teresa, beside her, the roar of battle all around. At 39 years of age, Mary had found the delivery considerably more difficult than the birth of her previous seven children.

Her husband, John, continued to work loading and unloading cargo ships on the quays despite his wife's poor health, despite the fighting all around him. From the banks of the river Liffey, he could see the gunship *Helga* ploughing her way menacingly up and down through gray-black waters, launching shells into a decaying city. Decay became destruction.

Determined to suppress any future attempts at revolution, troops poured into Dublin from across the Irish Sea. There were random arrests. Random searches. Random shootings. In early May, a squad of soldiers burst into Mary and John McGrath's home. Unable to get up from bed, Mary was dragged to the ground. When John returned home that evening, he found his wife dead on the floor, his newborn daughter, Teresa, crying by her side.

Unable to cope with the weight of raising a daughter on his own, John Mc-Grath sent his infant daughter west to his home village of Ros Dumhach on the Atlantic coast of Mayo, where Teresa was raised by her aunt.

~

Less than 100 miles down the coast from Ros Dumhach, Teresa McGrath's future husband was growing up in another isolated village on the west coast of Ireland. Like most of his peers, Peaitín Tom Mannion left home at a young age, looking for a better life in the United States.

That's where he was when he decided that he was going to the fight. Another low-paid Irish immigrant working on another Boston building site, Peaitín had been so enthralled by the 1926 heavyweight world title fight between Gene Tunney and Jack Dempsey that he decided to travel the 1,600 miles west to Chicago to witness the rematch.

The first fight had been an epic. A crowd of 120,727, the biggest in boxing history, stood in the pouring rain for 10 rounds to watch Gene Tunney give the heavyweight champion of the world a boxing lesson. Jack Dempsey lost his belt, and there was always going to be a rematch.

A year later, the two faced each other again, this time in Soldier's Field in Chicago. With a gate of $2.6 million, Tunney vs. Dempsey II was another record-breaker, but the fight took its place in boxing history for more than just the takings. It became known as the Battle of the Long Count.

For the first six rounds, Gene Tunney, whose parents came from Mayo in Ireland, was comfortably in control of the ring. In the seventh, however, Dempsey caught Tunney on the chin with four consecutive punches, hitting him a further four times before the champion slid off the ropes and onto the canvas. For the first time in his professional boxing career, Tunney had been floored. It's what followed that ensured that the fight is still being discussed to this day.

With the Queensbury Rules still being refined in the 1920s, new regulations had just been put in place before the Dempsey/Tunney fight. Boxers now had to retreat to a neutral corner before the referee could start his KO count. On the night of September 22, 1927, Jack Dempsey either forgot or ignored the new rule and stood above Tunney after knocking him out. The referee couldn't start the count until Dempsey went to the neutral corner and, by the time he did, Gene Tunney had already spent five seconds on the floor. Dave Barry had counted to nine by the time Tunney got up, having spent a total of 14 seconds on the canvas.

He went on to knock down Jack Dempsey in the next round, and although Dempsey didn't stay down, Tunney went on to win the fight by unanimous decision. Jack Dempsey never fought again.

Years later, by an open fire in Cill Bhriocáin, Ros Muc, a young Seán Mannion listened, hypnotized, to his father recount his witnessing of the Battle of the Long Count.

~

A few hundred yards down Snámh Bó road in Ros Muc is a small cottage with red windows and a red door. The thatch roof it once wore has since been replaced by corrugated zinc. Behind a whitewashed stone wall, rhododendron bushes and brambles compete to escape a feral garden.

The house, unoccupied, could easily be mistaken for a small vacation cottage, a refuge in wild isolated Ros Muc for a well-to-do couple from Dublin. But this cottage wasn't built as a vacation home. This was Peaitín Mannion's first home, built after fleeing from London with his new wife, Teresa McGrath, in 1939.

The Great Depression's decimation of the U.S. economy led to Peaitín crossing the Atlantic again in 1930, leaving Boston to settle into a new life in Britain. Another continent, another country, another building site. In London, he met Teresa, a young woman born in Dublin but, like himself, raised on the wild Atlantic coast of Ireland.

If Peaitín, as a construction laborer, held the stereotypical Irishman's job in 1930s London, Teresa fulfilled the employment stereotype on the flip-side of the gender coin. When she met her husband-to-be, she was employed as a cleaner and nanny by an upper-class family in central London.

By 1938, Teresa and Peaitín had married and had named their first child Mary, after Teresa's mother. It wasn't long, however, before the shadow of war cast a pall once more over Teresa's life. On September 1, 1939, Adolf Hitler's invasion of Poland left Britain with little choice but to go to war. Fearful of air attacks on London, authorities put in place Operation Pied Piper, a plan to relocate children from the city to other locations around England. When Teresa and Peaitín found out that their child was to be taken from them and relocated outside London, they took an overnight train across the country to Holyhead in northwest Wales and boarded a ferry to Ireland.

When the young couple arrived in Ros Muc, they moved into Peaitín's parents' home in the townland of Cill Bhriocáin. Peaitín's mother, Eileen, couldn't speak a word of English, and her newly acquainted daughter-in-law, Teresa, couldn't speak Irish. She soon learned the local language, however.

With Teresa expecting a second child, Peaitín realized they couldn't stay in the crowded family home much longer, and so he built the small house with the red windows and the red door on Snámh Bó road. The two-bedroom house soon filled up, Teresa Mannion conceiving 12 children. On October 6, 1956, she gave birth to Seán Mannion. Six pounds, three ounces, a white head of hair, and unusually large hands for a newborn baby.

When Seán was three years old, the family moved from the small house in Snámh Bó to the Mannion family house in Cill Bhriocáin. Seán doesn't recall anything from his time in Snámh Bó except for the day they moved, himself and his sister, Josie, running beside the donkey cart that carried all their belongings for the short half-mile journey up the road.

Seán's childhood in Ros Muc was little different from anyone else's in the village, but it was a childhood barely recognizable today. Among his pastimes, he and his friends would visit Cill Bhriocáin graveyard, examining headstones to see where the dead had originally come from. They would move entire haystacks from one field to another, simply to infuriate the local bachelor farmers. But there was no question about what the main pastime growing up in Ros Muc was.

"We used to box in much the same way that other kids played football," Seán said. "We used to spar in the fields, spar on the street, anywhere we could.

"Myself and the other boys used to spar in the Garraí Gamhna [a high-walled field that held stray livestock]. It was carnage in the Garraí Gamhna, we would spend hours sparring there until a grownup came around to tell us we had enough. That was our round. If no one came, we just kept on going."

Seán's brother, Paddy, worked in the local weaving factory, and he and his workmates chipped in and bought a pair of boxing gloves between them. Every weekend, staff members took turns to bring home the coveted gloves. Paddy's turn was a highlight in the Mannion household. Some years later, the eldest brother in the family, Tommy, sent two pairs of gloves home from Boston to his youngest siblings, Seán and Colm. There was little more than 18 months between the two.

"Colm and I were constantly boxing. In fact, Colm was probably a better boxer than I was but he didn't show the same interest. I remember getting mad one day when my father was commentating on my boxing style while we were sparring outside the house, and in my anger, I punched Colm straight on the nose and made him cry.

"I was about 11 years old and I still remember it to this day. It still hurts when I think about it. I threw away the gloves and started crying myself because

Colm was crying. I was mad at my father. Even so, we had the gloves back on the following night."

It was a busy time in the Mannion household. Even though six siblings had moved out of the house by the early sixties, Teresa was still attending to eight men. She had four sons at home, Seán, Colm, Briocán, and Paddy, along with her husband and two of his brothers, Tomáisín and Cóilín. Peaitín then received word from the United States that another brother of his, Michaelín, had had a stroke and had been checked into a nursing home. No brother of his was going to spend his final days in a nursing home, said Peaitín, and he traveled to the States to bring his ailing brother home to Cill Bhriocáin.

When summer came, there were even more staying in the five-bedroom house. Teenage students, mostly from Dublin, would travel to Ros Muc to learn Irish. Twelve students used to stay with the Mannions, and Seán and his brothers mostly got on well with them. One day, with the students away on a bus trip, Seán borrowed one of their bicycles. When the owner returned and found out that his bike had been touring Ros Muc without him, he tracked down Seán, gave him a few kicks and told him never to touch his bike again. Seán, furious, went to his father to complain.

"Don't come to me telling me that someone hit you," said Peaitín. "Why didn't you hit him back?"

"I can do that?" asked Seán.

"Of course you can. Why couldn't you?"

Seán went outside and found the teenage bike owner. The young Dubliner was taken aback when the smaller boy from Ros Muc started punching him. The student was about three years older than Seán, and even though he was stronger, young Mannion showed a prophetic tenacity.

"It took me a while, but I got the better of him in the end."

The late sixties and early seventies bore witness to one of those golden eras that tend to crop up in boxing every once in a while. In the heavyweight division alone, Muhammad Ali, Sonny Liston, Joe Frazier, and Floyd Patterson were at the peak of their powers. This extraordinary age in boxing was taking place in the United States and, while Irish boxing fans had traditionally gravitated toward the British sporting scene, a combination of emigration and television meant New York was closer to Ros Muc at that time than London.

During a wet January night in 1968, a rerun of a Muhammad Ali fight was being shown on Irish TV. In Ros Muc, Seán and Colm were sparring in the kitchen, imitating their hero on television. They were paying little attention to the actual fight, more interested in their own scrap, and the noise they were making was driving their parents crazy.

"For the love of God, will you two stop, or at least be quiet," shouted Peaitín at them.

But the two tiny boxers paid little attention to the living-room referee. On TV, Ali began to get the upper hand. It was a more evenly contested fight in Ros Muc.

Suddenly, on top of all the commotion, Paddy and Briocán burst into the house, both breathless, both with the same story.

"Michael Choilmín is starting a boxing club in the old school on Tuesday."

"If that's so," said Peaitín, looking over at his two youngest sons, both drenched in sweat, both wearing one oversized boxing glove each, "you two are definitely signing up."

2

ROS MUC

When Seán Mannion walked into the ring in Madison Square Garden on October 19, 1984, he had one word written on his waistband.

Rosmuc.

Around the globe, millions of boxing fans sat in front of televisions, waiting. In Jamaica and Ireland, they waited for Mannion vs. McCallum. In the United States and Syria, they waited for Hagler vs. Hamsho. But it was the same question on everyone's lips, regardless of where they were watching.

"Rosmuc?"

~

Sixty kilometers west of Galway city, on the cliff edge of Europe, is the village of Ros Muc. The first thing that strikes you when you get there is the poverty. Poverty of land, poverty of resources, poverty of jobs. Ireland's economic Celtic Tiger boom never made it to Ros Muc. The subsequent crash was barely noticed.

Driving through the area, you will see more local authority housing than in other rural areas. You will see more men on bicycles, not as a sport but as a necessary mode of rural transport. You will see abandoned factories, boarded-up houses. This was the Ros Muc that spawned Seán Mannion.

Right along the west coast of Ireland, from Cape Clear off the coast of Cork to the Rosguill Peninsula of Donegal, small pockets of Irish-language speaking areas survive among the mostly monolingual English-speaking majority. These Gaeltacht areas, as they are known, have maintained their linguistic heritage mostly through geographical accident. These are areas that have been too remote for industrial development to take hold, economically and culturally isolated from the rest of Ireland. Areas where language and poverty have interdependently coexisted. Areas like Ros Muc.

To say that Ros Muc is economically poorer than any other Gaeltacht area in the country is no exaggeration. It's also no exaggeration, or coincidence, to suggest that Ros Muc is linguistically richer than any other Gaeltacht area. It is a village that has been defined by want and lack over the years. A lack of jobs, clean running water, infrastructure. Ros Muc's deprivation can be more easily seen in the fact that there are only three long-term businesses in a village of 500 people. Two pubs and a shop.

Broadcaster and writer Prionsias Mac Aonghusa wrote that the area had reason to complain about every Irish government since the foundation of the Irish State in 1923. Despite Ros Muc being the strongest and purest Irish-speaking area in the country, he wrote, it was the area to have received least economic support from the state.

The association with poverty is nothing new for Ros Muc. In his 1943 autobiography, *Mise* [Me], the revolutionary Colm Ó Gaora wrote of his home village that it was a place where the impoverished drank their tea black and that many households had never owned a milking cow, a true measure of destitution in early twentieth-century Connemara. According to writer Críostóir Mac Aonghusa, it was one of the poorest places in Europe at the end of the nineteenth century.

Ros Muc has never been able to escape the shadow of poverty. When the *Irish Times* published a study comparing unemployment rates in Gaeltacht villages in 1996, Ros Muc's was 48 percent, over three times that of other neighboring Gaeltacht villages. When populations in Gaeltacht areas increased from 1981 to 1996, the population in Ros Muc actually fell by a staggering 25 percent.

It's little wonder, then, that when the world looks for impoverished Ireland, it settles on the small stony peninsula on its far-western shores. When the *New York Times* sought to analyze in 1991 the impact of the Maastricht Treaty on Ireland, they turned to Ros Muc:

> The people in this wind-whipped village on the bleak western rim of Europe are used to the hard life. They wrestle existence out of a place where big rocks seem to grow overnight in the fields and the soil is thin and poor, the sheep scrawny. A few miles out along an inlet, the Atlantic Ocean yields seaweed and mackerel for the few who have boats . . .

"There's a huge lack of confidence among the young people here," said Thomas O'Malley, who keeps a large shop in Ros Muc. "They feel that if anybody tries to haul himself up, he'll always be beaten back down again."

In the village, unemployment is at about 65 percent and the population is declining each year. Mr. O'Malley said he had to go to the next parish to get enough men for a football team of 20. The team has a 1–7 record.

Christo Walsh, who runs a shop and a pub, knows his market by making informal door-to-door surveys himself every few years. He estimates that 200 people have left in the last 10 years, putting the population at about 575. "When I was a boy," the 38-year-old merchant said, "we would have to line up 90 pints in advance along the bar every Sunday morning to handle the rush after Mass. Now maybe a half-dozen if we're lucky come in after Mass." The school he went to had 180 pupils, he said, but now has only 44.

Things didn't change much with the arrival of the Celtic Tiger. In 2007, with Ireland in the middle of the greatest financial growth in the country's history, Daniel Wood of the Canadian *Globe and Mail* newspaper observed that Ros Muc was "a place little altered by the economic boom that is sweeping the rest of Ireland."

Geographically, it's little wonder that Ros Muc has always been on the periphery. The R340 road that runs along Connemara's isolated coastline, connecting villages in a way that working sailboats once did, ignores Ros Muc, slipping by the peninsula instead of opening it up to the world. Instead, two minor roads serve as the only access to the village. On every side of the peninsula except to the north, there is sea. To the east, Camus Bay. To the west, Cill Chiaráin Bay. Stranded between them, the wet, boggy land of Ros Muc.

It's said that Saint Briocán sailed from the Aran Islands around 500 CE and built a temple in Ros Muc in the townland today known as Cill Bhriocáin [Briocán's Church]. According to folklore, people had settled in Ros Muc about 100 years before the saint's arrival. There are accounts of Ros Muc men standing with the High King of Ireland, Brian Ború, against the Vikings at the Battle of Clontarf on Good Friday, 1014.

The Battle of Clontarf is the first account we have of a fighting Ros Muc. There have been many accounts since. Historically disregarded by the state apparatus, it became apparent to the people of Ros Muc that they had little choice but to stand up for themselves. At the end of the nineteenth century, with English landlords still ruling the fate of Irishmen and women, the landowners of Ros Muc, the Berridges, evicted a number of families who couldn't pay their rent, and then destroyed their cottages. Defying the authorities and the potential consequences, the locals rebuilt homes for the evicted families overnight.

This inclination toward self-empowerment led to nationalism taking root in Ros Muc during the 1919–1921 War of Independence in a more significant way than in other areas of the west of Ireland. The man most responsible for this was Colm Ó Gaora, a Ros Muc–born republican who established a local branch of the Irish language revival movement, the Gaelic League, in 1902. It was this branch that brought one of the most significant revolutionary figures in Irish history, Patrick Pearse, to the area a year later. The 23-year-old Pearse was so taken by Ros Muc and its people that he built a cottage there on the shores of Loch Eiliúrach.

Pearse's influence led to a company of Óglaigh na hÉireann, or the Irish Volunteers, being established in Ros Muc in 1913. The Volunteers were a military organization, established as a response to the formation of the Unionist Ulster Volunteers in northern Ireland, its aim being to gain independence from British rule. Due to Pearse's high ranking and influence, the Ros Muc branch of the Volunteers was under the direct command of the Dublin head office, rather than the local Galway command.

It's understood that most of the planning for the 1916 Easter Rising was carried out secretly in Pearse's cottage in Ros Muc, and that all but one of the seven leaders who signed the 1916 Proclamation of Independence visited the cottage in the months leading up to the Rising.

As it happens, Colm Ó Gaora was the only man from Ros Muc who fought during the Rising. He was sentenced to 15 years for the attempted murder of three policemen in Cong on the Galway/Mayo border, and spent his first spell in prison in Dartmoor in England, along with future Taoiseach and President of Ireland, Éamon De Valera.

The Ros Muc antipathy toward British rule was further exacerbated by the execution of Patrick Pearse and his brother, Liam, immediately after the Easter Rising. Both were well known in the area, two men who visited Ros Muc on a regular basis and who went out of their way to speak Irish and to get to know the locals. If Patrick Pearse had a strong influence on Ros Muc and on its nationalist identity, his execution did nothing to diminish it.

The Volunteers grew stronger in Ros Muc with the coming of the War of Independence against the British. They also grew bolder. In April 1920, the Ros Muc Volunteers, under the command of Colm Ó Gaora, burnt the Royal Irish Constabulary (RIC) barracks in nearby Maam Cross to the ground. Shortly afterward, they struck again, burning the RIC barracks in Ros Muc itself. With no base in the area anymore, the police had to travel into Ros Muc by bicycle over the mountains from Maam, protected by the feared Black and Tans. The Black and Tans were an armed force made up mostly of British World War I veterans, brought to Ireland to assist and defend the RIC during the War of Independence.

Ó Gaora decided to attack the RIC and Black and Tan cycling column coming into Ros Muc and strip them of their arms and ammunition. On April 8, 1921, at Doire Átha Bhanbh just outside Ros Muc, the Volunteers sprang their attack from behind the willow trees. One soldier was shot and injured, and the Volunteers captured a rifle, two handguns, ammunition, and two bottles of poitín, an illegally distilled spirit that had been seized by the police.

That night, five truckloads of British soldiers traveled out to Ros Muc from Galway city for a journey of retribution that led to five houses and a shop being burned to the ground. Among the houses destroyed were Pearse's cottage and the Ó Gaora family home. But Ros Muc had no regrets. They rebuilt the houses. More importantly, the people of the small, isolated village had delivered their message to the might of the British army: we will stand up for ourselves, even if no one else will.

And stand up for themselves they did. Ros Muc has stood up for itself in all areas of life, from literature to language. Some of Ireland's finest writing, be it in English or in Irish, has come from Ros Muc. The likes of Pádraic Ó Conaire, Caitlín Maude, Patrick Pearse.

The area has stood up for itself culturally. When the people of the Gaeltacht felt they were being ignored by the national Irish language festival, Oireachtas na Gaeilge, it was in Ros Muc that the counter-festival, Oireachtas na nGael, was set up in 1987. When a campaign began to establish a Gaeltacht radio station, it was from Ros Muc that the first pirate broadcast of Saor Raidió Chonamara [Connemara Free Radio] took place in 1970. Again, when a campaign for a Gaeltacht television station took place, the first illegal broadcast came from Ros Muc.

Ignored by the state, the people of Ros Muc have had to stand up for themselves time and time again. It's little wonder that they tend to put Ros Muc ahead of everything else. That's why there was no corporate brand on Seán Mannion's waist when he walked into the Madison Square Garden ring. For Mannion, there couldn't have been a stronger brand to wear than Ros Muc itself.

3

PALE BOY

On a cold Tuesday night in January 1968, Peaitín Mannion, along with his two youngest sons, opened the doors of the old school in Ros Muc to a pulsating hall full of enthusiastic young boxers. Almost overwhelmed by the scene, an 11-year-old Seán ran to the back of the hall with his brother, Colm, to change into training clothes. When the other young boxers saw a togged-out Seán return to the fray, they began to laugh.

Standing in front of them was a small boy weighing little more than 70 pounds, wearing thick glasses, skin as white as the paint on the walls around him. Hearing the laughter, the pale face began to redden with embarrassment, tears welling in his eyes when he heard someone shout from the crowd.

"Stop laughing at him, maybe he'll be as good a boxer as you lads someday."

To this day, Seán Mannion remembers, appreciates, that voice.

Mannion would be the first to admit that he wasn't a particularly good boxer when he started out. He wasn't even the best boxer in his own family. Colm was the better fighter but Seán had a significant advantage over Colm, over the other boys in the club, over pretty much every boxer he ever met. He had an obsession, a fascination, with the sport that no one around him could match.

Seán didn't play football when he was young. He had little interest in the sea that surrounded his home. His heart broke every summer when the boxing club closed for the season. School was just something that came between him and the leather gloves. Every opportunity he had, he spent boxing, striving to improve.

"He was tough," said his first coach, Mike Flaherty, in a 1984 television interview for RTÉ. "He was incredibly brave, you couldn't frighten him. This was a great help to him when he was boxing away from home. Some of the other kids, you had to stay with them but Seán didn't want that. He didn't care, nothing worried him."

His dedication to boxing resulted in Seán constantly picking up injuries, even as a young boy. With no doctor to treat him, the remedy for an injured thumb was cold water and self-healing. At school the following day, he was often unable to pick up his pen. Eventually, his teacher lost patience with him.

"Young Mannion," he shouted at Seán, "it looks like you have a choice to make between boxing and school."

Taking him literally, an excited Seán answered "boxing." The punch he received for that answer was harder than any he had received in training the night before.

Within a year of its founding, Cumann Dornálaíochta na bPiarsach [Pearse's Boxing Club] organized its first boxing tournament. The head coach, Mike Flaherty, decided that Seán wasn't good enough for the tournament, and Seán was heartbroken not to be chosen for that first team. But for a small club in a small village, Seán faced stiff competition. Many of the boys that debuted in that tournament went on to greater things in boxing. Máirtín Nee boxed professionally in England, Colman Ó Flatharta established one of the strongest boxing clubs in Ireland, Michael Newell became the first man from Connemara to be shown boxing live on TV as he challenged for the Irish national title, Séamus Macken also fought for the Irish title, and Paddy McGrath fought as an amateur in Ireland, Britain, and the United States.

Watching ringside, Seán longed for an opportunity to get in there himself, so instead of the fighting, he focused on training. The club came together three nights a week, up to three hours each night. In the middle of the hall stood their trainer.

"Stand like this."

"Keep your hands up."

"Bring the left out front."

Mike Flaherty directed. The boys listened. The boys improved.

～

Mike Flaherty was a wanderer, never quite sure of his place. At the age of 14, he ran away from home to work on a farm 50 miles away. Once he was old enough, he joined the army, only to quit two years later. When he immigrated to the United States, he didn't settle in one particular city like most Irishmen, instead drifting across the country from Boston to Chicago and west again until he was stopped in California by the shores of the Pacific. Eventually, he married and settled down in Ros Muc, but even then regretted that he wasn't living on the other side of the bay, back home in Camus. A man who never settled, even in his own parish.

Flaherty's love of boxing came from his two stints in the Irish Army. After joining the Irish-speaking An Chéad Chath [First Battalion] in Galway in 1933, he was chosen for an athletics course at army headquarters on the Curragh in Kildare. With access for the first time to proper training facilities and coaching in disciplines such as boxing, gymnastics, wrestling, and running, Flaherty was in heaven. His natural sporting ability was given an opportunity to flourish, and when he returned to the barracks in Galway, he was assigned to the gym to train other soldiers.

Mike Flaherty loved the army. He loved the discipline. He loved the boxing. But he soon felt the need to roam. In 1935 he left for England, where he failed to settle once again. Two years later, Mike was back in the Galway barracks. Inevitably, after another two years, he began to feel the need to wander, but this time World War II ended his plans.

"When I had the two years in, the war had started," he said in an interview on RTÉ Raidió na Gaeltachta years later. "I could have left but to be honest, I was too embarrassed. They were looking for as many people to enlist as possible."

Flaherty certainly hadn't envisaged another seven years of the army, but the upside of being stuck in the same place was that it gave him the opportunity to build on his boxing. He went on to win the national Army championship and won the provincial Army title five times.

When a boxing club was founded in his native Camus, Mike Flaherty was invited to give an exhibition against Ireland's amateur heavyweight champion, Seán Thornton. Things were going smoothly, both fighters giving an honest display of defending and dancing, until Thornton caught Flaherty with a stinging punch to the ear. Exhibition or no exhibition, the Army champion wasn't going to allow another man to show him up on his home turf. Out of the exhibition suddenly emerged a fight, hundreds of spectators sitting on the green football field in Camus, looking up at two champions going toe to toe in the temporary ring. Strong punches. Powerful punches. Flaherty stuck to his motto. Boxing. Discipline. In the end, he emerged victorious in a fight in which there was supposed to be no victor.

Once the war ended in 1945, Mike Flaherty packed his bags again. After years of traveling across Ireland, Britain, and the United States, he returned to marry and settle down in Ros Muc in 1968. It was time to finally put the suitcase to one side.

But when Colm Sullivan from the newly formed boxing club committee knocked on his door and asked if he would become the club's trainer, Mike didn't realize what lay ahead. County champions, provincial champions, national champions, all from the little village in the west of Ireland. And a ringside seat in Madison Square Garden to watch one of those young boys from Ros Muc fight for the world title.

~

It was pitch black outside the community hall in An Cheathrú Rua, a few cars parked on the street, the flickering light of a candle barely visible in the pub window across the road.

Streetlamps would have shown heavy sheets of sideways rain in the orange gloam, pushed on by a southwesterly gale whipping off the Atlantic. But there were no street lamps in this corner of Connemara in 1969.

From the outside, it looked as if the hall was closed for the night. The front door was shut and no one to be seen from the outside. Only one window faced the road, and that window was black. Then, suddenly, a light appeared. A feeble, blue light. Weak as it was, the light seemed to awaken something within the hall. A noise, suffocated almost, fading in and out as the wind rose and fell.

Inside, there were about 100 people sitting around a boxing ring that had been erected in the center of Halla Éinne. They had been sitting quietly in the darkness until someone lit a paraffin Tilley lamp, then another, and another, until the room lit up and the audience's shadow could be seen dancing on the walls. The lamps rested on the canvas around the edge of the ring, just outside the ropes.

The electricity had cut out unexpectedly a few minutes earlier, just as one of the fights was about to begin. But all was right again. There was light. The boxing could continue. The audience spoke in hushed tones, muted by the dim light. It's not that there was anything particularly unusual about power cuts in Connemara in 1969, but people were accustomed to being at home by the fire when it happened, not waiting for a boxing match in a cold community hall in An Cheathrú Rua.

Standing in the ring was a thin, pale boy, his pale skin whiter still from the glow of paraffin lamps. Seán Mannion was 12 years old, and he was about to get into the ring for his first-ever boxing match when the power went. He was so nervous he hadn't even noticed the lights going out.

Standing across from him was his opponent, Martin Butler from Oughterard, the two of them pretty much the same height, pretty much the same weight. The bell rang. The boys came out. Three rounds and neither spared the other. Sitting ringside were Seán's father and brothers, cheering on the young boy wearing the white vest with the maroon stripe and green shorts. The colors of Ros Muc. The fight lasted six minutes. In Seán's head, it lasted little more than a second, but he would forever remember the referee raising his hand in victory afterwards. One fight, one win. Crowded by celebrating family afterward, his father's cousin slid a ten-shilling coin into his palm. When the boxing finished, they went out into the night for the van journey back to Cill Bhriocáin. Seán sat in the darkness of the van, feeling the coin in his hand, the medal around his neck. The journey had begun.

∼

Gradually, slowly, Seán began to improve. He had quickly realized that if he had any chance of matching passion with ability, he had to put the work into his boxing. That work began to pay dividends when, on his third attempt, he finally won the Galway County championship in 1972. In 1974, again at the third time of asking, he won the provincial championship, earning him a ticket to the national finals.

By this stage, Seán's boxing was beginning to impact the lives of his siblings at home in Cill Bhriocáin. He was away from home regularly, either training or fighting, and the additional workload around the house fell mostly on his brothers, Paddy and Briocán. Having escaped once again from working the fields beside the house, Seán was mockingly asked by Paddy if he actually thought he would one day fight in Madison Square Garden.

"Maybe someday I will," was all Seán answered.

Seán finished school in 1974; while he had enjoyed his first three years of secondary schooling in Ros Muc, he hated the final two years in neighboring Carna. Every morning, he reluctantly left home to take the bus west. As far as he was concerned, he didn't like the teachers and the teachers didn't like him. He took a particular dislike to a nun called Sister Pious. Hitting him was bad enough, insulting him in front of his classmates worse, but taking his boxing gloves from him was unforgivable as far as Seán was concerned. Years later, after returning from the United States after the world title fight, he met her in Carna.

"Who would you rather fight," she asked him, "McCallum or me?"

"Give me McCallum any day," he answered. "At least I could hit him back."

∼

Connemara has always had a rich boxing heritage, particularly at the amateur level. Given its standing historically as one of the poorest areas in Ireland, a reputation for fighting shouldn't come as much of a surprise. With poverty came the escapism of drinking and emigration, usually hand in hand. Young Connemara men, bound abroad by language, came together in pubs all over Britain and the United States, a reputation for hard drinking quickly followed by hard fighting. An 1867 cartoon in New York's *Harper's Weekly*, for example, depicted a St. Patrick's Day scene of scores of Irishmen brawling among themselves and police. Indeed, the number of Irish people being arrested in New York at the time for fighting and for drunkenness led to the police vans that took them away being christened paddy wagons. It was a similar tale in Britain, with journalist Katie Binns writing on bbc.co.uk in 2006 that during "the midyears of the century there were almost weekly references in the the *Bradford Observer* to assaults on the Police, common assault, brawling, drunkenness and disorderly behaviour. The hostile tone of the following extract from Bradford Observer reflects public opinion at the time: 'We understand that the low Irish resident in this town manifests at the present time unusual symptoms of pugnacity. There is a disposition to indulge in faction fights.'"

In his description of the life of an Irish emigrant living among Connemara people in England, Dónall Mac Amhlaigh makes multiple references to physical violence between his compatriots. His autobiography, *An Irish Navvy: The Diary of an Exile*, was written in the fifties and had enough references to fighting in it to suggest that punch-ups were as much a part of the Irish culture in Britain as was singing, with fights as likely to break out between workers on construction sites as they were in pubs.

The fighting wasn't confined to those abroad, of course. It would be neither stereotype nor exaggeration to say that there were few dances or social nights in Connemara that didn't end with a fight of some sort, certainly up until the 1990s.

The lights went out one night at a dance in An Cheathrú Rua during the late seventies, and by the time they came back on, three different fights had broken out around the hall. Around the same time, a publican in Ceantar na nOileán [The Island Region] had to fire a shotgun to stop a huge fight that broke out on his premises.

In many ways, Connemara was a fertile ground for fighting, and boxing cultivated that ground. By the late sixties, the sport had taken root and spread like wild ivy throughout the area. Among the reasons boxing had developed so strongly west of Galway city, according to Father Joseph Cooney of the Galway County Boxing Board, was that there were few proper playing pitches in the area (due to poor land), but there was a disproportionate number of community halls. The perfect space for sparring.

Some of Ireland's finest amateur boxers came from Connemara. Cóilín Ó hIarnáin from Carna, Michael Lally from An Cheathrú Rua, Peadar Breathnach from Camus, Antaine "Toto" Ó Gríofa from An Trá Bháin, and many more, all of whom won All Ireland titles at different weight grades. The likes of Mike Flaherty and Cóilín Breathnach won national Defence Forces titles. Máirtín Nee from Ros Muc won a county title and then moved to England, where he had 26 professional fights. And, of course, Seán Mannion.

But before Mannion ever laced a glove, one man stood above all others when it came to Connemara boxing. A man who developed a reputation both at home and abroad. And it wasn't always a positive reputation.

~

Máirtín Thornton from An Spidéal, not too far from Ros Muc, developed his boxing skills in the traveling carnivals of Britain, having emigrated from Ireland in 1936. Once suspended from elementary school for giving a fellow pupil such a bad beating that he needed medical attention, Thornton had a fearsome punch that compensated for his lack of speed and ring craft. He boasted of knocking out seven men in one day during his carnival days, with deluded carnival-goers taking on Thornton in an effort to win a prize they would never see. With some coaching from future world champion Freddie Mills, Thornton's huge punch went on to earn him the Irish heavyweight title and a world Top 10 ranking by *Ring Magazine*.

But it was Thornton's biggest fight that would see his downfall and infamy when, in 1945, he faced Bruce Woodcock for the Commonwealth and British heavyweight titles. The fight was held in Dublin, a city hungry for entertainment and diversion after the end of World War II. The fight, to be attended by celebrities, politicians, and British royalty, was to be broadcast live on national radio and, with tickets quickly selling out, there was a strong black market for seats. Everything was going well for London-based promoter Jack Solomons until just before the fight, as he recalled in his autobiography, *Jack Solomons Tells All:*

> Three days before the fight, Frank Conroy [Thornton's manager] informed us rather sheepishly that Thornton had some information to impart; something that might have an important bearing on the fight; something that might even prevent the fight happening! I urged that this was no time for quaint old local customs, tore round to the Shelbourne Hotel, and met Thornton outside that edifice.

Once again Martin looked as if butter wouldn't melt in his mouth. Nothing was wrong, nothing at all, at all. Except that if he did not get his dough right there on the spot he was no longer interested in Mr. Woodcock! Maybe I could sing songs or something to keep the crowd amused at the Theatre Royal.

Once again I gave him the horse laugh, the hearty laugh, the hollow laugh, and then the grin of a man who gets what he fancies for a death-cell breakfast. No good. Martin wanted his money, pronto.

"But don't you see," I pleaded, "I cannot pay you till after the fight. Suppose you get disqualified? I shall be responsible to the Irish Board for your purse-money. You'll have to trust me."

"Oi'm thrusting nobody at all. No money, no foight," he said.

"I'll hand the money over to Mr. Conroy. Will that suit you?"

"No, sorr. It's roight here in me hand oi'll be having it."

In desperation I dragged him round to the bank. There, after interminable entreaties, he agreed to wait until after the fight, provided his purse-money was handed over to the bank manager. Then, before I could write the cheque, he changed his mind again.

Thus was Solomons sunk for the first and only time in his career as a promoter. Grinning like a skull, I drew £800 in cash, gave half to Thornton and passed the other half to Conroy. This last arrangement was the only concession the Irish heavy-weight would allow me.

I stumbled out of the bank like I was going to a hanging—my hanging. If the newspaper boys back home got to hear of this, I thought, they would rib me to pieces. And supposing that fool Irishman got himself disqualified! I alone would have the responsibility of handing that £800 over to the Boxing Board.

Thornton wanted the money up-front because he knew something Jack Solomons didn't. He knew that there was a strong chance of him being disqualified after the fight. He said nothing, put the £400 in his pocket, and smiled as he walked out of the bank.

Máirtín Thornton went on to reinvest the money, betting £500 in total on Bruce Woodcock to win their fight, and once the bell went in the Theatre Royal in Dublin for the first round of the contest, it was obvious what he had done. There was no effort whatsoever from the Irish champion. The crowd erupted in fury when they saw Thornton quitting after only three rounds. Someone threw a bottle at him, missing the boxer and smashing inside the ring.

"THORNTON THREW IN THE THIRD ROUND," reported the *Irish Independent*. "Martin Thornton left the ring at the Theatre Royal last night to the accompaniment of loud jeers and cat-calls from the crowd which fifteen minutes earlier had afforded him a tremendous reception. . . . The sad feature of the fight—if one could call it a fight—was that Thornton never really seemed to make an effort to win."

"Mr. T'ornton seemed to show no desire whatsoever to hit Mr. Woodcock," wrote Jack Solomons. "The lethal punches Martin had thrown in earlier fights were evidently back home in the bank."

The boxing commission suspended Máirtín Thornton without disqualifying him entirely, but he would only fight once more. Years later, Thornton admitted that he had put money on Bruce Woodcock to win the fight.

Despite, or perhaps because of, his infamy, Máirtín Thornton remained a hero in Connemara. Thornton had put Connemara on the boxing map in a way that no other person had ever done before. There, he even had the Máirtín Thornton Award for best tournament boxer named after him. The prize, won by a young Seán Mannion, was a fortnight's training in London with Jack Solomons. Mannion turned down the prize.

Seán Mannion was about to become Connemara's new boxing hero, and he was going to do it on his own terms. He certainly wasn't about to travel to England for boxing lessons.

If Seán Mannion was going to leave Ireland, he was only heading for one place.

∼

In 1974, there was nothing unusual about a 17-year-old boy from Ros Muc leaving home and moving to Boston. In fact, it would be more unusual not to. The next logical step after finishing school was always emigration.

Seán's sister Josie had come home from the States for that summer and, come the end of July, Seán traveled back across the Atlantic with her. It wasn't a particularly tough decision to make. Seán already had seven siblings living in Boston, along with most of his friends from school and from the boxing club.

He moved in with his brother, Paddy, and after overcoming the initial shock of the big city, began to settle down. Boston and Cill Bhriocáin were two very different worlds, but he soon fell into the Irish American way of life, working as a construction laborer during the week, heading to Irish dances on the weekend where he would meet his former neighbors from home.

His remaining time was soon consumed by boxing. Paddy brought Seán to Connolly's Gym on the third floor of the Ellis Building in South Boston. The first thing you noticed when you walked into Connolly's Gym was that, unlike most gyms of the time, it was clean. Inside the door was a lounge with a few chairs, where old guys from the neighborhood hung out, reading newspapers, discussing fights and fighters.

The boxing ring was to the left as you walked into the gym. Heavy bags hung from the ceiling, the rat-tat-tat of the skipping rope forming a noisy symphony with the snap of the speed ball. Looking down over it all was a photo of the onetime middleweight world champion, Paul Pender, a cousin of the owner, Jimmy Connolly.

Through the gym, Seán began to pick up fights. At an amateur tournament in the Boston city center, Seán and Paddy McGrath, also from Ros Muc, signed up on that night and both ended up fighting boxing royalty. Seán knocked out Rocky Marciano's nephew in the first round. Paddy stopped Jack Dempsey's grandson in the third.

That December, Seán's uncle died back home and Seán returned to Ireland, planning to stay no more than a few weeks. But when he arrived home, Peaitín asked him to stay and fight for the national title, given that he had earned his place earlier in the year with his provincial win.

Seán stayed and, in January 1975, traveled to Dublin for the All-Ireland title fight. The National Stadium was, and still is, the epicenter of amateur boxing in Ireland, but with the stadium closed for renovations, the tournament was held in Dalkey in south county Dublin. Things started well—he beat Tom Ward from Roscommon in the quarterfinals—but was beaten by Brian Byrne in the semifinals. Byrne was a classy boxer who went on to win the All-Ireland title that year, and represented Ireland at the Montréal Olympics the following year.

Defeated, Seán returned west to Connemara. By the time he had reached Ros Muc, he was sure of two things. He preferred living at home than in the United States, and he had no intention of crossing the Atlantic again without a national title to his name. Fortunately for him, a job arose in an area not renowned for job opportunities. A generous grant from the Gaeltacht development agency, Gaeltarra Éireann, led to the opening of the ABM factory in Ros Muc. ABM was a steelworks company, welding truck frames and scaffolding. It was the only industrial employment in the area, and inevitably, the company moved on five years later, leaving a devastated Ros Muc behind.

But in 1975, ABM needed skilled employees, and six workers were sent from Ros Muc to Ráth Chairn in county Meath for a training course in a sister factory. Despite being on the other side of the country and a world away from Ros Muc in terms of good land and agriculture, Ráth Chairn had close links to the Connemara Gaeltacht. The area was settled by Connemara people in 1935 as part of a government scheme to transplant Irish speakers around the country, creating new Irish-speaking communities. Seán and his colleagues weren't long settling in.

After a long day learning the finer points of steel welding, the six Ros Muc men trained with the local Girley Boxing Club. Gradually, Mannion's friends headed back west, but Seán and another trainee, Tommy Conroy, stayed on. The amount of time they spent training led the boxing club to provide them with a caravan hooked up with electricity from the gym. Sleep. Work. Boxing. That was the sum total of life for the "odd couple," as they had been christened in Meath.

That November, Mannion opened another shot at the All-Ireland championship by winning the Golden Shamrock, as the Leinster provincial title was known. In May 1976, he traveled to the National Stadium in the best shape of his life, weighing in at 140 pounds. His first opponent, Ferris from Dublin, was easily dispatched in the quarterfinals. The semifinal wasn't as straightforward. Kenny Beattie was from White City Boxing Club in Belfast, a four-time All-Ireland winner who would represent Northern Ireland at the Montréal Commonwealth Games in 1978. Beattie fought well in Canada and reached the finals, only to be defeated by a young Jamaican named Mike McCallum.

The fight between Mannion and Beattie was a bruiser, both boxers punching accurately, both defending well. When the third round was over, neither knew who had won. But it was Seán's arm that the referee eventually lifted in the air.

The National Stadium was full for the All-Ireland final. Pretty much all of Ráth Chairn had traveled to Dublin, along with a big crowd from Ros Muc. Mannion's opponent was Johnny Thornton from Drogheda, but Seán didn't seem too concerned beforehand. He had an inkling that the real final had been his fight with Kenny Beattie. He was right.

When the bell rang, Johnny Thornton, wearing red shorts and a black vest, was first out of his corner. Seán wore a yellow vest with black shorts, his tousled hair tumbling below his ears. There was little science in Mannion's boxing for that fight. He had watched Thornton's semifinal win, and figured that the route to victory was unremitting attack. Again, he was right.

Thornton advanced, but soon began to retreat. The man from Ros Muc came at him furiously, throwing wild hooks with both left and right. By the second round, Seán had his opponent on the ropes, Thornton with his head down and hands up in an attempt to ward off the blows coming his way. By the time the referee stopped Mannion's attack to give the Drogheda man a standing count, Thornton's face was smeared in the blood pouring from his nose. The referee restarted the fight, but stopped it again within 10 seconds. This time, for good. Seán Mannion was the new junior champion of Ireland.

Back in Ros Muc, watching his son win the All-Ireland title live on TV, a tear rolled down the rivulets of Peaitín Mannion's face. Peaitín, dying of cancer, never thought he would see the day when his son would become champion of Ireland. When Seán arrived back home the following day, his father greeted him as Connemara fathers do.

"You did alright," Peaitín said. "You should have beaten him more easily."

He looked at his son and at the medal around his neck. The two of them began to cry. Peaitín died a year later, and before the coffin was closed, Seán slipped his All-Ireland medal in beside his father's resting body.

By the time Seán fought his last fight in Ireland, he had won the Galway and Meath county championships, as well as the Connacht and Leinster titles and the All-Ireland. He had represented three of the country's four provinces internationally, Connacht, Leinster, and Ulster. He won the Galway County Sports Award in 1976, the first man from the Gaeltacht heartland to do so. Apart from representing Ireland in the Olympic Games, which were three years away, Seán had little else to achieve in amateur boxing. It was time for the next step.

He had long known what that next step would be. Years earlier, while training in the old school, he would often hear of amateur boxing and professional boxing and had no idea what the two terms meant.

"I'll tell you," said Peter Conroy, one of boys from the boxing club, as they sat on the walls of Cill Bhriocáin graveyard. "Amateur is what you're doing now, but they'll give you money when you're fighting professional."

"By dad," said a 12-year-old Seán, "I'm going to turn professional someday."

And so, on June 28, 1977, Seán Mannion boarded a plane at Shannon Airport to start a new life as a professional boxer in Boston, Massachusetts.

4

BOSTON, IRELAND

Pat Hegarty was the first man to sell draft Guinness in Boston. After emi-grating from the west of Ireland, Hegarty bought the Red Fox tavern on Dorchester Avenue on July 21, 1965, and changed the name to the Blarney Stone. Pulling that first pint was a proud moment.

The Blarney Stone was where Seán Mannion used to hang out when he first moved to Boston. It was where his Irish friends and family gathered to drink, sing, fight. In the early eighties, you had a greater chance of bumping into an Irish speaker from Connemara in the Blarney Stone than you had walking down Shop Street in Galway.

But nothing stays the same. You won't hear any Irish in the Blarney Stone today. By the early nineties, Pat Hegarty was selling 50 percent less beer than he had been a decade earlier. The demand for live Irish music had evaporated. No more Patsy and the Shamrocks, no more John Connors and the Irish Express. In the end, Hegarty had little choice but to sell up.

Today, the Blarney Stone is a café bar, selling Argentinian Malbec and spinach-and-kale salad. The Blarney Stone has changed. Boston has changed.

~

Looking around Boston today, you could easily be under the impression that it was always an Irish city. The small island on the other side of the Atlantic has left its mark everywhere. On the Boston Celtics, on the flags hung from houses in South Boston and Dorchester, on the surnames in the Senate, on the Catholic churches, on the pubs. Even the mayor's parents are from Connemara. But things weren't always so.

Boston was a strong Protestant city up until the end of the nineteenth century, a city run by the Brahmins, the elite descendants of the Puritans who had arrived from England in 1630. The Brahmins had little time for the impoverished Irish immigrants arriving in their city by boat. Even as early as the 1830s, long before the vicious gale of the Great Famine filled the sails of coffin ships bound for Boston, there was a tension between the Irish and the Americans.

"This was an overwhelmingly Protestant city where the vast majority of people traced their origins to England," according to Kevin Cullen of the *Boston Globe*, "and then in two generations, the majority of citizens in Boston were not just Irish, but Catholic. To the Brahmins who ran the city, it was that latter thing that was more disturbing to them.

"It wasn't that they were Irish, because there had always been a sort of tradition of Irish Presbyterianism in Boston. They were the merchant class here in Boston. But it was the idea of all these unwashed Catholics. Because you know, at the end of the day you could wash them, you could send them to school, but you couldn't change their faith. And that was very disturbing to them."

Riots between the Protestant ascendancy and the Catholic blow-ins became increasingly regular. In August 1834, rumor spread that the nuns of the Ursuline Convent in the center of Boston were involved in bloody rituals and were even sacrificing babies. When a hostile crowd gathered outside the convent, the Mother Superior had to open her doors to the Protestant politicians and assure them that there was no basis to the rumors. It did little to quell the tension, however.

"If the Catholics get the upper hand of us, they will crush us to the earth," someone shouted outside, according to the *Jesuit or Catholic Sentinel* newspaper report of the incident in 1834.

Later that night, the crowd returned with torches and with intent. Pushing nuns to one side, they ransacked their way through the convent. Tombs were broken into, coffins split open and, finally, the convent torched. When the Brahmin firemen arrived, they stood by and watched the flames devour the convent instead of making any efforts to extinguish them.

As the Irish population in Boston increased, so did tensions. Three years after the burning of the Ursuline convent, trouble flared again when firemen returning to their station came across an Irish funeral in the city center. It was reported that one of the firemen said something derogatory to the funeral crowd, and that a fight broke out. With the Brahmins considerably outnumbered, two of the firemen were badly beaten. When they finally managed to make it back to the station, their fire chief was outraged. He ordered all brigades to head to Sea Street for revenge.

"The Irish have risen upon us and are going to kill us."

When the firemen caught up again with the funeral, a full-blown riot broke out. The Yankees were in the majority and chased the Irish down as far as Broad Street, where most of the new arrivals had settled. Broad Street was destroyed, as historian Edward Harrington recounts in Peter F. Stevens's *Hidden History of the Boston Irish* (2008):

> Wherever the marauders broke in, they smashed windows and doors, stole whatever they coveted, and then proceeded with savage thoroughness to destroy everything else. Clothing was torn to shreds, shoes were cut to pieces; furniture and household goods of all kinds were thrown into the streets. Featherbeds were ripped up and their contents scattered to the winds in such quantities that for awhile, Broad Street seemed to be having a snowstorm . . . the pavement in spots . . . buried ankle-deep in feathers.

In the end, it took 10 infantry companies to stop the riots. Houses had been destroyed, hundreds injured but, astonishingly, given the severity of some of the injuries, no one killed. Fourteen Irishmen and four Yankees were brought to court on charges relating to the riots. Three immigrants were sentenced to jail. All four Protestants were found to be not guilty. No more than in every other area of Boston city administration, the Yankees had control of the courts system in the 1830s. But things were about to change.

At the time, Boston was different from most U.S. cities when it came to immigration. In other places, new arrivals came slowly, steadily, and from a broad range of countries. In Boston, however, the Irish flooded into the city in the 1840s and continued to arrive at this pace for the next 40 years. By the time the Italians, the Russian Jews. and the Lithuanians began arriving in the 1880s, the Irish had control of the city apparatus.

In 1820, there were only 2,000 Irish-born residents in Boston. Ten years later, that figure had increased to 7,000. By 1855, there were 44,000 Irish men and women in Boston, and 70,000 by 1880. For the first time in the history of the city there were more Irish than Brahmin in Boston, and the first Irish mayor was elected in 1855.

Hugh O'Brien was from Cork, and had made his money as publisher of the *Shipping and Commercial List*. Despite an understandable resistance among the Yankee elite, O'Brien's tenure as mayor surprised many. He widened streets, developed new parks and built libraries, all the while reducing taxes. It helped that O'Brien was a conciliatory figure, courting neither side of the political divide openly. His election as mayor, however, marked the beginning of an era of Irish domination of the Boston political scene.

In 1906, John F. Fitzgerald was elected mayor, father of Rose who would later marry Joseph Kennedy and give birth to the Kennedy political dynasty. If Hugh O'Brien was reluctant to side with his own people, Fitzgerald, or Honey Fitz as he was known, showed no such reticence. Fitzgerald was a master of cronyism, to the extent that when there were no jobs to be given out to Irish constituents, he made them up. Tea warmers. Tree climbers. Rubber boot repairers.

Honey Fitz left his mark on Boston in a big way. As congressman, he drove the legislation that delivered America's first underground train system to the city. As mayor, he was responsible for the development of the zoo, the aquarium, and the Red Sox stadium, Fenway Park.

But when he stood for office for a third term, it was a fellow Irish candidate who ensured he didn't get re-elected. James Michael Curley threatened to go public with a story that Mayor Fitzgerald had been having an affair with a 23-year-old woman named Elizabeth "Toodles" Ryan. Fitzgerald withdrew from the race, leaving Curley to put a political legacy in place that would see him elected mayor of Boston four times between 1914 and 1950.

James Curley's father, Michael, was from Oughterard in Connemara, county Galway. He immigrated to Boston at the age of 14, where he married another Galwegian, Sarah Clancy. They had two sons, James and John, but Michael Curley died when James was only 10 years old, suffering a heart attack while attempting to lift a 400-pound rock as a bet. Suddenly shorn of their father's income, the boys and their mother were dropped into a world of poverty and were brought up in the Boston slums. Sarah took a job as a cleaner, and it wasn't long before James himself started working, initially in a drugstore, in a piano shop, and then for a blacksmith.

But as he grew older, James Michael Curley became drawn to politics. Tall, well-built, and with a strong voice, he had the attributes needed. He also had little reluctance in using his fists, an important attribute in Boston politics at the time.

At the age of 24, Curley was elected to the city's Common Council and spent much of his time assisting new immigrants to the city. He went a step too far in his assistance, however, when he sat for a civil service exam for a post office job on behalf of one of his constituents. Curley had checked beforehand on what the maximum penalty would be if caught, and after determining that all he had to lose was being banned from sitting future exams, went ahead with the deception.

Not only was he was caught, he soon found out that he had missed a particular statute that led him to spending 60 days in prison. Boston's conservative elite let it be known that they were embarrassed and outraged by the James

Michael Curley scandal. Curley didn't seem particularly embarrassed himself, however. He wrote in his 1957 autobiography, *I'd Do It Again: A Record of All My Uproarious Years*,

> Although my sentence was not scheduled to expire until noon, I was released fifteen minutes before that hour on the first Wednesday in January . . . I stepped into a waiting carriage and proceeded to City Hall where a friend warned me that Daniel J. Whelton, President of the Board of Aldermen, planned to declare my seat vacant [due to his penal conviction].
>
> It was relatively warm for a January day, and the large window directly behind the presiding officer's chair was open. I took the first seat nearest Whelton in the council chambers, and just before the meeting opened, stepped up to him and said: "I understand that you propose to move that my seat be declared vacant."
>
> "Yes," he said, "I do."
>
> "Well," I answered, "I just want to inform you that if you present such a motion, you will go through that window." The window was on the second floor, and he apparently realized it would be a rather uncomfortable landing on the hard surface below. He glared at me, rapped for order and proceeded with the business of the day without making any reference to me.

Curley's supporters had a standard answer whenever the exam fraud was raised at a political rally: "He did it for a friend!"

James Curley was elected to the U.S. Congress in 1910, but the real prize, as far as he was concerned, was mayor of Boston, which he achieved four years later. By this time, Curley had developed a political character imitated in Boston political circles for generations after. He wore a long black Chesterfield coat and a grey hat. His accent evolved to become a strange mixture of Irish and Harvard, with a broad "a" and an almost silent "r," exemplified in caricature by Mayor Quimby of *The Simpsons* and in real life by the Kennedy family.

He soon put a new political structure in place that undermined the ward system that had existed in the city up until then. With the new system, Curley was in charge of everything. When he got up in the morning, there was a queue outside his house looking for indulgences. There was another queue waiting for him when he arrived at City Hall. And that's exactly what he wanted. Thousands of Bostonians personally indebted to James Michael Curley. All the more reason for them to vote for him.

At the time, Boston's mayor wasn't allowed to stand for two consecutive terms, but Curley's lobbying and patronage ensured his replacements were underwhelming incumbents that were easily displaced when he could stand again in the next election. Once back in office, he raised taxes from the upper classes to pay for huge public works, employing many of the city's poorest people. Tunnels were bored, hospitals built, beaches developed, along with libraries, playgrounds, subway stations, parks, and new roads.

No more than Honey Fitz, Curley had no reluctance in using the system to consolidate his own political ambition. Irish people were given high-ranking jobs, there were persistent suspicions about his election results, and he was repeatedly brought before court on charges related to dubious political practice.

Curley was convicted of fraud in 1937, and would have spent time in prison if it wasn't for the thousands of ordinary Bostonians that donated to pay his fine of $42,629. He was convicted again in 1946 on a charge related to mail fraud, and served five months in prison before being pardoned by President Harry Truman.

When James Michael Curley died in 1958, it was the biggest funeral Boston had seen up until then. Over a million people stood on the side of the road as his cortège made its way to the graveyard. Among the many stories told at the funeral was one Curley often told himself. After his father had died, James's mother got a job as a scrubwoman, so called because she spent the day on her knees scrubbing floors. Curley walked into City Hall on his first day as mayor to see a woman on the floor, scrubbing.

"Curley remembered his own mother scrubbing floors on Beacon Hill and in the Back Bay, and told the cleaning women that they should be on their knees only to pray to God," according to William Bulger's 2009 biography, *James Michael Curley*. "He ordered long-handled mops for all the city's cleaning women, and issued an order that no scrubwoman was to get on her knees in City Hall."

James Michael Curley's political legacy was to consolidate the Irish grip on Boston politics, developing a system of patronage in which jobs were given to friends, to relatives, to Irish people. A legacy that ensured that it was a person of Irish heritage in almost every high office in the city.

While Boston politics has changed considerably, now reflecting the more diverse makeup of the city, as well as becoming less violent, the Irish connection remains strong. In January 2014, Martin J. Walsh was inaugurated as Boston's 54th mayor. Connemara was well-represented at that inauguration: Walsh's mother is from Ros Muc, his father from Carna. Seán Mannion's brother happens to be married to the mayor's aunt. Walsh, who spent his childhood summers exploring the fields and byroads of Ros Muc, has an incredible backstory. Diagnosed with cancer at the age of seven, doctors gave him six months to live. Later, he overcame the very Connemara disease of alcoholism, and hasn't had a drink since 1995.

Today, a Bostonian of immediate Connemara extraction holds the highest office in his city. "My home is Dorchester, Massachusetts," said Mayor Marty Walsh, "but I am also from Ros Muc and Carna."

~

Around the time of the Broad Street riots, most Irish immigrants to Boston lived in crumbling tenement buildings by the city-center wharfs. Across from these buildings, on the other side of the Fort Point Channel, was South Boston. At the time, South Boston was pretty much cut off from the city itself, a place where cattle grazed and few people lived. But in the early nineteenth century, South Boston was annexed by the city of Boston, and work began on building roads and houses. The peninsula was mapped out in grid format, streets running parallel and perpendicular to each other, named after numbers and letters.

"If you look at South Boston geographically," wrote Kevin Cullen, "it was an island before bridges were built to it from the mainland in the 1840s, just when the famine was sending so many Irish over. So it was always geographically insular, and it was always culturally insular too."

The Irish didn't move into South Boston straightaway. Instead, they would row across from Boston in small boats in order to work in the new factories opening there, escaping the South Bridge toll. Businesses included razor blade manufacturer, Gillette, along with steel and glass works, printing companies, and boat builders. But when the North Free Bridge was built in the 1830s, the Irish began to flood into South Boston.

From the middle of that century until the start of the 1900s, South Boston's population grew from 23,000 to 67,000, and most of them were Irish. On the east side of the peninsula, looking out on the sea were the houses of the upper class, large buildings with generous gardens. On the west side, closer to the city center and beside the factories, were the Irish.

In 1847 alone, over 37,000 Irish immigrants came to Boston as a result of the Great Famine, and South Boston's population almost doubled in two years. Narrow, densely populated streets popped up all over Southie, as it became known. Catholic churches were built. There were so many Irish people in the area that the place was divided by counties. Galway people settled on A and B streets, Cork people on D, and so on. A strong community developed. A religious community, a working community, a criminal community. Every facet of life. An Irish community.

When the following generations of Irish immigrants arrived, settling down in South Boston wasn't a straightforward option anymore. There was little space left in the area, as few people tended to move out. First-generation Irish immigrants raised their families there, and their children in turn raised their families there.

The Irish community in Southie kept growing, and when emigration from Connemara to Boston flourished again during the 1960s and 1970s, there was no space for them among their antecedents. These new Irish immigrants settled in Dorchester, south of South Boston, and south of the Boston city center.

No more than South Boston, Dorchester was originally an agricultural area with a few large houses built by the upper classes, until the development of Dorchester Avenue in 1805, connecting the Boston city center with then-rural Milton. Only the wealthy had the resources to live that far out from the city, but with the arrival of the streetcar—a train carriage pulled by horses—the population skyrocketed.

Most of the new arrivals were Irish immigrants. At the start of the twentieth century, 70 percent of those living in Dorchester were born overseas, the number of residents increasing from 7,000 to 200,000 in 30 years. So many people were moving into the area that a new style of housing called the triple decker was built. The triple decker was a large house divided into three or six parts, over three floors, with at least one family living on each floor.

When the next tsunami of immigration came across the Atlantic during the 1970s and 1980s, most of them, especially those from Connemara, moved to Dorchester. By the middle of the 1970s, there was no question about it: Dorchester was the most Gaelic and Irish part of Boston. Walking down Dorchester Avenue, past Fields Corner, you would bump into Irish people everywhere you went.

"South Boston is always thought of as the most Irish section of Boston, but there would have been more Irish-born people living in Dorchester," according to Kevin Cullen. "When you said you were from Dorchester, you had to specify more and if you were Irish working class, you would identify yourself from a parish. So you say you were from Saint Brendan's, or Saint Ann's, or in Sean's case he moved to Saint Mark's originally, which would have almost always had Irish-born priests.

"It would have had a very vibrant Irish community there, a lot of guys in the construction industry, a lot of guys in roofing, a lot of guys in painting. And so what was typical of that era is Irish kids would come in, they used to call them Aer Lingus carpenters because they decided to be carpenters on the Aer Lingus flight over. And there were generally two routes to getting a job; you either went to the pub, the Eire Pub in Adams Village, the Centre Bar closer to Saint Mark's, or you would go and hit up the priest and say, you know, where can I get some work?

"And generally, when Irish kids came here, particularly in the 70s and 80s, they had work just like that. There was always work. And they generally didn't have trouble finding it."

Many, if not most, of the Connemara population in Dorchester were living and working illegally in the United States, but it was rarely an issue. They would get up in the morning and work among their own people. They would go home in the evening among their own people. They would socialize at the weekend among their own people. Dorchester was a home away from home for them. Irish shops, Irish restaurants and, most of all, Irish pubs. The Blarney Stone. The Emerald Isle. Nash's. Ned Kelly's. The Tara. Mickey's Place. Scruffy Murphy's.

But that Dorchester is no more. If you walk down Dot Avenue today, there's little chance of bumping into an Irish person. Even less of a chance that you'll hear Irish. Around Fields Corner these days, you're more likely to hear Vietnamese.

The Irish started leaving Dorchester in the early nineties. Some of them headed home, many moved farther south to Quincy, as far south as Marshfield even. Retiring from work and looking for a quieter life. Or raising families and looking for better schools in the suburbs. Even if the schools weren't better, they were most likely safer at that time. In 1990, 152 people were murdered in Dorchester alone.

Today, the Emerald Isle is closed, its name in faded green paint lingering for years on Dot Avenue until the building was finally gutted and divided into retail units. The bar that was once the Tara is now a beauty parlor. Mickey's Place is a Vietnamese electronics store, and Ned Kelly's is a gay club and restaurant called dbar.

Today's Dorchester Avenue is a long way from the Dorchester Avenue Seán Mannion so proudly walked down in 1977, his bag on his shoulder and his dreams in his fists. Miles from home, but yet still home, with a new chapter in his life about to start.

5

THE SOUTHPAW

Brockton was a tough town back in 1978. It still is today. A 30-minute drive south of Boston, the statistics back up its reputation for crime and violence. In a place where you have a 1-in-24 chance of becoming a crime victim, Brockton is ranked among the top 100 most dangerous cities in the United States. Unsurprisingly, it's the kind of place that inspires fighters. They call Brockton, among other things, the City of Champions. It's no exaggeration.

Rocky Marciano, born and raised in Brockton, was the only world heavyweight champion to go undefeated throughout his entire career—49 victories in 49 fights. Marciano retired in 1955, having successfully defended his title six times.

Brockton was also home to Marvelous Marvin Hagler. A 13-year-old Hagler moved to Massachusetts with his mother after their family home was destroyed in the 1967 Newark, New Jersey, riots. Hagler would go on to become one of the greatest middleweight boxers of all time, inaugurated into both the International and World Boxing Halls of Fame in 1993 and ranked the Fighter of the Decade for the 1980s by *Boxing Illustrated*.

Marvin Hagler was 15 when he first walked into Goody and Pat Petronelli's new gym on Ward Street in 1969. Rocky Marciano, who died in a plane crash that same year, was a friend of the Petronellis and a hero of Hagler's, and it wasn't long before Brockton had a new champion under the direction of Goody and Pat. The gym soon gained a reputation as a conveyer belt of classy American boxers, producing the likes of Hagler's half-brother, Robbie Sims, who would go on to become the U.S. middleweight champion, and Pat Petronelli's son, Tony, another future U.S. champion.

Seán Mannion knew all about Brockton from his old copies of *Ring Magazine*, and one of the first things he did when he arrived from Ireland in 1977 was to head on a pilgrimage to the City of Champions. He and a friend drove south from Dorchester after work one evening, found the crumbling building that housed the Petronelli gym, and walked up three flights of creaking wooden stairs before opening a door into boxing heaven.

The first thing that hit them was the sound. A snapping drumbeat of punch bags and speed balls. Immediately in front of them stood a tired-looking boxing ring, the worn blue floor fenced in by red, white, and blue ropes. To the left, four windows looked out over Brockton. On the other side of the ring stood a line of wooden chairs, and a table struggling under a mountain of boxing gloves. Behind the chairs, heavy bags hung from the ceiling. The paint on the walls, once white, now almost entirely obscured by posters of history's greatest fights and fighters.

With a deep breath, Seán inhaled all that was around him. Hagler, Petronelli, Sims. Goody and Pat's sharp voices cutting through the heavy, sweat-drenched air. This was it. This was pro boxing. This was what he had wanted since he was 12 years old, since he lay in his bed in Cill Bhriocáin, eyes closed, beating Muhammad Ali in his dreams. From the days when his mother would travel to the train station in Galway once every three months to buy a copy of *Ring Magazine* for her son.

"Hey, any of you guys a southpaw?"

Seán looked up. Tony Petronelli was looking down at him and his friend. Petronelli was preparing for a fight against Jim Montague, a dangerous left-hander from Northern Ireland.

"I am," answered Seán.

"Cool, will you gimme a round?"

Seán didn't hesitate, climbing into the ring in his work clothes and boots against one of the finest boxers in the United States. Petronelli had won five U.S. national titles by that stage of his career, and had fought for the world super lightweight title, losing to the legendary Wilfred Benitez.

"Okay, Irish, let's go, one round."

The one round came and went. They looked at each other. Another round. The sparring session lasted four rounds in total, and neither held back. Petronelli looked at Mannion when they were finished.

"Who the fuck are you?"

Seán told him.

"Well, come back tomorrow and bring a pair of shorts next time."

Seán was back at 7:00 p.m. the following evening, this time with his boxing gear. The two went eight rounds together. Eight hard rounds.

"You're wasting your fuckin' time fighting amateur," Tony Petronelli told the young Irishman once they had finished. "Turn pro, man."

He didn't have to say it a second time.

~

If you close your eyes and try picturing a postcard-perfect New England autumn scene, you'll probably see North Easton. Tree-lined streets with golden leaves falling gently. Traditionally painted shopfronts. A white wooden church in the center of the town. Only 15 minutes' drive west of Brockton, North Easton feels like a million miles away from the rough, tough City of Champions.

Paul Mitrano lived in North Easton. Mitrano was the rich guy in town, owning two Chevrolet dealerships, a greyhound track, half of the local bank, real estate all over Massachusetts and Puerto Rico, as well as a beautiful house in Easton. But Mitrano wasn't the type of reclusive millionaire to hide his wealth behind a New England picket fence. Come summer, for instance, he would buy every kid in Easton tickets to see the Boston Red Sox, bussing them to the baseball game in Fenway Park.

Paul Mitrano had it all, except for one thing. Although he had adopted his wife's son from a previous marriage, he had no other children of his own. Mitrano used boxing and boxers to fill the void in his life, sponsoring and managing fighters such as Ted Whitfield and Dublin's George O'Neill, always on the lookout for the next Rocky Marciano or Willie Pep. He would put boxers up in his own home or in other houses nearby. Future World Boxing Hall of Famer Joey Giambra, who was taken on by Mitrano and given a place to live in North Easton, remembered him as a father figure who regularly addressed him as "son."

Paul Mitrano was a regular visitor to the nearby Petronelli gym, watching boxers go through their paces, talking fights with Goody and Pat in their office, behind a glass door that bore their names painted in gold lettering. Mitrano noticed a new guy sparring in the gym one evening, and asked who he was.

"That's Seán Mannion. He's not one of ours, but he sure gives our guys a good workout."

The following day, on the building site where Seán worked as a laborer for Clifford Construction, he was approached by his boss, Dan Clifford.

"A friend of mine, Paul Mitrano, saw you sparring last night."

"Yeah?"

"Yeah, he says you're pretty good. He's got an offer for you."

Mitrano wanted to manage Seán. As part of the deal, Seán would get free accommodation in North Easton, along with a car. It would mean an end to early morning starts on building sites. He would be paid a regular income by Mitrano, and have his training overseen by the Petronellis. Structured sparring with Marvin Hagler, Robbie Sims, Tony Petronelli, and the rest. In Brockton. The City of Champions. Seán Mannion was still only 21 years old and hadn't even turned pro, but had just had his destiny handed to him.

Seán said no.

Seán Mannion, sometimes intentionally, sometimes accidentally, was a man of principle. His principles and his loyalty stood to him right throughout his life. People tend not to speak ill of Seán Mannion because of this, despite some of the more colorful incidents in his past. And yet, in many ways, his principles also stood against him. For Seán, the most important things in life, more important than everything else, himself included, were Ros Muc, family, the Irish language, Connemara, friends, Ireland. If any one of these six things cropped up in a decision Seán had to make, they were given priority, regardless of the implications for Seán Mannion himself. Mitrano's offer was the first challenge to these loyalties, these principles, in terms of his boxing future.

The Principles vs. Seán Mannion. Seán never stood a chance. If he went with Mitrano, he'd have to abandon his family and friends in Dorchester. His Irish enclave. His fellow Irish speakers. He'd also have to abandon Jimmy Connolly.

When Seán Mannion first arrived in Boston in 1974, he knew immediately that Jimmy Connolly would be his trainer and manager. An Irish name above the gym door. Irish blood in the owner's veins. There could be no other.

When he returned to the United States in 1977, Seán was only ever going to start off his professional boxing career in one place. Even when he received a better offer from elsewhere. Even when Jimmy Connolly failed to fulfill the terms of their contract. Even when he heard that Connolly had threatened him with a gun. Because Seán Mannion was a man of principle. For better or for worse.

~

When Seán Mannion flew into Logan Airport in June 1977, there would be no returning home after six months. Seán Mannion had come to Boston to stay in Boston.

His brother Tommy found him a job in construction, and another brother, Paddy, gave him a bed in Dorchester. Around him were siblings, relatives, and friends. Pubs, dances, music. All Seán was missing from home was boxing, and he wasn't long filling that void.

Jimmy Connolly had since moved to the Michael F. McDonough Gym under the courthouse on West Broadway, in the heart of South Boston. The Municipal Court, or the Muni as it was known locally, was an imposing red-brick building where the abundant criminals of Southie faced their justice. The same men who would then go downstairs to engage in a more legal form of violence, punching bags, speed balls, each other.

Directing the violence was Connolly, a trainer and manager who knew his way around the boxing business. He had trained his cousin, Paul Pender, who won the world middleweight title in 1960 after beating Sugar Ray Robinson, one of the greatest boxers in history. Connolly spent time training Micky Ward, a future world title winner immortalized in the movie *The Fighter*, as well as many other Boston boxers. He even joined up with the World Wrestling Foundation in the mid-1980s to train Mr. T!

More importantly for the young boxers in his gym, Jimmy Connolly had contacts. He worked with his brother Billy and, together, they could get you fights. Billy was an impressive cut man, the kind of guy that could curdle blood if his reputation was to be believed.

"There were times when he was almost disappointed you didn't get cut," said Danny Long, a former sparring partner of Seán Mannion. "If you got cut in the mouth, he used to shout 'eat it, eat it,' he'd make you eat the Vaseline!"

The Connolly brothers had strong Irish connections. Their mother, Mary, was from Four Roads in Roscommon, their father of Galway descent. William and Mary Connolly lived in Mission Hill, Boston, raising four sons and two daughters. Jimmy was born in 1936 and joined the Marines after graduating from Mission Hill High School at the age of 17. Having achieved the rank of corporal, Jimmy left the Marines for the Boston Navy Yard in 1956, and when that yard built its last ship 18 years later, Jimmy turned to boxing full time.

Connolly knew he had a good boxer in Seán Mannion from the moment he first walked into his gym in the summer of 1974, and was disappointed to see him return to Ireland a few months later.

"Jimmy seemed to stay up to date on him when Seán was in Ireland, even I knew about him before I ever met him," said Danny Long. "I remember Jimmy talking about him, this kid from Ireland, and he told us he won the Irish title."

Jimmy's admiration for Seán was evident to all in the gym, and his young protégé felt the same way about him.

"For me, it seemed like there was no one on earth as good as him, what with the talk about him and the talk he had himself," said Mannion. "He could tell a good yarn and he had good connections if he used them properly."

"He looked like a little altar boy," remembered Connolly in a 2009 TG4 television documentary, "but he'd get in there and kick the crap outta ya if you gave him the opportunity and a lot of guys didn't like that because they were going up the ladder themselves. They were looking for easy opponents. Seán Mannion was not an easy opponent."

While the relationship between the two started out well, it wasn't long before tensions began to surface.

"He used to bad-mouth you when you weren't around," said Danny Long. "I remember one time he was bitching about Seán, waiting for him to come into training. He pulled his jacket aside, showing us he had a gun tucked into his pants. 'Where the fuck is that fuckin' Irishman?' he said, 'I bet you he's fuckin' drunk. If he comes in here, I'm going to pop two shots in his kneecaps.'

"Next thing, the door opens and Seán comes into the gym. 'Oh hi, Seán,' Connolly says, nice as pie, 'let's get you set up with Danny for a sparring session.'

"That's the kind of guy he was, nice to your face but could bad-mouth you all day long."

Long was a good boxer, with 31 wins out of 38, and was a regular sparring partner for Seán.

"Too regular in the end," he laughed. "We used to spar each other all the time. Seán was a very tough fighter, fast on his feet, and he used to catch me a lot at first with them sharp, stinging punches. But we sparred so many times I got to know every move he was going to make, and I'm sure he got to know every move I was going to make. In the end, we knew every move the other guy had, it was almost a waste of time."

By this stage, Mannion still hadn't decided if he was going to turn pro or not, a lifelong dream colliding with the reality of a decision on which there would be no going back. Seán had a shot at qualifying for the Olympics if he stayed in the amateur ranks, but leaving aside the fact that the games were still three years away, he wasn't even sure of a place on the Irish team, let alone a medal.

After his return to the United States, Seán had five amateur fights between 1977 and 1978, but when Jimmy Connolly wanted him to fight in the U.S. amateur Golden Gloves championships, Seán told him that he couldn't see the point. He had recently won the Irish title, and with the 1977 Golden Gloves having just been held (where a young man from Detroit called Tommy Hearns won the 139-pound title, and another young man fighting out of Miami, Mike McCallum, won the 147-pound category). Seán would have to wait another year. In the end, it was the time gaps that made his mind up for him. Three years to the Olympics. A year to the Golden Gloves. That and Tony Petronelli's advice. It was time to turn pro.

According to Massachusetts State Athletic Commission regulations, a contract between a boxer and his manager could last no longer than three years.

This wasn't long enough for Jimmy Connolly, however, so he drove Mannion down to New York where a four-year contract could be legally signed. Under the terms set out, 33 percent of any future purses would go to the manager (Connolly), 10 percent to the trainer (from Connolly's stable), and the remainder to Seán. Seán Mannion signed his first boxing contract, without any independent legal advice, in the offices of the New York State Athletic Commission in Manhattan. He spent the rest of the afternoon as a tourist in New York City with Jimmy Connolly, heading down to Times Square, heading up to the top of the World Trade Center, heading out to the Statue of Liberty. Bizarrely, Seán says he remembers Connolly, a reformed alcoholic, bringing him to visit a former drinking buddy of his in Manhattan. The friend turned out to be the actor Peter O'Toole.

Seán Mannion became a pro boxer at the age of 21, and was raring to go from the start. He would get up every morning at 5:30 a.m. and run a set route in his work boots. From Lower Mills in Dorchester to Adams Street to Milton Square and back home. From there to a day of sweat and graft on the building sites of Boston, sweltering under a summer sun or shivering in nor'easter snow. It was tough work. Down to Southie in the evening to Connolly's gym, sparring, skipping, throwing punches. More tough work. But it would soon be worth it.

Seán Mannion's first professional fight took place on June 28, 1978, exactly one year to the day he got off that plane at Logan Airport. When Jimmy Connolly told him that a fight had been arranged, Seán didn't ask him who his opponent was, what kind of boxing record he had, or even where the fight would be held. He had already agreed to leave those kinds of details to his manager.

"You do the management," Seán had told him, "and I'll do the fighting."

Mannion's first fight, held in the Providence Civic Center in Rhode Island, was against Danny Torres of New Jersey. Also on the card that night was a young man called Mustafa Hamsho, originally from Syria but living in Brooklyn. Mannion and Hamsho would share the same card once more on a decisive night in 1984, both fighting for world titles in New York's Madison Square Garden.

The fight night was being organized by Anthony "Rip" Valenti, the biggest boxing promoter in New England and the man who put Boston on the boxing map in 1940 when he brought Joe Louis to the Boston Garden for a world heavyweight title fight against Al McCoy.

Valenti started out in boxing management in 1920 after opening his front door in Boston's North End one morning and tripping over a young boy lying on his porch. The boy was Sammy Fuller, a 13-year-old who had been thrown out of his home by his stepfather. Fuller moved in with Valenti for nine months and won the world light welterweight title in 1932.

It soon became apparent to Valenti that the money in boxing wasn't to be made in management, but in putting together fights. He made $3,300 on his first fight night, but the Great Depression hit him with a haymaker. Rip Valenti organized 15 cards between 1933 and 1934 and lost over $20,000.

Things improved for Valenti after that, but there always seemed to be downs along with the ups. He signed a young Marvin Hagler before having to hand him over to Bob Arum and Top Rank, whose tight control on the U.S. boxing scene meant that they could effectively decide if Hagler was to get any decent fights or not. Some Valenti fight nights turned a profit, others didn't. Finally, at the age of 84, eight months from his deathbed, Valenti made his money. When Marvin Hagler fought Thomas Hearns in 1985, Bob Arum gave Rip Valenti the contract to show the fight on 22 cinema screens all over New England. Valenti made $1.8 million on that night.

There were no riches to be made on Seán Mannion's first fight, however. He would make $125 from his six rounds with Danny Torres. That was $72 for Seán, $53 for Jimmy and Billy Connolly. Jimmy drove down to Providence, Billy beside him in the front seat, Seán sitting in the back, resting after a long day on a building site in 90-degree heat.

The debut went well. In the audience were three cars' worth of Mannion supporters. In his corner with the Connolly brothers was an old friend from Na Piarsaigh boxing club, Paddy McGrath.

By the third round, Danny Torres was in trouble. Seán could see that he had the winning of the fight and went on the attack, fists flying in from left and right, honing in on the ribs, liver, coming inside Torres's guard, waiting for that chin to open up. Suddenly, however, the referee jumped in between them. He had noticed that one of Mannion's laces had come undone and made him go back to his corner to have it re-tied.

"Fuck that, I had him there," Seán told his cornermen.

"You have him, whatever happens," Paddy McGrath answered. "Patience."

Seán took his advice. The fight went the designated six rounds. The first time the man from Ros Muc had ever fought six rounds. It was a majority decision by the judges. Seán Mannion had won his first fight as a professional boxer.

Seventy-two dollars. He didn't care. It was a start. But Seán Mannion made sure that he never walked out of his corner with loose laces again.

6

THE MOB

Tucked away in the bottom-right corner of the front page of the *Irish Times*, October 20, 1984, was a short report on Seán Mannion's WBA world light middleweight title fight held in Madison Square Garden the night before.

Across the top of the page, spread over four columns, was a large photograph of guns and explosives. M-16s. Hand grenades. A Browning machine gun. AK-47s. All on display in Irish Garda police headquarters in Dublin. Under the photo, the caption read:

"Some of the arms seized from the Marita Ann off the Kerry coast on September 29th which were put on display at Garda headquarters in Dublin yesterday."

No one reading the paper that October morning would have realized that there was a connection between the two stories, the boxer at the bottom and the guns on top. But there was. The actions of two young men living in Boston, but both from the tiny village of Ros Muc, who had attended the same school and who were related to one another, had made the front page of the *Irish Times* on the same day.

Patrick Nee was born in Ros Muc, county Galway, in 1943. A cousin of the Irish heavyweight boxer, Máirtín Nee, and a distant cousin of Seán Mannion, he, like Mannion, went to school in Ros Muc before Nee's family immigrated to the United States in 1952. Pat's mother, Julia, would say that the biggest mistake of her life was not throwing her son overboard the ship *Brittanic* as they sailed from Ireland to Boston.

"If I could have seen the future, you would have been on the bottom of the Atlantic," she told her son years later.

The Nee family settled in South Boston, and Pat adapted to his new surroundings quickly. By the age of 14, he had become a member of the Mullen Gang, stealing from trucks that were being loaded on the South Boston docks. After a spell in Vietnam with the Marines, Nee returned to Southie. He wasn't long home before his brother, Peter, having also recently returned from the war, was murdered.

It was said locally that Peter had been killed by another ex-Marine, Kevin Daley, after a scuffle outside the Coachman Bar in South Boston. Seeking vengeance for his brother's death, Nee shot Daley four times with a Colt .38 on a rainy night in November 1969.

"I was fortunate it was a really rainy night, so he never heard me come up the alleyway," said Nee. "When he got out of his car and closed the door and he turned around, I was standing there, and I says: 'Your fucking turn.' And I shot him five times.

"I had hit him over the heart, under the heart, I blew out his right lung, I shot him twice in the stomach, I kicked his teeth out and I spit on him. I wouldn't do that now, what with forensics, but back then, it wasn't a big dig."

Kevin Daley survived, however, and having identified his assailant, Pat Nee was arrested soon after. When the day of the court hearing arrived, Daley was brought in before the judge in a wheelchair. Nee, sitting beside his lawyer, looked confident. The prosecutor opened the questioning, according to Nee's 2006 autobiography, *A Criminal and an Irishman*.

"Can you identify the shooter in the courtroom?" asked the prosecutor.

Daley looked at Nee, the two well-acquainted from Southie and from the night that left Kevin Daley in a wheelchair for the rest of his life.

"Well, now, taking a good look at him, up close and all I know this is not him," said Daley.

"Are you sure, Mr. Daley?" asked a perplexed judge.

"Yes sir. I can't say that this is the man who shot me."

Pat Nee was released and, if anything, emboldened by his attempted murder charge.

Shortly afterwards, a street war erupted in South Boston between the two major crime gangs there, Nee's Mullen Gang and the Killeens. In 1972, the Mullens killed gang kingpin Donald Killeen, resulting in a merger of sorts between the two forces, under the stewardship of Howie Winter of the Winter Hill Gang.

As new members of the Winter Hill Gang, Pat Nee was now teaming up with former Killeen rival James "Whitey" Bulger, extorting drug dealers and running betting and loan rackets. There was little love lost between Nee and Bulger, however. Before coming under the leadership of Howie Winter, Bulger had attempted to kill Nee, and Nee had attempted to return the favor. Neither had succeeded.

When Winter was imprisoned in 1979, Bulger took over the leadership of the gang, leading to a murderous domination of the Boston criminal underworld that would eventually see him fleeing Boston in 1994 after being revealed as an FBI informer, and later sentenced to two consecutive life terms plus five years after being arrested in 2011. While Nee was implicated, but never charged, in a number of Bulger-related killings, he began to focus on a new venture following Whitey's takeover of the Winter Hill Gang. He began putting together the largest arms haul ever seized from the Irish Republican Army.

By September 1984, Pat Nee had accumulated 7.5 tons of guns, explosives, electronics, hand grenades, and other material. A fishing boat, the *Valhalla*, was purchased to ship the weapons from Boston to Ireland, where the $1.2 million haul was transferred to another fishing vessel, the *Marita Ann*. On board the *Marita Ann* was Martin Ferris, who would later be elected to Dáil Éireann, the Irish parliament, as a member of Sinn Féin. The Irish Navy was lying in wait for the shipment from the United States, however, and the *Marita Ann* and its cargo were seized off the coast of Kerry. Martin Ferris and his crew were sentenced to 10 years in prison. The FBI eventually caught up with Nee, and he was given 18 months.

It wouldn't be the last time Patrick Nee would see the inside of a prison. He wasn't a year out of Danbury Federal Correctional Institute when he was arrested again while attempting to rob an armored truck. This time, he was sentenced for 37 years. He was out again after 10.

But back in 1977, when Seán Mannion first came over to Boston, Pat Nee, along with Whitey, ruled Southie with a very strong arm. Nothing happened on the streets and in the projects of South Boston without Nee knowing.

Sure enough, Mannion wasn't long in the city when Nee came by his gym for a chat. Two guys from Ros Muc, a long way from home, both of whose livelihoods depended on very different forms of violence. Seán, working the punchbag, didn't notice Nee and his colleagues entering the room. Everyone else noticed, however. A blanket of quiet fell over the relentless thud of punch bags and skipping ropes.

"Hey Seán, howya doin'?" asked Nee. He introduced himself. They discussed family. They discussed Ros Muc.

"Seán, if any of these fucks here, or anyone else for that matter, fucks with you, you give me a call. You got that?"

Seán nodded, but the "You got that?" wasn't meant for him. It was meant for the rest of the gym. They got the message. Don't fuck with Seán Mannion.

"When Seán came over in 1977, he was around some people that mightn't have had his best interests in mind," said Pat Nee, recalling the time. "There were a lot of drug dealers in the gym, bringing all kinds of heat on the place, scumbags, wiseguys that would try and make money off Seán.

"When the gunmen get involved, you get a problem, but those were guys that we could and we did handle. Just the fact that they seen us come in to see Seán and knowin' that we're both from the same place in Ireland was enough."

Pat Nee wasn't exaggerating about wiseguys and drug dealers. It seemed that half of Whitey Bulger's gang was training with Seán at the time. And Seán was getting plenty of offers to join up as yet another Whitey henchman.

One of those Whitey gang members was John "Red" Shea. It was clear early on that Red had most of the abilities needed to become a boxer. He was light and quick on his feet, and he wasn't long racking up significant underage victories. By the time he was 14, he was the New England Junior Olympic Champion, which he went on to win three times. Shea had two things going against him when it came to a potential boxing career, however. He had a short temper, and he couldn't resist the trappings that came with a life of crime. Red Shea was selling cocaine for Whitey Bulger, and he was in no way reluctant to use his fists, or anything else for that matter, in making his way in the world of drugs.

"On the one hand, boxing was tremendous for me, it taught me so much, it gave me confidence, skill, focus," said Red Shea. "But I also met a lot of characters that had been associated with Whitey Bulger and it's pretty much where it all began for me in getting into the Irish Mafia.

"In the gym, I was associating myself with the guys who were associated with him. And the biggest thing was drugs, and that's what I started getting into, because the money was easy, and good. And with all that, there was a power that came with it, a strength, and a sort of respect, you know, who's who of the neighborhood.

"Most of the guys that were associated could obviously handle themselves, because I met them in the gym, sparring, boxing and Seán boxed some of them too."

Shea was sparring with Seán one evening when the Ros Muc man raised the question of cocaine.

"Red, you should stay away from those drugs, they're going to be nothing but trouble for you."

"Look, Seán, I'm going to be a millionaire by this time next year."

"Yeah, Red, but you're going to spend the rest of your life looking over your shoulder."

It's unlikely that Red Shea was thinking of Seán's advice on August 10, 1990, but when Seán picked up the *Boston Globe* the following day, he wasn't surprised by what he read: "In a sweeping blow to the criminal organization of reputed underworld figure James J. (Whitey) Bulger, a federal grand jury has indicted 51 persons on charges including distributing cocaine, conspiring to operate a criminal narcotics enterprise and filing false income tax returns."

The list of arrested Whitey Bulger accomplices read like a who's who of Seán Mannion's boxing circle. "Red" Shea, who tried to flee from the police that night. Paul "Polecat" Moore, who was a senior figure in the Bulger infrastructure. Kevin McDonald, or "Andre the Giant" as he was known in Southie, was Seán's bodyguard when Mannion was preparing for his world title bout in New York. He was arrested with a loaded shotgun and a .38-caliber Smith & Wesson by his bed.

But while Seán used to spar with Red Shea, the age and weight gap meant that he sparred more often with the likes of Polecat Moore, Frank MacDonald, and Danny Long. Long ended up with the Boston Police Department when he finished boxing. The other two didn't.

Six feet tall and 200 pounds, Polecat Moore could challenge anyone in Jimmy Connolly's gym. But like Red Shea and Andre the Giant, he ended up as another Whitey acolyte caught in that August dragnet. Sentenced to nine years for drug dealing, he began to question his loyalty to Whitey Bulger after some time alone in his cell and offered to testify against Bulger. The authorities didn't think twice about the offer, and Polecat was released. In an article from August 1991, the *Boston Herald* called Moore and his testifying associates "a Dream Team of rat witnesses."

"Moore was a top drug dealer in South Boston but was reportedly disillusioned with being a 'stand-up guy' for Bulger after his wife wasn't 'taken care of' when he went to prison on drug charges. 'He knows where some serious bodies are buried,' one source said."

But of all the friends and foes, colleagues and criminals that used to frequent Jimmy Connolly's gym in order to spar with Mannion, Frank MacDonald was the one with whom Seán got on best. Frankie MacDonald's story was also the most tragic of them. A quality boxer, Frank was a bit of a hero in Southie, one of the few from the area known for something other than crime, respected not only as a boxer but as a trainer, coaching the likes of Red Shea and Joey DeGrandis.

"I can't think of any other reverence that existed in the [South Boston] neighborhood like the reverence for successful, good boxers and my brother

Frankie would be one of those people," said Michael Patrick MacDonald, author of *All Souls: A Family Story from Southie*. "I have a strong image of him running around the neighborhood and little kids, especially in the Projects, coming out of the woodwork to see him, or to chase after him, or to throw punches and to imitate that spirit, I guess. And so he was really looked up to."

Frankie MacDonald wasn't involved in drug dealing, but the same couldn't be said of his entourage. The Tank won pretty much every amateur title available to him in Massachusetts and New England, with Polecat Moore and "the boys," as Whitey's troops were called, in his corner. He won the Junior Olympics title. He won the Golden Gloves four times. Frankie was good, and he was only getting better. A serious workout for Seán whenever they sparred.

"When are you going pro, Frankie?" Seán recalls asking.

"I gotta get out of South Boston first, Seán. There's no future in Southie."

Seán didn't pay too much attention to the answer. They kept sparring. Eight rounds. Jimmy Connolly shouting at them from the other side of the ropes.

"Don't stand still. Keep movin'. Keep fuckin' movin'."

Another tough session. Seán changed back into his work clothes after finishing up, said goodbye to Frankie, and headed back home to Dorchester. He would never see Frankie MacDonald again. Two nights later, Seán arrived home to his sister's house on Silloway Street after a training session. The house was empty. His sister, Eileen, and her children had gone back to Ireland to visit family in Ros Muc, and her husband, Mike, was working the night shift. Seán took a shower, ate some pork chops that were left in the fridge, and sat down in front of the television.

"A man has been killed in an attempted robbery of an armored truck in Medford," said the newsreader. He didn't give the name of the dead man, but mentioned that acid had been used to burn off the deceased's fingerprints.

Seán soon got the call. The man killed in Medford was Frankie. Frank the Tank MacDonald, 24 years old.

Frankie mightn't have been dealing drugs, but he was a man in a hurry, and a man in a hurry is known to take shortcuts. He was in a hurry to get out of Southie, to get out of the projects. He hated the small apartment in which his mother was living, in which she was raising 10 children by herself. He hated the guns. He hated the constant unease. Frankie was in a hurry to fulfill uncomplicated dreams. A house in the suburbs for his mother. Tickets to Disney World for the kids. An escape from Southie.

It was Frankie's brother, Kevin, who was meant to do the robbery that day, but when he couldn't go, Frankie jumped in. An easy job, simple, straightforward. Money. Escape.

At the time, Frankie himself had surrendered to the cocaine blowing through the streets of Southie. Not selling it, but using it. Lots of it. Cocaine gave him courage. When Kevin pulled out of the Medford robbery, Frankie didn't feel the slightest reluctance in replacing him. Three of them—Frankie, a friend of his called Ricky, and another 19-year-old guy—drove the 20 minutes northwest to Medford.

All three involved in the Wells Fargo robbery had a specific role. One of them was to shove a gun into the security guard's back. Another was to wait in the getaway car. It was Frankie's job to jump into the back of the truck and grab the money. That's exactly what he did. But when he leapt back out, the Wells Fargo driver shot him in the back. Frankie made it into the car, still clutching the money, bullets fizzing all around him.

It wasn't the bullet in the back that killed Frank MacDonald. That turned out to be a relatively minor injury. The coroner informed the family that strangulation marks had been found around Frankie's neck and that his fingerprints had been burnt off with acid. The gang managed to steal $100,000 from the Wells Fargo truck that day, and they weren't taking a chance on an injured member being picked up and questioned.

A while later, Red Shea came down to the MacDonald home in South Boston with a large wad of cash. Ten thousand dollars. Funeral costs, said Red later. He gave the money to Frank's brother, Johnnie. Johnnie looked at Red, then at the roll of cash in his hand. He stood up and threw it into the bay.

Frankie's death affected Seán in a big way. He lost a sparring partner and a friend. The killing only added to the Ros Muc man's hatred of the drugs all around him, reaffirming his rejection of the opportunities to join Whitey Bulger's "boys."

Seán remembers being asked on a number of occasions to meet Whitey Bulger in his infamous Triple O's Lounge. Boston's Irish mob always needed muscle, but Mannion refused the Boston Godfather's invitations. John "Red" Shea recalls as much.

"Seán's not a mean person. I heard that Seán was asked to probably join the Irish Mafia, again I don't know that personally, but from what I hear, he was asked, Seán could never do that. He doesn't have the disposition, he's not that type of person to be mean like that. And, yeah, I'm so glad that he never made that decision."

"I didn't want anything to do with that stuff," said Mannion, "ruining people's lives, pushing drugs on kids."

Seán steered clear of Bulger, their only one-on-one encounter being when a speeding Whitey crashed his car into Mannion's one night while coming off

L Street in Southie. Bulger didn't stop, and Mannion, not realizing who the driver was, chased Whitey through the streets of South Boston. Eventually, Bulger pulled over.

"Do you realize you hit my car?" asked Mannion through the window of Bulger's Chevrolet Malibu.

Bulger didn't say much, apologized, and threw a roll of cash at Mannion. Five hundred dollars.

"That was more than what the car was worth," said Seán. "It only dawned on me when he pulled away who I had been talking to. I don't think I would have chased him down if I knew it was Whitey!"

Bulger wasn't the only mobster to throw cash Seán's way. Four years after his first visit, Patrick Nee recalls arriving back in Connolly's Gym, looking for Mannion.

"There's a guy going to call you from Leavenworth Prison in Kansas, he's from Limerick. He wants to write an article about you, he writes for the Irish paper down there."

Looking to get in touch with Seán, the Limerick man had contacted the former head of the Winter Hill Gang, Howie Winter, who was also in Leavenworth, serving time for fixing horse races. Winter, who had previously gotten Pat Nee to arrange a phone call between him and Seán so that he could wish him good luck coming up to a big fight, asked Nee to sort things out. Nee headed down to the gym.

"Sound," said Seán, "I'll talk to him, no problem."

"Thanks," replied Nee and handed Seán $100.

"Ah Jesus, Pat, I don't want any money for it."

"Take it, Seán."

"No, really Pat, it's okay."

"Seán, take it. It's not from me, that's what they told me to give you. You gotta take it."

Séan took the $100.

The two spent another while in the gym talking, discussing life, relatives, Ros Muc. When Nee left, the other boxers ran over to Mannion.

"Do you know who that guy is?"

"Why wouldn't I know him?"

"But do you know who he is?"

"Of course I know him, he's my cousin."

"But do you know who he really is?"

"Look, I've been talking to him for the last fucking hour. Yes, I know very well who he is, don't you worry."

When the crowd around Seán dispersed, Jimmy Connolly came over to him. "What did he want?"

Seán looked at him.

"He came here to make sure that nobody fucks with me."

It was obvious to Seán that everyone in the room was afraid of Patrick Nee. It was also obvious to him that everyone in the room was now treating him in a different way. Seán Mannion had their respect for something other than boxing.

Pat Nee remembers the incident, laughing off any suggestion that he provided Mannion with protection.

"He's from Ros Muc, I'm from Ros Muc. We were climbing to the top in our respective fields, you know. I would have done anything for Seán, but Seán was a tough guy in his own right. He didn't need me. He could take care of himself on the streets."

7

A NEW STAR

"**Y**ou won't get far, Seán."

Seán Mannion was stalked by a little voice in the back of his head from the moment he took the decision to turn pro. A negative, persistent little voice. A voice that didn't plan on helping him in any way.

"You'll be back home within the year, Seán."

Seán Mannion had only ever had the one dream. Pro boxing. Now, faced with the reality of having become a professional boxer, he was beginning to have doubts.

When Mannion started boxing in the United States, the weight divisions in which he traded punches were the most competitive, not just of the time, but possibly in boxing history. Marvin Hagler, Sugar Ray Leonard, Wilfred Benitez, Thomas Hearns, Mike McCallum, Roberto Duran . . . it was a roll call of greatness. And it was an unusual roll call in one respect. There was no dominant nationality or race in middleweight boxing at the time. Black, white, Mexican, American, Irish, Italian, Puerto Rican, Panamanian. The weight divisions from welterweight to light heavyweight were brimming with the best boxers in history, and a young man from the west of Ireland was attempting to break in and leave his own mark on the era.

Seán Mannion's second fight, within two weeks of his first, was in the Boston Garden, far from Ros Muc but among his own people in his new home town. Tony Petronelli was topping the bill that night, fighting Northern Ireland's Jim Montague. Montague had taken the U.S. boxing scene by surprise when he beat Petronelli two months earlier, and the U.S. champion was looking for revenge in his own backyard. He would get his retribution, winning by unanimous decision. Seán had helped Petronelli in his preparation for the first Montague fight, sparring with him in his work clothes, but this time around, he had his own fight to focus on.

Being only his second pro outing, Mannion's fight against Tommy Pyke was always going to be a big deal for him. But the fact that it was being held in Boston, in front of his friends and family, added to its significance. He was going to have to look good in this one. No slip-ups. Sitting in the dressing room waiting for the first fight of the night to finish, Mannion started to wind himself up.

"This fucker is not going to beat me. This fucker is not going to beat me in front of my own people."

By the time he left the dressing room, Seán Mannion had worked himself into a frenzy. The arena reciprocated. When he walked into the Garden, the noise hurtling down from the banked seats slapped him across the face. Home to the Boston Celtics and Bruins, the Garden was initially designed as a boxing arena, and you could tell on that July night in 1978. There was a fury to the welcome Seán received as he bounced up toward the ring. A Connemara man fighting in the Boston Garden. This was a big deal for the Boston Irish. Mannion climbed up the steps and slipped under the ropes into the ring.

"This fucker isn't going to beat me in front of my own people."

The bell rang for the first and last time. The man from Ros Muc came out of his corner like an Irish Jake La Motta, arms low, fists wild. Within 90 seconds, Tommy Pyke lay on the flat of his back, arms splayed out by his side. Standing over him, Seán Mannion's fury and adrenalin evaporated into exhaustion. It was over. The crowd, louder than they had been all night, had just discovered a new hero. Prostrate on the damp canvas, Pyke knew that his first pro fight would be his last. He would never enter a boxing ring again.

Instead of savoring the victory, however, Mannion's anger quickly returned. By the time he was back in the dressing room, he was spitting profanities, punching walls.

"What the hell's the matter with you, Seán?" asked Tony Petronelli. "You just won!"

"That son of a bastard they got me wasn't even able to stand up," answered Mannion. "In front of my own people."

"Look Seán, calm down," said Petronelli, reason in his voice after the accumulated experience of 40 pro fights. "In a few years' time, you'll be more than happy to get one of those guys again."

After the Pyke win, fights started coming Seán's way with the speed and frequency of his own left hook. The following month, he was back in the Garden to take on Steve Coupe, a fight that couldn't have been more different from his previous bout. There were no wild rushing blows here. Coupe's reputation as a heavy puncher ensured a night of dancing out of reach for Seán, staying light on his toes, using the width of the ring to pick off punches. The fight went the six rounds, another Mannion victory against another boxer who would never again grace the ring.

It was three fights in two months for Mannion after that. Two victories against Jose Ortiz, a Puerto Rican from Connecticut, but it was at the fight against Steve Hughes that he caught his first glimpse of the big time. It was the biggest crowd Seán had ever fought in front of, 6,208 boxing fans squeezed into the Cumberland County Civic Center in Portland, Maine. Indeed, it was the biggest crowd ever to have attended a boxing match in Maine, all there to catch a glimpse of the Olympic gold medal hero, Sugar Ray Leonard. Another 7 million people watched the fight on TV and saw Sugar Ray beat Bernardo Prada of Colombia.

Seán and Danny Long had traveled up together from Massachusetts, Seán having been assigned Sugar Ray's brother, Roger. Long beat his man, but with Roger Leonard injured, Seán's opponent was one of Sugar Ray's sparring partners, whom he beat with reasonable ease. It would be a very different outcome when he would finally face Roger Leonard the following month.

"What kind of boxer is this Roger Leonard guy?" Seán had asked Jimmy Connolly.

"Ah, he's okay, but you're not going to have much of a problem with him," was the answer. The wrong answer as it turned out.

It wasn't long before Mannion found out that Roger Leonard was better than okay. Like his Irish opponent, Leonard hadn't had much professional experience. Seán had six fights, six victories. Roger had three fights, three victories. But Sugar Ray's older brother had an exceptional amateur record. Shortly before turning pro, Roger won the U.S. National Amateur Athletic Union (AAU) welterweight championship. He had been a four-time U.S. Air Force champion. Years later, Sugar Ray Leonard admitted to Mannion that his older brother would probably have been the better boxer of the two if it hadn't been for drugs and alcohol. Roger started out with drink, but finished his boxing career in a storm of heroin, from which it took years for him to escape.

Despite his addiction problems, Roger "The Dodger" Leonard, who had Sugar Ray and his cousin, O'dell Leonard, on the same card that December night, had little difficulty with Seán Mannion.

"He beat the crap out of me," remembered Seán. "I couldn't get near him. Any time I'd make a move on him, he hit me three times before I even knew it. He was fast and he could box."

"It was a big day for the Leonard family from the Baltimore area at Spring-field," reported the *Nashua Telegraph* on December 11, 1978. "Ray Leonard's brother, Roger, 158 pounds, won the unanimous six-round decision against Sean Mannion, 154, of Boston, displaying strong jabs and hooks in his third professional bout."

According to the official fight record, Mannion weighed 154 pounds that night. According to himself, however, he weighed no more than 145 pounds. Whether he did or not, Seán was adamant that he was way too light to have given Leonard any sort of decent challenge. Being underweight coming into the fight, he said that his manager had two options: deceive the boxing com-missioner, or cancel the fight. Connolly went with deception. With Leonard fighting at light middleweight, Mannion was taking on an opponent two weight classes heavier than him, and he said that he felt it that night.

Seán's first defeat left him rattled. A stain on his boxing record that he could never erase. He kept telling himself that it was just a bad night. That's all it was. One bad night. Six days later, he was back in the ring, this time in Rhode Island, beating Jesse Rogers in six rounds. The fights kept coming, and so did the victories. By the time Seán had put in his first year as a pro, he had racked up 11 victories in 12 fights, four of them knockouts. The boxing world began to notice the new guy.

In April 1979, Seán bought the latest edition of the venerable boxing publica-tion, *Ring Magazine*. The greatest welterweight on the planet at the time, Wilfred Benitez, graced the cover, having just won the world title for the second time (at the age of 17, Benitez was the youngest man ever to have won a world title). *Ring Mag-azine* was Seán Mannion's bible, the magazine he read in bed as a kid back home in Ros Muc. The magazine that sparked in him a thousand dreams of greatness. Now, it was his face staring back at him from the pages that saw him discover and adore the likes of Muhammad Ali, Emile Griffith, and Joe Frazier. There he was on page 18, his raised fists taped in white, a pair of Everlast shorts around his waist.

"IRISH" SEAN MANNION, NEW WELTERWEIGHT SENSATION was the headline. "Outside the ring, Mannion is easy going and gentle, but he's a tiger from bell to bell once inside the ropes," reported *Ring Magazine*. "He comes to fight and doesn't back off to anyone. That's what makes him a drawing card, and he's acquired many fans. He is handsome, twenty years old, unspoiled, has a gentle disposition, and is single, which accounts for much of his female following."

Mannion's pro boxing career had gotten off to a great start, and it was about to get a whole lot better. For the first time in his fledgling career, he was about to be given top billing on a fight night.

Seán had a bout set for early November, but when his would-be opponent suffered an injury a few days out, Jimmy Connolly told him to stick with the training in case something turned up. And something did. Something big. Seán Mannion vs. Jimmy Corkum in the Hotel Bradford Ballroom, Boston.

Jimmy Corkum was a man on the way up, and Seán Mannion was looking to knock him down. Corkum's management had little inclination for letting their man get in the ring with Seán, however. By 1979, Jimmy Corkum was ranked the 10th best light welterweight in the world, and fifth best in the United States. He wasn't going to take any chances fighting a dangerous boxer like Seán Mannion when there were easier ways to continue his climb to the top.

Tired of having his requests for a fight rejected, Seán headed to Corkum's home gym in Brockton and took a sparring session against a small-time boxer who wasn't up to much. With Corkum and his manager, Vinnie Vecchione, looking on, Mannion made sure that his opponent gave him a good beating. The plan worked. Shortly afterwards, Jimmy Connolly received a phone call from Vecchione offering a bout against Corkum.

$\sim$

Vinnie Vecchione was a mobster with a .22 bullet permanently lodged in his shoulder, following an attempt on his life. He was also a boxing man, and in a town like Brockton, that was a big deal. Vecchione owned a gym there, and was infamous for having ignored a young boy who had come by three days in a row, looking for a trainer, in the early seventies. Recounting the story in the *Boston Herald*'s obituary for Vecchione in 2009, Ron Borges described how, finally, the boy gave up and went across the road to Goody and Pat Petronelli's gym.

"Hey, that's how it goes," said Vecchione about the time he let a young Marvin Hagler slip away. No boxer ever managed by Vinnie Vecchione won a world title, but in 1995, he was awarded Manager of the Year for what was possibly an even greater achievement. As the obituary put it, "for a few short years in the 1990s, he was the greatest manager that ever lived."

Vinnie Vecchione spent the nineties carefully nurturing a heavyweight boxer named Peter McNeeley, steering him clear of potentially dangerous bouts, accepting small money fights in lieu of bigger payments for bigger challenges. The cautious approach worked. By 1995, Peter McNeeley was ranked number three in the world by the World Boxing Council despite being described by Michael Katz of the *New York Times* as "a guy who can't even fight a little bit." Vecchione and McNeeley ignored the mocking. Their reward would come.

On March 22, 1995, Mike Tyson was released from prison after serving three years of a six-year sentence for rape. Don King was looking for an opponent for Tyson's big comeback, and Vinnie Vecchione had just the guy. Mike Tyson vs. Peter McNeeley quickly sold out the MGM Grand Garden in Las Vegas, along with $50 million worth of pay-per-view TV.

The fight lasted 89 seconds before Vecchione jumped into the ring to save McNeeley from the most dangerous boxer on the planet. McNeeley had already been knocked down within seconds of the fight starting, and having been downed and dazed a second time, his manager decided to intervene.

It wasn't a popular intervention. The crowd was furious that Mike Tyson's glorious comeback had been cut short by a flat-capped mobster seeking to rescue his own man. Rumors spread that the Mafia was behind the early stoppage, with big money having been gambled on a first-round finish. Vecchione didn't care about the rumors. He knew his guy was in trouble and felt like he had no choice but to step in and save McNeeley. As it happens, they actually saved each other. For the first time in both their lives, boxing had given them real money—$700,000 from the fight, and another $100,000 for a Pizza Hut TV commercial in which a slice of pizza knocked out McNeeley!

Peter McNeeley may have been his first big payday, but Jimmy Corkum was Vinnie Vecchione's first big hope. Vecchione had started out as an apprentice to the legendary New England boxing promoter, Sam Silverman. But when Silverman died in 1977, Vecchione lost his appetite for the fight game and wanted to leave boxing.

"I'd have quit but for one thing," he said in an interview with the *Boston Herald*'s George Kimball in 1995, staring at a photo on his office wall. "This kid here, Jimmy Corkum. I wasn't going to walk away and abandon my fighter."

~

Jimmy Corkum was only 21 years old when he fought Seán Mannion, but was already marching a path to greatness. He was 19 when *Ring Magazine* ranked him 10th in the world in his division. A television company followed him around as part of a fly-on-the-wall documentary about his life. Newspapers heralded him as the next great thing, and with reason. Having won the New England Golden Gloves as an amateur, he had 40 pro victories—23 of them KOs—by the time he met Seán Mannion. The older Mannion, by contrast, had only had 13 pro fights. There was no question about who was the favorite for this fight. The *Boston Herald* predicted an easy win for Corkum, saying that the man from Brockton was just too good for the young Irishman from Ros Muc. If the next "great white hope" was to spring from Massachusetts, consensus had it that his name would be Corkum, and not Mannion.

The Hotel Bradford was jam-packed. Brockton vs. Dorchester. USA vs. Ireland. Rip Valenti had no problem selling tickets for this one. There were five fights on the card that night and, after Danny Long won his fight in a first-round KO, it was Mannion's turn. The headline act.

Seán got up off the wooden bench in the makeshift changing room and headed out toward the crowd. He didn't feel nervous. He felt no anger. Only calmness. So calm that he actually surprised himself when he noticed it. The noise as he approached the hall had a volume that made you feel it as well as hear it. In the ballroom, the wooden dance floor was obscured by a newly erected boxing ring and seats filled to capacity. Both Brockton and the media might have been in agreement about the outcome, but having actively sought out Corkum, Seán felt more confident than usual coming into this fight.

"Heavy favorite Jimmy Corkum of Brockton, a premed student at Stonehill . . . figured to flatten Mannion," wrote the *Boston Globe*'s John Ahern in November 1979.

Seán looked across the ring. With his Irish and Jewish ancestry, Corkum was wearing shorts with a shamrock sewn on one leg, the Star of David on the other. He was standing beside his manager, Vecchione, talking, laughing. Laughing? Before the fight?

"Nobody laughs at me," said Mannion to himself.

The bell rang.

Seán Mannion started the fight with a rasping fury, nailing Corkum repeatedly with his left, refusing to let the Brockton boxer recover. After three rounds, Jimmy Connolly told his man that Corkum was adapting to his style and that it was time to switch from left to right, from southpaw to orthodox. Not many boxers can make the switch naturally, but years of practice, first under Mike Flaherty and then under Connolly, had given Seán a fluency in both fists that took Corkum by surprise. At the start of the sixth, Mannion switched once again, back to the left. The fight would soon end, with the *Boston Globe* reporting afterwards in a piece titled "Mannion KO in 6th shatters Corkum," that the "likeable Irishman with the delightful brogue took over in the first moment of the fight and never let up, pounding the tough Corkum with right-hand leads when he fought from the standard stance and with solid lefts when he went southpaw. It was a relentless attack, a never-ending bombardment that culminated in a knockout that was a devastating end to a rugged war."

No one saw this one coming. Mannion's fans went wild. Briocán, Seán's brother, raced into the ring, lifting his brother in the air.

"Get him the fuck out of the ring," shouted Connolly at Seán, "or he'll get you disqualified."

Jimmy Connolly didn't like it when Seán's brothers were around him, and he had told him as much. That night against Corkum, Connolly had been annoyed initially by Seán having Paddy work in his corner and now, here was another brother with him in the center of the ring.

While Briocán celebrated, Corkum lay stretched out on the canvas, badly cut. He had fallen three times that night, but there would be no resurrection for Jimmy Corkum. He was 21 years old, a glorious boxing career seemingly in front of him, but after his defeat to Mannion, he would never fight again.

Overnight, it seemed, Seán Mannion had turned from being a scrappy neo-pro to having developed a reputation as a crafty, clever boxer. He had earned just $750 for the win against Corkum, but the fight had added significantly to his reputation. The newspapers back home in Ireland began to pay attention for the first time. "Mannion Now Star of U.S. Boxing Big-Time" was the headline in the *Connacht Tribune* on November 16, 1979.

But despite the newfound glory, despite the recognition and acknowledgment, things didn't get easier for Seán Mannion. Other boxers weren't exactly clamoring to get in the ring with him. There were, after all, easier ways to earn a living as a fighter than taking on a southpaw who could take and give a punch, and who had yet to be knocked out. By its nature, boxing is a risky sport, and taking a chance against Seán Mannion wasn't good risk management.

The record spoke for itself. By that stage, taking on Mannion should have come with a career health warning. In little over a year, Mannion would be the last opponent for Tommy Pyke, Steve Coupe, Jimmy Corkum, and Patrick Maloney (Mannion's next opponent after Corkum, who was stopped after seven rounds with deep cuts under each eye). None of them would ever enter a ring again after facing the Irishman. Two years later, Sean would fight Ricardo Camoranesi from Argentina. Another man who would never again don a pair of gloves.

Seán didn't have a particularly big punch, but he worked constantly at getting around that, developing a stylish durability that he kept adapting. He studied fights, boxers, watched videos, read books.

"He was very much like Mike Tyson in that respect," said Peter Kerr, a Glasgow man who used to be in Seán's corner. "He was constantly studying, reading, watching anything he came across that had to do with boxing."

"Seán was a real student of the game," said Tony Cardinale, Seán's former attorney, who went on to become a renowned boxing manager and organized crime lawyer. "He kept coming up with different angles of attack, different ways of hitting guys."

In the newspapers, he was described as an "artiste." Maybe he didn't have a big punch, but he could certainly take one. During fights, Mannion would often give the impression that he was in trouble, lying on the ropes, his hands held high to protect himself. But more often than not, the ropes were part of the plan, absorbing punches until suddenly getting off the ropes and letting off an uppercut when least expected. One under the chin, wobbling the legs of an opponent already tired from his attempts on Mannion while he lay back with his arms up. That's when Seán's attack would begin. It was little wonder that he saw no queue of opponents lining up to take him on.

"Chasing these guys was rough," remembered Jimmy Connolly in a 1999 interview with the Irish television station, TG4. "A lot of people didn't want to fight Seán Mannion, not because he was a heavy puncher, but because he was a dangerous guy, because he had a lot of ability. He would just dazzle these guys."

Seán had bigger problems than coming up with opponents, however. He was finding it increasingly difficult to keep both lives going, the life of a professional boxer and the life of a construction worker.

"People didn't understand," he said. "At the time, I was getting up to run every morning, then going to work on a construction site and heading to the gym in the evenings. After a while, I could do neither properly but I had no choice. I had to stick with them. I was exhausted."

Only a year into his career as a professional boxer, Seán was already burned out. He started missing work days. If he was working, he started missing training sessions. The rumors began to spread. Seán Mannion was hitting the bottle. Hard.

Seán, 23 years of age, wasn't even drinking at the time. He couldn't escape the rumors, however, and they would stalk him for the rest of his life.

8

DRINK

S even and Seven.

That was Seán Mannion's first drink. Eighteen years old, at an Irish dance in Forest Hills in Boston, fresh across the Atlantic from another world 3,000 miles away. Seagram's Seven Crown whisky with 7-Up.

When his head started to dance in time with those around him, he figured that the second Seven and Seven was probably two too many.

Seán Mannion was, and still is, known in the United States for his boxing. But in Ireland, and especially back home in Connemara, Mannion's reputation was defined by something else. Not training. Not boxing. But booze. Stories of his drinking spread early on like seeds in the wind and, like seeds, they grew, much to the irritation of the former U.S. light middleweight champion.

"I drank, no question about it, and I drank more than my fair share," admitted Mannion. "But the stories about me drinking while I was in training always bothered me. Certainly, I could spend a week or two after a fight drinking, but not while training. You don't get to be a world title contender if you're always drinking.

"I remember being in the Blarney Stone pub in Dorchester after the Mike McCallum fight when these two guys from home came up to me. 'You did well in the world title,' said one of them, 'but if you weren't drinking the night before, you would have beaten him.' 'Don't I know,' I said back to him and I just left it at that. Drinking the night before? I had just spent the guts of two months training up in the Catskill Mountains.

"People say to me that if it wasn't for the drink I'd have won the world title. That's ridiculous as I wasn't drinking at all at the time. People don't understand that I was up against a man who would go on to become one of the top 10 boxers of all time. I had to be at my best then.

"People will always talk regardless of what you do. It's the Irish attitude of trying to put you down. You won't hear it from the American, but you'll hear it from the Irishman."

Remarkably for a man of his drinking reputation, it would be five years after that first drink in Forest Hills before Mannion would consume alcohol again. Seán was 23 years old, at yet another dance, this time in the Freeport Hall in Dorchester. Three of his sisters bought him a vodka and orange to see what effect it would have on their baby brother. Seán vomited bright orange in the gym the following day and figured it would be best to stay away from the hard stuff. So he turned to beer.

And so it began. A week, two weeks, three weeks of unrelenting training. Followed by a fight. Followed by victory. Followed by celebration. The celebration would often last as long as the training that preceded it. Seán would hit the Blarney Stone or the Emerald Isle or the Twelve Bens, drinking, partying, celebrating. A release from the imprisonment of boxing's unyielding tempo. A tempo that didn't stop, that didn't concede until the final bell rang out and the referee did or didn't lift his arm in the air. Every day that same tempo. Get up in the morning to a city fast asleep. Run. Home. Shower. Work. Home. Gym. Shower. Dinner. Sleep. Get up in the morning to a city fast asleep . . .

Seán Mannion used drink to smash that tempo apart every time a fight finished, and he was no exception of his era or of his weight division. By 1982, the great Sugar Ray Leonard was caught up in a world of alcohol and cocaine. Roberto Duran struggled to control his weight due to his near-addiction to food and drink. The world's youngest world champion, Wilfred Benitez, was effectively finished as a boxer by the age of 25 because of drug use. Even Marvin Hagler, one of the most committed and dedicated athletes in the sport of boxing, was stalked by rumors of drink and drugs.

"Irish" Micky Ward was well aware of the damage drink and drugs did to a boxing career. His half-brother, Dicky Eklund, lived in a destructive haze of crack cocaine and alcohol, in and out of prison before an eight-year sentence sobered him up long enough to train Micky to a light welterweight world championship. Life for the two in Lowell, Massachusetts, was as dysfunctional as its portrayal in the movie *The Fighter*, and Micky remembers Mannion disappearing on drinking sessions with his half-brother.

"They trained together, they sparred together, they did a lot of drinking together. Seán and Dickie would be sparring with me on a Thursday and all of a sudden you wouldn't see either of them again until Tuesday. Seán, when he trained, trained his ass off, but he liked to have a few drinks.

"If Seán did the right things he was supposed to do, he'd be a world champion, no doubt. But he didn't."

For the first half of his boxing career, Mannion managed to control his drinking. Perhaps the beer stopped him from ever gaining total control over his weight, but it didn't come between him and his work in the ring. That would come later. But if Seán Mannion didn't have a problem with drink at the time, drink certainly brought problems his way.

Seán would be spotted socializing in one of Dorchester's many Irish bars. A guy who was supposed to be able to take care of himself. Inevitably, the challenge would come. A shoulder as someone walked by. Or a few sharp words. Or a fight involving one of Seán's friends breaking out. Instead of staying out of the way, Mannion would have to put his friends, relatives, Ros Muc, Ireland, whatever, first. It didn't really matter. Honor, his incurable disease, had to be defended.

"I think he would agree he could have been stricter about his training, especially later on," said Mannion's close friend and former boxer, Michael Newell. "His boxing peers had more focused routines, training night and day, and they wouldn't drink alcohol either. Seán liked a drink, maybe too much for a man in his line of work."

Early in 1980, Newell and Mannion were out for the night in Fields Corner in the most Irish part of Irish Boston. Leaving the Emerald Isle bar, a group of young American men started shouting abuse at them. It had happened before, but the two had just walked away. Seán turned to his friend.

"I'm not walking from these guys anymore. They think we're fools."

The two boxers faced the crowd.

"They were good for nothing," recalled Seán. "Each time we hit one of them, they would fall to the ground, get up and run away."

The fists kept flying until one of the gang pulled a knife on Seán. He ducked as he saw the shine of the blade coming at him but didn't manage to escape entirely. Seán was stabbed in the arm, just above the elbow, a scar as a reminder to this day. He punched the guy with the knife, knocking him to the pavement, but was soon knocked to the ground himself by a smashed bottle over his head. Michael Newell took care of the guy with the bottle.

"I remember them, sure, it would happen often enough," said Newell. "Seán never looked for trouble, he wasn't a brawler even when he had drink in him. We would go out and have a few drinks and people would start on him because he had a name and was well-known.

"Fields Corner was quite wild back then. There were people who were known for fighting and drugs. They would come into the Blarney Stone where we would be and we wouldn't always get along. There was trouble at times."

～

In March 1980, Seán Mannion traveled to Nova Scotia in Canada to fight former Canadian and Commonwealth welterweight champion Lawrence Hafey. Seán had been fighting regularly up until his victory over Jimmy Corkum, but boxers began avoiding him after he beat Brockton's great white hope. He had only had one fight in almost five months by the time he met Hafey, a considerable slowdown on the pre-Corkum average of a fight every four weeks.

The Hafey fight was held in Halifax just before St. Patrick's Day and, even though it went the distance, Seán was awarded a majority verdict for his first ever ten-rounder, with the newspapers reporting afterwards that Hafey "blocked more punches with his face than his gloves."

Seán flew back to Boston with his two brothers, Paddy and Tommy, a happy man after taking his share of the $1500 purse. He had found the training tough, but it was beginning to pay dividends. Once again, it was time to celebrate, and he and his friends decided to make a weekend of it in honor of the patron saint of Ireland.

Sunday night, March 16, Seán and a bunch of his friends were drinking in the Centre Bar in Dorchester. A squat, low building on the corner of Centre Street and Dorchester Avenue, the Centre Bar had a foreboding look about it. Painted black on the outside and with bars on the windows, the only exterior hint of it being an Irish pub was the provincial coats of arms painted on the walls.

Seán recalled sitting at a messy, rowdy table. Men, women, American, Irish, English speakers, Irish speakers. Industrial laughs and industrial language. An old man from Roscommon, whose daughter was sitting by Seán, sat at the counter, listening. He had had enough.

"Watch your language, girleen," he said down to his daughter, reprimanding her in front of her friends.

One of the Americans at the table jumped up and tried to hit the elderly Irishman. Mannion, distanced from the melee by where he was sitting, let off a punch across the table in an attempt to defend the old man. He hit the American. Glasses fell and peace shattered. The American guy's friends turned on Seán. Fists flew. A table united in banter and laughter quickly divided itself into two camps: Irish vs. American. When staff tried to get Seán to leave the bar, he was in little mood to cooperate. Like a clichéd Irish celebration of St. Patrick's Day, punches flew, skulls cracked, and blood spilled. In the end, Mannion was thrown out. Furious, he sat down on a low wall opposite the pub, blood pulsating through his veins, rage enveloping his senses like a dark shroud. When the police arrived shortly afterward, a young woman from the Centre Bar pointed across the road.

"That's him over there."

The police ran toward him, but the man from Ros Muc was too angry to walk away quietly. Seán punched and dropped the first cop to make it as far as him. Unsurprisingly, the fallen man's colleagues didn't take kindly to this. They jumped on Mannion, batons raining down through the darkness of night, seven policemen punching and kicking and hitting the man described by *Ring Magazine* as "an easy-going and gentle type outside the ring."

But there was nothing easygoing about Seán Mannion that night. He kept throwing punches, tearing the shirt off a policeman in the process. He was pulled down to the ground but managed to get back up. One of the cops dragged his hand across Mannion's mouth in an attempt to pull him back down again. Mannion bit his hand. The cop screamed. The batons descended again. He was soon back on the pavement.

Seán was given a brutal beating, his shirt torn off, a gaping wound in his head, and with worse to come. In the paddy wagon back to the police station on Gibson Street, one of the policemen stayed on his knees in front of a handcuffed Mannion for the entire journey, punching him in the stomach.

When they arrived at the station, the duty officer noticed that one of the policemen was bleeding, his hand cut.

"What happened to you?" he asked.

"This fuckin' Irish pig did it," he replied, rubbing his bloody hand in Seán's face.

Seán looked at him, angrier than he had ever been in a boxing ring.

"You'll pay for that when these cuffs come off," he told the cop.

He wasn't joking. When the handcuffs were eventually removed, he punched the officer right there and then. He knew that his window of opportunity would be small, so he let off as many punches as he could in a quick-fire staccato attack. It seemed like every cop in Station 11 jumped in to stop him. Batons, fists, feet. Seán Mannion was badly beaten by the time the duty officer managed to stop the mini-riot. He was thrown into a cell for the night.

The following morning, Briocán came down to Gibson Street to have his brother released on bail. Seán was so badly hurt that he could barely walk out of the station. He had been charged with seven offenses: drunk and disorderly, assaulting a police officer, resisting arrest, damaging police property . . . the list was long and the implications grave. There was a significant chance that Seán would get prison time. Worse still from his perspective, there was a stronger chance that his boxing license would be revoked.

Mannion spent the next few months in and out of court, his case being adjourned on each visit. Finally, it was decided that his case would be heard in four weeks. Seán closed his eyes when he heard the date. There would be no more dancing around the seven charges. This was it. His dreams held ransom by a night of madness.

On his way out of court that day, remembers Seán, he heard someone call him.

"Hey, you're Seán Mannion, right? What are you doing here?"

Mannion explained the situation. The stranger paused for a moment.

"Do you know the names of these cops?"

"It's right here," Seán answered, handing him the charge sheet.

"Mind if I write them down?"

The man took the sheet, jotted down the information, said his goodbyes and left.

A month later, Mannion was in court again, his boxing future in the hands of the legal system. The judge sat down. The charge was read out. One charge. One charge?

"A mistake," muttered Seán to himself.

But it was no mistake. Seán Mannion faced only the one charge. The least serious of all seven charges. Drunk and disorderly. The other charges had been thrown out. "Continuance without a finding," said the judge. Even that single drunk and disorderly charge had been laid to one side as long as Seán managed to stay out of trouble over the coming year.

Seán Mannion walked out of court an unburdened but puzzled man. No prison. No boxing license revoked. Unburdened, puzzled, and ecstatic. He could only guess that the stranger he had met four weeks earlier had something to do with it. Two months later, he met the same man again. He introduced himself to Seán this time. Italian, he said. A huge boxing fan. A huge Mannion man, he said. Mafioso, Seán found out later. Mafioso and one of the most senior figures in the New England trade union scene.

Shortly afterward, Seán was told that one of the seven police officers involved in arresting him that night was furious at the decision to throw out six of the seven charges. When he threatened not to cooperate with the decision, he was allegedly transferred out of Station 11 in Dorchester to another district in adjacent Roxbury.

One would have assumed after his stroke of good luck in the courts that Seán Mannion would have learned his lesson forever. One would have been wrong.

~

A stream of sunshine forced its way through smoke-stained glass, through metal bars, illuminating particles of dust dancing in the heavy air, falling, pouring, onto a table of drink.

Seán Mannion and his youngest brother, Colm, were spending a Saturday evening drinking in Dorchester with a friend of Colm's from home. The pub door opened, flooding the bar with an uncomfortable reminder of the sunny day outside. Another Connemara man, Michael [not his real name], who happened to be going out with Colm's drinking buddy's sister, walked in. Colm's friend, no fan of his sister's new love interest, flared up immediately, trying to provoke Colm into teaming up with him and teaching the new arrival a lesson. Seán sighed, turned to him, and told him to shut up. But it was too late. The threat had been made, and the threat had been heard on the other side of the room.

Michael, who had come in to meet his own sisters, picked up a bottle from the counter and threw it at the three sitting in the corner. The bottle smashed on the table, right between Seán and Colm, covering them with fragments of glass. Seán stood up. The bottle thrower ambled over, smiling, hand in pocket and a reputation for carrying a knife preceding him.

"I hit him and I got lucky," said Seán, "knocking him out with the first punch. He fell back into one of the seats, his hand still in his pocket. 'I'm going to get done now one way or another,' I said to myself so I hit him another good few punches."

Michael's two sisters came running over, screaming at Seán, trying to stand between him and their brother.

"If you're going to hit our brother, you're going to have to hit us."

"I'm not fucking hitting you," said Seán when he noticed Michael getting up, hand still in pocket. He threw another punch. Someone shouted that it was time to leave before the police arrived. On his way out the door, he noticed the Connemara man stirring again. One more punch for good measure.

The following day, Seán Mannion was served with a court summons. Court day arrived. Deja vu. He walked into Dorchester District Court alone. In front of him was a mass gathering of the plaintiff's family. The charge was read out. The court was informed that Michael had received 59 stitches as a result of Seán's punches. Giving evidence, Michael's sister said that Seán had threatened her children in a South Boston gym.

Seán jumped out of his chair.

"I've never even seen your kids," he shouted at her.

The judge told him to be quiet. Seán didn't hear a thing. The yelling continued between the woman on the stand and the defendant, both trying to shout the other down. Seán was thrown out of the courtroom. The case was adjourned.

Mannion heard later that the woman's children had been among a group of young kids looking for autographs at his gym a few days earlier. When they came home with Seán Mannion signatures, their mother tore up the slips of signed paper and threw them in the fire.

The case dragged on over six months. Allegations and denials. Testimony was given that Seán used a bottle, along with his fists, to inflict damage. He insisted that he had used only his hands. Two men from the west coast of Ireland, born and raised across the bay from each other, going toe to toe in a Boston courthouse. With Seán's pro boxing license once again in jeopardy, some of Michael's friends pushed him to withdraw the charge. Finally, he conceded.

The hearing was about to start when Michael stood up, Seán remembers.

"Your Honor, I want to drop the charges."

Judge Paul H. King looked at him, his face red with rage at what he had just heard.

"What did you say?"

"Your Honor, I said, I want to drop the charges."

"Do you realize that you have wasted the court's time and the Commonwealth's time?"

"That's right, your Honor," Michael answered.

The court room descended into laughter. Everyone but the judge. He looked at Seán. He despised him. There was a history between Seán Mannion and Judge Paul H. King. Mannion had been dating King's grandniece, and the judge didn't consider the boxer an appropriate date. But even without a history, it's unlikely that King would have looked favorably on the Irishman.

Judge King wasn't a particularly patient or compassionate dispenser of justice. "What did you do to make him hit you?" he asked a woman who had been a victim of domestic abuse. "Maybe if you tried running around the block a few times a day, you wouldn't have time to write bad checks," he told an overweight man who had the misfortune to come in front of him. "Who's that bimbo?" he remarked about another woman. "No wonder we lost the war," he said as he dismissed a Vietnam veteran.

In the end, the State Supreme Court had heard enough of Paul H. King and his undiplomatic ways, and he was removed from his post as Dorchester District Court judge. But despite the fact that he had been accused of setting extra-high bail for black defendants, of urinating in public, and of driving while under the influence of drink, he wasn't removed entirely from public office. King finished out his career in the Boston suburb of Stoughton, dealing with civil cases.

On that particular day, however, he lost his shot at Seán Mannion, and Mannion knew that he was a lucky man. When they left the courthouse, Seán and Michael Newell celebrated by stopping into every bar on Dorchester Avenue. When they came as far as the Blarney Stone, they headed in for a bite to eat. Who would walk in but the man who had just asked King to throw out the case.

"Seán, give me a bite of that steak," he shouted over.

"Take care of yourself, you bastard, unless you want another 59 stitches," was Mannion's answer.

They both laughed. Michael made his way to the counter and ordered a drink. Seán kept his eye on the knife pocket.

~

Sometimes, Seán Mannion doesn't want to see that he has a drink problem. But he can see it alright. He will deny it sometimes. He will admit it sometimes. But the clarity can be painful.

"I'm so happy when I'm not drinking because it's lovely to be at home and not be hungover or anything like that. Not wanting to go out for another drink, looking for the cure. I know years ago I could give up the drink for three months, and when the three months were up, I'd be back on it again. But when it gets a hold on you, it's different.

"People who don't have a problem with drink don't understand how difficult it is, it's like a disease. Sometimes, something could be bothering you and you'll think of having a couple of pints. 'I'll only have two,' I'll say, but the first one's the worst, that's the one that kills you. You'll always wake up the next day worse than the day before.

"I'd say I have problems when it comes to drink. There are a lot of people who won't admit that they have a problem but I'm saying that I do and I can't speak for anyone else."

Seán's sister, Ann, has tried to help him with his alcoholism for years, witnessing how his difficulties in dealing with his world title loss, and with the loss of family members, has trapped him in a cycle of being on and off the drink.

"He'll tell you that he's able to do it himself," said Ann. "I tell him he should dry out or go to the AA but he doesn't believe in it. He went to an AA meeting at home a long time ago and he was a long time sober. And then when he's not drinking and he thinks of all those things, he feels like he needs another drink.

'That drink will do me no harm, I'll just have the one.' But that's the disease, in your head again.

"He has admitted to me a couple of times that he's an alcoholic. And he tried, here [Boston] and at home, to sober up. And he did for a while but something always happens that drives him back to the drink.

"Drink is an awful sickness. At least if you had another illness, you could cure it. But the drink is something that affects the whole family."

~

Seán Mannion had five big fights outside of the ring, according to himself, and alcohol played a part in most of them. But his drinking had a greater impact on his fights in the ring than those outside. He didn't drink while training (not until after the world title fight, he insists), but if he didn't, it's reasonable to assume that the beer drinking didn't help once he'd return to the gym after the long sessions.

Unsurprisingly, his manager used to get particularly worked up about his fighter's drinking.

"If I find the next guy who buys Seán Mannion a drink, I'm going to shoot him," Jimmy Connolly said to Seán's friend, John Grealish, in the gym one night, opening his jacket and showing Grealish the handgun he was carrying.

"You might as well shoot me so," Grealish answered.

Seán came into the gym the following day after hearing about the conversation. He strode over to Connolly.

"Fuck you Jimmy," he said. "Now I'm going to have to buy my own beer."

Whenever Connolly had set up a fight for Seán, his first port of call would be the Blarney Stone. Usually, that's where he would find his fighter.

"Seán, you have a fight in two weeks, you gotta get into shape."

And Seán would return to the gym. And Seán would ensure that he was fit. And more often than not, Seán would win the fight.

"I've never seen another human being in the gym that could get into condition as fast as he could," said the former Boston boxer and trainer, Jimmy Farrell, in a television interview with TG4. "He could get in condition, he'd come in looking a little rough, and he could get in better shape in two weeks than anybody."

That didn't matter much to Jimmy Connolly, who didn't hold back on his assessment, regardless of whether Mannion was drinking or not. "Seán's a washed-up alco," Seán's sparring partners recalled him saying, "he's always drunk." The story got around and pretty soon, there were references about his drinking in the Boston media.

"At the Horseshoe Tavern, Mannion plays darts with his friends. He has established a new code of sociability.

"'If you want to be my friend,' Mannion tells them, 'don't buy me a beer.'"

That's how the *Boston Globe* finished "He's All Irish—Except For the Nickname," an article about Seán preparing for a big fight in 1982. Deserved or not, he now had the reputation of being a boozy Irish boxer. Looking back at his boxing career, it's difficult not to wonder if things would have turned out different if he hadn't been drinking.

"I don't know about that," said Tony Cardinale. "Sure, there were times when I wished he trained harder but the nights he put his mind to it, this guy was a life taker.

"Either way, I don't think it would've turned out much different. It's always the same, win the world title and nobody cares what you do outside the ring. Lose your one shot at being world champion and everything you ever did is examined."

9

EL NINO

There was nothing angelic about Ruby "The Angel" Ortiz.

Ortiz was an up-and-coming boxer, born among the mangrove forests of Salinas, Puerto Rico, before moving to New York where he lived with his girlfriend, Miriam Quiles. Unusually, Ortiz had two boxing nicknames. He was also known as Ruby "The Snake."

Shortly after 11:00 p.m. on a warm Brooklyn night in June 1977, "The Snake" shot Miriam Quiles once in the head, killing her instantly. Three of Miriam's four children, aged between 10 and 15, were in the apartment at the time.

Ruby Ortiz called the police and sat in the apartment waiting for them, his girlfriend dead on the floor, the gun flung across the room. Miriam Quiles was 30 years old, Ortiz was 22. He later said that he had tried to shoot himself afterward but that the gun had jammed.

But by April 1980, Ortiz was back in the ring, fighting Seán Mannion in New York's Madison Square Garden complex, having been acquitted on technical grounds.

Mannion had just had his own problems with the law coming into the Ortiz fight, with a court case hanging over him after beating up seven policemen three weeks earlier. As a result, Seán was struggling to make weight from the moment the fight was set. The beating he had received from the Dorchester cops on St. Patrick's Day weekend forced him to put his training on hold, and he was ten pounds over the set limit coming into the welterweight fight.

In a desperate effort to shift the pounds, Mannion headed down to New York a week ahead of time. He set up camp in Gleason's, New York's most storied boxing gym, where his sparring partner was a young boxer called Tony Danza.

Danza, who had just gotten a role in a new TV comedy series called *Taxi*, struck up a friendship with Mannion, sitting ringside with Seán's sisters for the 1984 world title fight and later inviting Seán onto the set of *Who's the Boss* where Danza, the sitcom's star, introduced Mannion to the audience.

But the last-minute training couldn't save Mannion from "The Snake." At the end of 10 tough rounds, the referee lifted Ruby Ortiz's arm in the air after a split decision, much to the fury of the Irishman. To this day, he finds it difficult to accept the decision, despite claiming that he felt weak going into the ring after losing 10 pounds in 10 days.

"He didn't beat me but he got the decision," said Mannion. "It was difficult to get a decision against a Puerto Rican in New York at that time."

This was the first time that Seán had, in his own view, unjustly lost a fight. Looking back through his record, he reckons that there were 5 suspect verdicts in his career of 57 pro fights. He was a beneficiary of one of those decisions, taking a win he felt he didn't deserve against Robert "Boo Boo" Sawyer of Washington, D.C., and losing four he should have won.

At this stage of his pro boxing career, most of Seán's fights had taken place outside of Boston. There were two downsides to this. First, it meant that Mannion was usually fighting in his opponent's hometown, with the accompanying danger of hometown crowds influencing hometown decisions. It also meant that Seán had a pretty difficult time creating the momentum and growth needed to build a fan base. Incredibly, it would be another six years after the 1979 Jimmy Corkum fight before Seán Mannion would again fight in Boston.

Much of the problem came down to his manager falling out with the high princes of Boston boxing, Goody and Pat Petronelli. Without the Petronellis on your side, trying to find good fights in Massachusetts was a waste of time.

The fallout had come from seemingly nowhere.

"We're not going down to those bloody Italians anymore," Jimmy Connolly said to Seán one day.

And that was that.

Not only did the sudden dispute between the two boxing camps leave Seán without hometown fights, it meant that he no longer had access to sparring sessions against some of the best boxers in the world, despite them being on his very doorstep. Seán had just spent two years sparring with Marvin Hagler, Robbie Sims, and Tony Petronelli and now, all of a sudden, Connolly had decreed that they wouldn't be driving down to Brockton anymore.

"The Petronellis don't want Connolly fighters on cards with their fighters," said Connolly in an interview with the *Boston Globe* in June 1983. "I don't know why. I've never figured it out. I always gave them sparring partners and cooperated with them in any way."

To make matters worse, the *Boston Globe* reported shortly afterward that Connolly had also fallen out with New England's biggest boxing promoter, Rip Valenti, after Valenti failed to find a place for Mannion on the Marvin Hagler–Tony Sibson world title card. When Connolly complained to Top Rank's matchmaker, Teddy Brenner, Brenner approached Valenti.

"I told him that Connolly could shove it," the *Boston Globe* reported a furious Valenti as having said in an article titled "Mannion's Big Chance," adding that "Valenti's comment on the Connolly-Petronelli relationship: 'Around here, everybody is jealous of everybody else's fighters.'"

The dispute between the Petronellis and Connolly also meant that Mannion couldn't even get fights on his own Dorchester doorstep, as his manager had also fallen out with the local Freeport Hall promoter, Jimmy Farrell, according to the *Boston Globe* article.

"We had a falling out over fighters," said Farrell. "He wouldn't let me use his fighters on my cards if Petronelli fighters were on the card."

The Farrell-Connolly relationship had already been soured by Connolly failing to live up to his promise to provide him with a fighter for a Freeport Hall card. In the end, Farrell filled the gap on the night with a boxer plucked from the spectators, who then went on to win his fight!

With Massachusetts now a boxing wasteland for Mannion, Connolly had to look further afield for fights, forcing him to strike up a relationship with New Jersey–based Lou Duva.

One of the legends of modern boxing, Duva was a wisecracking, business-smart trainer and manager to heavyweight champions such as Evander Holyfield, Michael Moorer, and Lennox Lewis. Infamous for doing whatever it took to protect his boxers during fights, or for telling referees exactly what he thought of their decisions, Lou Duva was a small man who had little compunction about running into the ring to throw a punch at a boxer twice his size. His swearing was so bad at times that TV broadcasters would turn off the microphone when showing Duva in the corner between rounds.

"I'm cursing only in Italian now," he told *Sports Illustrated* after that decision in 1989.

He once described an overweight George Foreman, who had been labeled as fit as a fiddle coming into a world championship bout against Holyfield, as looking more like a cello than a fiddle.

But there was more to Lou Duva than cheap laughs and bad language. Duva was also a fight promoter, and he and his son, Dan, had set up Main Events, a boxing promotion company seeking to take on the two giants of U.S. boxing, Bob Arum and Don King.

In 1977, Lou and Dan started using Ice World, a skating rink in Totowa, New Jersey, as a venue for Main Events fights. Things started off small, organizing bouts between local boxers, but it all changed with the emergence of a new TV sports channel, ESPN, in 1979. ESPN needed something to show, and Lou Duva was given a month's contract to organize fights that would draw a TV audience.

The month went well, the contract was extended and, by August the following year, Seán Mannion was on his way to New Jersey for the inaugural ESPN American Boxing Championships, his first-ever fight on live television and his first shot at a pro title. Mannion met Steve Snow in the semifinal bout, and knocked his opponent out in the fifth round.

The Irishman was up against Tony Suero in the final, another young pro who'd had a bright start to his career. Seven fights, six wins, and one draw. Mannion gave Suero a pounding over seven rounds of intense fighting, but with Seán seemingly ahead on points, Suero caught him with his head in the eighth and final round.

Seán's forehead split open, blood gushing. The fight was stopped so that a doctor could have a look at the cut, but it didn't need much of an examination. It was obvious to everyone in the Totowa Ice World, along with the ESPN viewers at home, that the fight was over. It was obvious to Seán as well, blood coursing down over his eyes, furious at what had happened and skeptical of how accidental the head clash with Suero had been.

There was no questioning Seán's bad luck. The Associated Press reported on September 18, 1980, that "Tony Suero, 20, of Vineland, survived a heavy beating," having "delivered a deep cut above Mannion's right eye in the eighth round. Mannion, a 147-pound native of Ireland, continued to fight after the blow, but blood was streaming down his face so rapidly, he was forced to quit."

The red blood had left another black mark on Mannion's record: his third loss in 18 fights, his second in five months. His first shot at a title, on live TV, but the Suero butt had put an end to that. The following day, Mannion traveled to Chicago to attend a friend's wedding, annoyed that he didn't have an ESPN belt to show off, but 11 stitches to his forehead.

That was September 1980. The cut to his head meant that it would be January 1981 before Seán would fight again, a long run-in to Christmas for Mannion that saw few visits to the gym. By his next fight, against Ralph Doucette, he had gained over 10 pounds, necessitating a switch from welterweight to light middleweight.

Idleness was Seán's enemy. With no fights scheduled, he had fallen out of the rhythm and rigor of boxing, and into the rhythm of the pub. The Twelve Bens. The Blarney Stone. The Emerald Isle. Friends, family, socializing with the same people all the time. And while Seán Mannion drank bottles of Budweiser through the winter of 1981, the likes of Marvin Hagler invited only isolation to his training camp in nearby Cape Cod. No people, no temptation, only focused training. Not the kind of environment that Seán would have enjoyed.

Peter Kerr, a Scotsman married to a Ros Muc woman, had come into Mannion's corner by this stage, but his most important role was taking care of Seán outside of the ring, saving him from himself and from others.

"It was my job to get him to bed at night and to get him up in the morning but the biggest problem with Seán was trying to keep people from him," said Kerr. "Nobody worked harder once he got himself into the gym, he was always focused on making the weight once he was in the gym, but he could really blow himself out of shape in between fights.

"When he had a local fight, you could sell 600 tickets, but all 600 wanted to go on the piss with him afterwards."

Mannion vs. Doucette was one of seven fights on the card in the St. Stanislaus Hall in Nashua, New Hampshire, on January 10, 1981, but things weren't going very well for the promoter, Ralph "Ace" Duresky. Every fight seemed to be finishing early, and it looked like the punters were in for a short night's entertainment. There had only been two bouts that hadn't finished in a KO, and all the other fights had finished in either the second or third round. Duresky approached Mannion just as he was making his way into the ring.

"Hey Seán," Mannion recalls him saying, "if you got the beating of this guy, will you carry him along for a while? People are starting to feel shortchanged here, and I'm getting a lot of hassle."

Seán thought about it. Doucette's record suggested that he wouldn't pose much of a problem, but there was always a risk. A whole busload of Mannion supporters had traveled up from Boston to New Hampshire, and he wanted to ensure that they had cause for celebration on the journey home. Still, though, he couldn't help but oblige the promoter.

The first round started off well. Mannion had a read on his opponent within the first minute, and he pulled back a bit in his fighting. But by the time the round was coming to a close, Doucette had started to give off a few crisp punches. The bell went. Seán trudged back to his corner.

"Fuck this," he muttered to himself.

The official fight record has the contest finishing in three rounds. It didn't. Seán went out at the start of the second round having changed his mind about what he had promised Duresky.

"He [Doucette] was coming toward me when I caught him with a right hook," recalled Mannion. "Clean out. He was out for at least five minutes. I think that he was probably the only person I ever knocked clean out like that."

An easy win. Easy money. Even so, there was still no sight of the jackpot. Seán received $500 for the night, a little over half that when it had been shared out. His faith in his manager was rapidly eroding.

"When is the big fight coming, Jimmy?" Seán would ask him in training.

"Soon, Seán, soon."

Always the same answer.

The venues started getting bigger, certainly, but the purses didn't increase much. A fortnight after beating Doucette, Seán had his first fight in Atlantic City, the east coast boxing headquarters of the time. Vegas-on-Sea. Seán Mannion vs. Robert Sawyer in the Playboy Hotel and Casino. One of Sugar Ray Leonard's regular sparring partners, Sawyer came out of the corner and hit Mannion with two clean punches to the nose. That set the tone for the rest of the fight, with Seán constantly on the back foot. By the time the eight rounds were up, Mannion had two black eyes and a strong inkling that he had lost the bout. He hadn't. He was awarded a split-decision win, but even after looking back at the fight on TV, Seán reckoned that it had finished level, at best. This was the first time he had ever gotten such a decision.

His relief didn't make the long journey back to Boston any shorter, however. Six hours down to New Jersey in the car with Jimmy and Billy Connolly, six hours home. Boxing promoters paid for flights as part of the deal, but Connolly preferred to drive. A waste of time, thought Seán to himself, stewing in the passenger seat. The tension between the two ratcheting up by the day.

Mannion had one more fight organized by Jimmy Connolly before he finally lost his patience. Hector "Papo" Figueroa, a tough Puerto Rican who would win the New England welterweight championship in his next fight, went the distance in a 10-round fight against Mannion. A reasonably straightforward win, Seán presumed, once the fight finished. A draw, decreed the judges.

He would be given a second shot at Figueroa, but at the time, Mannion was beginning to tire of boxing. Silly decisions going against him. A manager who wasn't getting him decent fights. Twenty-two pro bouts with the biggest purse only coming to $1500. It was time for change. Seán picked up the phone and called Jimmy Connolly.

CHAPTER 9

"Jimmy, I'm sorry but I'm not getting enough fights, and I'm not getting enough money."

He hung up, and then called another number. Lou Duva.

Seán recalls that Duva offered him a fight straight away, eight rounds against Tony Braxton in Ice World, Totowa, on January 21, 1982.

"How much are you looking for the fight, Seán?"

"Two thousand dollars," Seán muttered hesitantly. There was silence for a moment.

"Ok, Seán, no problem. But I gotta little extra proposition for you. If you come down here now as sparring partner for Bobby Czyz for the next few weeks, I'll pay your flight, lodgings, and food."

Seán almost cried with delight when he put down the phone.

Bobby Czyz was an atypical boxer. A member of Mensa, a student of Nietzsche, and an atheist, Czyz didn't fulfill the usual boxing clichés. But a boxer he was, and an incredibly successful boxer at that, winning world titles at two different weights. He was, according to Evander Holyfield, the strongest man he ever fought.

Seán Mannion and a friend of his from Ros Muc, Noel O'Donnell, headed down to New Jersey to help Czyz prepare for his fight against Marvin Hagler's stepbrother, Robbie Sims. Mannion and O'Donnell shared a room in a Holiday Inn next door to Ice World, with $40 a day to spend on food. As the day went by, the room began to shrink. O'Donnell would stretch back on the bed, smoking a cigarette, looking over at Seán about to tuck into his room service steak dinner.

"Don't eat those, Seán, they're not good for you," Mannion recalls him saying.

Seán would leave the fries to one side. O'Donnell would eat them.

"Go out for a run, Seán, like a good man."

"Fuck off, Noel, why don't you go for a run yourself?"

A mixture of humor and irritation, broken up by the tough sessions with Czyz.

In one of their sparring sessions, Seán knocked Bobby Czyz to the floor.

Lou Duva shook his head.

"Jesus, he's not going to like that," he said to O'Donnell, Czyz lying on the ground, furious that a lighter man had put him on the canvas.

"Maybe not," O'Donnell replied, "but there's fuck all he can do about it now."

After three intense weeks in Totowa, Seán Mannion was ready for Tony Braxton, and Bobby Czyz was ready for Robbie Sims. Five days before the fight,

Seán headed back up to Boston for the weekend. He had just gotten in the door when the phone rang. Lou Duva.

"Seán, I got a problem. My main event on Thursday night has fallen through, the guy I had to fight Nino Gonzalez is injured. Will you do me a favor, will you fight Gonzalez?"

"All right," said Seán, reluctant as ever to refuse anyone, "but the money has to go up if it's a main event and it's a ten rounder."

"How much?"

"Another thousand."

Sourcing his own fights, Mannion had just secured $3,000, the biggest sum he had ever gotten for a bout, and double his previous max. He still had a management contract with Jimmy Connolly, and Connolly would get his own cut of the money. But it was an eye-opener for Seán in terms of the opportunities out there, in terms of earnings and fights.

It wouldn't be an easy $3,000, however. When Mannion vs. Gonzalez was announced, Nino was the clear favorite, and with good reason. Two fights prior to the Mannion fight, Nino Gonzalez had fought Roberto Duran. This was Duran's first fight after the infamous "No más" incident against Sugar Ray Leonard where he quit mid-fight for no apparent reason. But the Panamanian legend wasn't lacking in confidence as he prepared to get back into the ring.

"He's a good fighter," Roberto Duran told Michael Katz of the *New York Times* in a preview piece on July 7, 1981, "but he's going to die like a duck."

It seemed Katz was of a similar view.

"There is little suspense here as to the outcome," he wrote in a piece for the *New York Times* titled "Duran Back, but Is He Ready?" "Duran should win, but winning will not be enough."

Duran was under pressure, not just to beat Gonzalez, but to beat him convincingly, given the whispers that followed him after unexpectedly quitting the Leonard fight. Among the things Duran was accused of after that fight was fear. It was fear that led him to quitting, that led him to throwing in the towel despite the fact that he hadn't even been hurt. Fear? Roberto Duran? The man who, as a 14-year-old in Panama, reportedly knocked out a horse with a single punch? The man who had won 30 fights in a row, 19 of them KOs, by the time he won his first world title in 1972? The greatest lightweight of all time, according to *Ring Magazine* and the Associated Press? Fear seemed an unlikely explanation.

Whatever the reason for his infamous "no más" ("no more" in Spanish) utterance, the fight against Nino Gonzalez was his first opportunity to show that all was fine with Roberto Duran, that he was as devastating and brutal in the ring as ever, and that there was no question of fear. Duran's comeback fight was held in Cleveland, Ohio, and predictably, he won. But there certainly wasn't anything devastating or brutal about the win. He was given the decision after 10 rounds, but it was far from convincing.

"A gift, not a decision," derided the local newspaper, the *Plain Dealer*, in a report the following day.

"Never mind the decision, look at the movies," Gonzalez's trainer, Billy Annese, told Michael Katz of the *New York Times* in his fight report. "Nino landed six times as many punches."

"I really, really thought I won the fight," Gonzalez himself told Katz.

He lost, but it didn't matter much. Roberto Duran was back, and Nino Gonzalez was now ranked the world's seventh best boxer in his division. Provided he won his next two fights, Gonzalez would face the winner of Wilfred Benitez vs. Roberto Duran for a shot at the WBC light middleweight title.

Gonzalez would take on Seán Mannion in the second of those two fights after what seemed like a straightforward win against John Symonette from Florida. But what can appear to be straightforward in real life can be as murky as the bog lakes of Ros Muc when it comes to boxing, and the fight Gonzalez had with the man who called himself John Symonette was one of those opaque tales that only boxing could conjure.

When Nino Gonzalez needed a credible but beatable opponent after the Roberto Duran fight, his promoter reached out to a Florida-based trainer called Georgie "Tiger" Small. Small had a reputation for coming up with good fighters, and offered up John Symonette.

"He told me John Symonette was a two-time Golden Gloves champ, the Nassau junior middleweight champ, the Florida junior middleweight champ," said Nino's promoter, Nelson Fernandez, in an extensive piece in the *Miami News* in November 1981. "He said I wouldn't find him in the record books, though, because most of his fights had been in the Caribbean. He told me he'd give Nino a hell of a fight. We agreed on a purse of $800, plus expenses and airfare."

But Nino Gonzalez would never fight John Symonette. Instead, Georgie Small offered the fight to a 19-year-old nobody called Tony Torres, who had never won a fight in his life. Torres accepted Small's offer of $500, but on the flight to New Jersey, Small told him that he would have to pretend he was someone else. Someone called John Symonette. Small didn't tell him why.

"I didn't know what was happening, but I needed the money," the *Miami News* reported Torres as saying. "I figured I had to go through with it if I wanted to get my plane ticket to get back home."

"The night of the fight, I wore my brother Johnny's old robe," said Torres. "I had to tape over the Torres part so you couldn't see it. I got in the ring first. I wasn't too nervous. I figured I was fighting a guy just like me. I stood there and waited for my opponent and suddenly the lights went dim.

"The theme music from *Rocky* started playing from the loudspeakers and the spotlights started shining back to the dressing room door. Cable television was there. I started wondering. The crowd started moving around and some started chanting, 'Nino . . . Nino . . . Nino.'

"I watched this guy comin' to the ring and that's when the announcer started in, 'Ladies and gentlemen, the seventh ranked junior middleweight in the world, Nino Gonzalez.'

"Well, I started to feel sick. I said 'oh, oh, I'm in big trouble this time.' I knew Nino Gonzalez. I watched him give Roberto Duran a tough fight a couple of months ago on TV. They said he had lost only twice in 26 fights. A lot of fear suddenly came in me. I was nervous. If I woulda' known it was gonna be Nino, I never would have gone up there."

Sitting ringside was Bob Lee, president of the U.S. Boxing Commission. He figured out pretty quickly that things weren't quite right, as the *Miami News* reported.

"It was clear to me the minute he saw Nino he was petrified. I can see why. Nino's a big favorite up here and when he came into the place with music, the whole crowd cheered. It must have seemed like it was 1,000 people against one at about then. When the bell rang it was tip-toe through the tulips for the Symonette kid. I don't think he ever got offensive.

"I yelled at Georgie Small and told him if the kid didn't fight, he was not going to get paid. Nino gave him a love tap in the ribs and the kid collapsed. George was standing on the stool, yelling for the kid to get up. He did and managed to swing a couple of times, Nino hit him a few more times, then once on the shoulder and that was it. The kid went down again. We stopped the fight. Nino never hit him like he could."

Torres thought that his jaw was broken during the fight, but Georgie Small wasn't hanging around any hospital in case the boxing commission wanted to catch up with him. He put Torres on a flight back to Fort Lauderdale, but didn't give him any money for the journey. Torres bought a bag of chips with his one remaining dollar and thumbed a lift from the airport to his home in Homestead, Florida. It was midnight by the time he got home, tired, hungry, and still dizzy from the three strangest days of his life.

~

Unsurprisingly, Gonzalez severed his ties with Nelson Fernandez after the Torres fight, and went back to Lou Duva for his next bout against Seán Mannion. The one fight that stood between him and a shot at the world title.

The reception Gonzalez received from the crowd in the Ice World auditorium that night was incredible. Little surprise. Gonzalez was fighting in his home state. Gonzalez was the hero from TV, who had gone 10 rounds with Roberto Duran. Gonzalez was ranked number seven in the world. The fight notes that night predicted that Nino would stop Seán by the seventh round. It wasn't a reflection of how poor Mannion was, noted the program writer, but of how good Gonzalez was.

Waiting for his brother, Paddy, in the dressing room, Seán was wearing a new pair of boxing shorts. Galway maroon in color, Ros Muc written on the left leg.

"Where the fuck were you until now?" he roared when Paddy sauntered in shortly before fight time. Like many brothers, they didn't always get on.

Paddy had gotten stuck in snow and traffic on his way down from Boston, and he was in a hurry to get out of the dressing room, having come in to pick up tickets for friends of the Mannions. Still furious, Seán kicked a chair across the room as Paddy walked out.

By the time Paddy returned, his brother was lying on a couch in the corner of the room, his ankle in pain from his cantankerous kick. He could barely stand up.

"If it's that bad," said Paddy, "maybe we should just postpone the fight."

"I've come this far," said Seán, "we might as well go a few rounds and get some money for it."

The tightly bound laces on Seán's boxing boots managed to keep the swelling down, but he was in agony as he walked out to the ring. The Connemara supporters cheering their man didn't notice the limp. Sitting in the crowd, Seán's friend, Máirtín Conroy, clung to a rosary, knuckles white, beads bedded in his palm, anticipation and anxiety as Mannion took on one of the world's great up-and-coming boxers.

"This is the first time I've seen an Irishman wearing red," said the ESPN commentator when he saw Seán's maroon shorts. That was enough to ensure that Mannion would never wear them again. Too much talk as he grew up in Ros Muc of British redcoats in Ireland to want to be associated with that particular color. Green shorts only from then on.

Seán hauled himself into his corner, not being able to put weight on his right leg. In the ring, he lay back on the ropes, giving his ankle some respite, waiting for Gonzalez.

Mannion was informed by the same indicators that poor Tony Torres had picked up on—that Nino had left the dressing room. The *Rocky* music pumped up. The crowd went crazy.

"Come on, Nino," said someone sitting beside Máirtín Conroy.

"Shut the fuck up," retorted Conroy, rosary still in hand, oblivious to being in Gonzalez's home state arena.

The bell went. The ankle was forgotten. If Nino Gonzalez thought that it would be plain sailing with favorable winds all the way to a WBC world title fight, he was about to realize that there was a storm ahead. Mannion came at him like a gale. Gonzalez struggled to give off clean punches. When he did, the crowd bayed its appreciation, but his blows had little impact on Seán that night. It didn't take the TV commentators long to pick up on the fact that Nino was in trouble.

"There's an upset in the making here, a big upset."

Left, left, right. Again. Left, left, right. Gonzalez's face began to turn red. He lifted a fist, gesturing at Mannion to come at him, taunting him.

"Seán is more than willing to oblige," noted the commentator.

And he was. Mannion accepted the invitation and by the end of the fifth round, had complete dominion over his New Jersey opponent.

As the rounds went by, Gonzalez became increasingly anxious. He couldn't make headway against Mannion, and frustration began to get the better of him. He started to punch low. Low and dirty. The bell for the end of the sixth round was clearly gone when he let off a big right, catching Mannion off guard. Mannion took it as a compliment.

"The only time he could hit was after the bell," he told the *New Jersey Herald* afterwards. "He wasn't able to hit me during the fight. No way."

By the start of the seventh round, the local fans had turned against their own man.

"Let's go, Seán," chanted the Ice World crowd. "Let's go, Seán."

"The visitor has won the hearts of Nino Gonzalez's fans," said ESPN. "Suddenly, Seán Mannion is the fan's delight and he really earned it."

When the referee announced Mannion's victory, Paddy ran into the ring, lifting his brother up into the air, both having forgotten about the sprained ankle that would leave Seán on crutches for the next six weeks. A comfortable victory on points, one judge scoring eight rounds out of ten in his favor.

Seán Mannion was back. The victory over Nino Gonzalez was big news, coast to coast, in U.S. boxing. In their fight report, "Mannion Ruins Gonzalez' Hopes for a WBC Championship Fight," the *Los Angeles Times* called it the biggest victory of Mannion's career. The *Times* reported that "the loss virtually erased Gonzalez' hopes of fighting the winner of this month's bout between World Boxing Council junior middleweight champion Wilfredo Benitez and challenger Robert Duran" and that "Mannion, 26, a native of Ireland, dominated the fight until the seventh and most dramatic round."

For the first time in his career, Seán Mannion was ranked in the world top ten. He had heard nothing from the newspapers back home in Ireland since beating Jimmy Corkum two years prior, but suddenly, the Ros Muc man was back in the news.

"Mannion Punches Way into Rankings," read the *Connacht Tribune* headline on February 2, 1982. "Is on Verge of a World Title Chance." The article reported "that odds were a lop-sided 4–1 against Mannion winning according to ringside estimates. With this win, Mannion is now ranked among the top ten world class fighters in his division and automatically becomes a contender for the Junior Middleweight Crown."

Things were rarely that simple when it came to Seán Mannion, however.

10

THE LAWYER

Tony Cardinale's office is situated in a stand-alone building on the banks of the Reserved Channel in industrial South Boston. From the lawyer's desk, you can see the copper spire of the Gate of Heaven as it looks down on its Southie congregation from the top of Telegraph Hill.

Tony Cardinale, well known not just in South Boston but throughout the United States, is no ordinary lawyer. It was his investigative work that revealed the biggest scandal in the history of the FBI—their role in protecting and facilitating Whitey Bulger, one of the most dangerous criminals in the United States at the time.

Cardinale is one of the best-known Mafiosi lawyers in America. John Gotti. Gennaro Angiulo. "Fat Tony" Salerno. "Cadillac Frank" Salemme. Some of the most dangerous and most powerful men in U.S. criminal life. Cardinale has defended them all.

Tony Cardinale was also Seán Mannion's lawyer.

In the early 1980s, Cardinale took on a case involving four boxers training out of Jimmy Connolly's gym in South Boston, who had been working as bouncers at a nightclub called the Rathskellar. The Rat, as it was better known, was the epicenter of the Boston rock scene, hosting the likes of REM, Aerosmith, and Metallica, and it was up to the four to keep a lid on what could often be a boisterous venue. It turned out, however, that the four boxers were pretty boisterous themselves, and Cardinale ended up defending them after they were charged with beating up an entire softball team who had refused to leave the Rat while celebrating a win.

When the case came to court, Cardinale made all four wear glasses, shirts, and cardigans. He filled the courtroom with young men from South Boston and sat the four defendants among the crowd at the back of the room. The case was thrown out after the softball players failed to pick out the four Rat bouncers.

This was how Tony Cardinale met Seán Mannion. Traipsing his way up and down the four flights of stairs to Connolly's gym in order to meet his clients, the lawyer's keen boxing eye quickly picked up on the Irishman. Cardinale may have gone on to become one of the highest profile lawyers in the United States, but he was born into boxing.

Tony Cardinale was raised in New York City, growing up among boxers and movie stars in a restaurant called Delsomma's on 47th Street. Delsomma's was owned by Frankie Cardinale, Tony's father, and by four of his uncles, with the likes of Frank Sinatra, David Mamet, and Sidney Poitier among the regular customers. But with three of the Cardinale brothers having been former pro fighters, and with Frankie still involved in training, boxing trumped the silver screen when it came to conversation in the restaurant. Rocky Graziano would drop in regularly, along with the likes of Willie Pep and Ray Arcel, the heroes of the time. In Delsomma's, if the story didn't involve 20 square feet of boxing ring, it wasn't of interest.

The Cardinale family lived nearby, on the third floor of an apartment building in the Hell's Kitchen neighborhood. Back then, Hell's Kitchen had a reputation to go with the name, with things deteriorating badly in the early 1960s. The summer after Tony finished seventh grade, the muggy, hot streets of midtown west Manhattan made for a dangerous playground, with gangs attacking each other in broad daylight.

"There were confrontations between groups of Puerto Rican kids and the kids I hung out with," remembers Cardinale.

The confrontations soon escalated. A friend of Tony's was stabbed in one incident. A few weeks later, another friend was killed. That was it for Frankie Cardinale. He had seen enough of Hell.

Frankie found a house to rent in the hills of eastern Pennsylvania and, a month later, announced to his family that he had bought a place in Totowa, New Jersey, 20 miles from Hell's Kitchen. Lou Duva was a good friend of Frankie's, and if Frankie couldn't live in the capital city of boxing, he was, at the very least, going to live next to the biggest players in the sport.

The move to suburbia came as a shock to young Tony. Verdant lawns. Towering sycamore trees. Space. After a childhood in midtown Manhattan, this was a whole other planet. He took up boxing and American football. Football won out in the end, bringing with it a sports scholarship and a shot at a law degree. It was Suffolk University Law School that brought Tony Cardinale to Boston.

Boxing disappeared in Cardinale's rearview mirror once he had settled into a life of law in Boston, until the day he received a call from a Welsh heavyweight by the name of "Irish" Jimmy Smith. There was nothing Irish about Smith, but the prefix tended to sell more fight tickets than "Welsh."

Tony knew all about Jimmy Smith. After all, he was the protégé who broke his father's heart. Years previously, Frankie Cardinale was Jimmy Smith's trainer, and Frankie protected his delicate potential with the care and focus of a parent hovering over a toddler who had just figured out walking. Cardinale spent a year training Smith before bringing him anywhere near a ring. But when he finally did, Jimmy was ready. Ten fights, ten wins and ten KOs. Managers and promoters quickly noticed the new heavyweight in their midst. When the legendary promoter, Bob Arum, inquired about Smith, Cardinale sensed that his legacy as a boxing trainer was about to be secured.

And then one day, the legacy evaporated. Tony Cardinale told the story of Jimmy Smith and his father, Frankie, walking to the gym together when Smith told him that he didn't want to train that day.

"Why not?" asked a puzzled Frankie.

"I just don't want to."

"Look Jimmy, I've just invested the last two and a half years in you. Why don't you want to go to the gym?"

"I don't want to box anymore."

Just like that. The answer hit Frankie like a punch to the liver. He looked at Smith in a mixture of disbelief and disgust. It wasn't as if Cardinale didn't understand the commitment that a life of boxing took. If anything, he knew it more than most. You could see it in his face. His nose askew, scar tissue folded around his eyes. He knew that this was a tough world, but he couldn't understand how someone would want to walk away from two years of hard work, with glory and riches on the other side of an open door. When he recovered from the shock, he asked Smith why.

"I just don't want to end up looking like you."

"Irish" Jimmy Smith walked away from boxing, his face intact, his pockets empty. Frankie Cardinale heard little again about his errant protégé except for the occasional rumor that Smith was sleeping rough. Eventually, the Welshman saw the error of his ways, but Frankie told him to hightail it when he came around looking for a way back into the ring. Smith headed north to Boston looking to pick up a few fight dollars, and that's where he stumbled across the son of his former trainer.

After Tony Cardinale sent Smith down to Jimmy Connolly's gym, he started to get to know the other boxers there. Many of them were part of Southie's criminal culture, and their reprobate ways meant that there was always plenty of demand in the gym for Cardinale's legal services. It was on one of these legal visits that he got acquainted with Seán Mannion. Cardinale got to know Seán well and ended up as his lawyer, but with a broad remit advising him on matters both inside and outside of the ring.

His work with Mannion opened a lot of boxing doors for Tony Cardinale, and he would go on to represent the likes of Joey DeGrandis, who fought three times for the world title; José Rivera, who won the world title twice; and he would manage John Ruiz, who became the first Latino ever to win the world heavyweight title, which he did in 2001.

~

By early 1982, Seán Mannion's relationship with Jimmy Connolly was as frigid as the January gales whipping in off Dorchester Bay. Mannion had just cut his own deal with Lou Duva for the Nino Gonzalez fight, and his manager was not pleased. For Seán, however, it was more evidence that Connolly had been selling him short for years.

"It's not easy to get fights for you, Seán."

Seán secured the Gonzalez fight with just one phone call.

"There's money to be made, Seán, but not yet."

Seán earned more money in the one fight he himself had organized than Jimmy Connolly had ever made him. He returned to Connolly's Gym in South Boston with the bitterness and reluctance of a man who had just discovered that he had been shortchanged for years.

There was no hiding the animosity between the two any longer, even in front of the other boxers in the gym. Conversations became a clipped mess of swear words, every exchange couched in contempt. Small stuff became big stuff. Big stuff became huge. Big stuff for Seán usually involved family, and when Connolly told him that he didn't want his brother, Paddy, in his corner anymore, Seán threatened to quit.

Paddy Mannion had little boxing experience when he first started working Seán's corner, and he and his brother were constantly arguing ("Paddy and Seán were forever at each other, but Paddy would swear to Saint Peter that it was himself who was right," observed their sister, Eileen). Still, Seán wanted, needed, his brother in his corner because he wanted one of his own people with him, and he wanted to have Irish spoken in his corner.

His native language confused more than his opponents. "That's the strongest Irish brogue I've ever heard," said one television commentator, who thought the brothers were speaking a particularly obtuse variant of English between rounds. Gradually, Paddy would pick up the boxing expertise needed, but he was never entirely comfortable with his role in the corner. "To be perfectly honest, it wasn't me he needed but an outsider," said Paddy. "We used to have great *craic* together but we were always at each other's throats. I didn't enjoy that. I remember walking into Madison Square Garden as a trainer for a world title fight, asking myself what the hell was an amateur from Ros Muc doing there?"

Seán managed to get his way and Paddy remained in his corner, but his win against Gonzalez did nothing to improve his relationship with his manager. Connolly's revenge involved spreading rumors about Seán's drinking, telling anyone who would listen that the Ros Muc man was "over the hill."

By this stage, the four-year contract between the two was coming to an end, and Seán Mannion needed a lawyer to secure his future in the ring. When Tony Cardinale walked into the South Boston gym, Seán knew that he had his man.

Jimmy Connolly also knew that he had his man, however, and wasn't about to let go easily of a potential cash cow like Seán Mannion. Despite the ongoing antagonism between the two, Connolly offered his prize fighter a new three-year contract with improved terms and conditions. Unsurprisingly, Seán was skeptical, but Cardinale suggested that they sit down with Connolly to discuss what future management under him would look like. By the time the talks had finished, Connolly had swayed Seán with a beautiful new vision of big fights for big money. A new contract was drawn up and signed.

"He was a fantastic talker," said Seán, shaking his head ruefully. "He promised world-class fights, he promised lots of money, he promised contacts that would find classy opponents. But it was all a bloody lie. The contract was no sooner signed than we were back to the old shite again."

But one thing had changed. After beating Nino Gonzalez, it seemed like it didn't really matter who was managing Seán Mannion anymore. There was no longer any difficulty in finding fights. As a valuable commodity, bigger and better boxers were coming to Seán.

One of them was the U.S. light middleweight champion, Gary Guiden. Guiden, ranked sixth in the world, had won the title in 1981 after knocking out Sugar Ray Leonard's cousin, O'dell, in four rounds. For Mannion, taking on Guiden was a big deal as it was his first shot at a national pro title and a big leap closer to getting that almost mythical world title shot.

Bob Arum's Top Rank was promoting the bout, and the promotional focus was on the Irishman. With the fight set for Atlantic City on St. Patrick's Day, Top Rank was targeting the substantial Irish population on the East Coast. The fight would also be live on TV.

Seán Mannion knew that the fight against Guiden was a huge opportunity, and he trained accordingly. For the first time, one of the big U.S. newspapers carried a long feature on Seán, much to the delight of the promoters. In "He's All Irish—Except for the Nickname," the *Boston Globe*'s Steve Marantz wrote that Mannion was "so Irish that he psyches himself by listening to the music of Patsy and the Shamrocks, who can be found at the Blarney Stone on Dorchester Avenue."

> Mannion's 24-year-old Irish heart gets more inspiration from Paddy Mannion, his older brother and cornerman. When Sean slumps on his stool, Paddy splashes water over his face and says, "Cuinne suas do lamha."
>
> That's Gaelic for "keep your hands up." During a tough fight, the Gaelic instructions cut through the fog in Mannion's head. "Gaelic is my first language," says Mannion. "It means a lot to me to hear it in my corner."

The feature piece finished by noting that, by beating Guiden, Mannion would have a shot at WBA light middleweight champion Davey Moore.

After the newspaper hit the streets on Saturday, Seán's name was on the tip of every tongue in Boston. By Sunday, however, it was all over.

"I had put in so much work with my trainer at the time, Paddy Quelly from Clare, that I felt invincible, that I couldn't be beaten," said Seán. "I had never felt as prepared for a fight in my life. Then, on Sunday night, I was sparring with Danny Cronin in the gym when he hit me on the cheek."

Danny Cronin was a light heavyweight renowned for his heavy punches. He was one of Seán's regular sparring partners, and although he only ever had 10 pro fights, he used that big punch to knock his opponent out in eight of them. Cronin also brought that punch to sparring sessions, reinforced by his old, oversized gloves.

"Those bloody gloves were like rocks," laughed Seán.

"When we used to get into the ring together, it was war," said Cronin. "It didn't matter what fight was coming up, neither of us ever held back."

Sure enough, it was more scrap than spar when the two teamed up in Connolly's gym, and when Danny Cronin caught Seán on the left cheekbone, Seán's face swelled up immediately, his right eye closing up. Jimmy Connolly jumped into the ring between them.

"Stop," he screamed at the two boxers, according to Mannion. "Stop for Chrissakes, stop."

Connolly feared straight away that the Guiden fight would have to be cancelled and that they would lose their shot at the U.S. title. He grabbed Seán by the head and turned it to one side to inspect it. "Ah, it's not so bad," he said, trying to reassure himself more than Seán, "you'll be alright, you'll be alright."

Seán pulled his head from Connolly's grip. "For fuck sake, Jimmy, I can't even see out of it."

It was pretty clear that Seán wouldn't be alright. He was brought to hospital, where they confirmed that his cheekbone had been fractured. Seán Mannion wouldn't be seen live on TV on St. Patrick's Day after all.

Although he didn't volunteer the information, Seán knew that it wasn't Danny Cronin's fist that had broken his cheekbone. A few years earlier, Mannion had received a stray kick to the face from a friend of his during a street brawl on Field's Corner in Dorchester. It was the kick that had fractured the cheekbone, and Cronin's oversized glove just happened to find that weakness.

The U.S. light middleweight title fight between Seán Mannion and Gary Guiden was rescheduled for May, not in Atlantic City but on the other side of the country, in Caesars Palace, Las Vegas. With the influx of TV money, Vegas had become the New York of boxing, and Caesars Palace the new Madison Square Garden.

Seán should have been over the moon coming into the rescheduled Guiden fight, but he wasn't. It was a big-time contest on a big-time stage, but for Mannion something was amiss, and he couldn't quite put his finger on it. Maybe it was having lost the initial momentum of the big St. Patrick's Day buildup. Maybe it was fighting away from his East Coast friends and fans. Whatever it was, it led to a flat six-week, pre-fight buildup for Mannion, and a rare feeling of unease going into the ring against Gary Guiden.

Not that you'd notice any unease in the first round against Guiden, however, where he gave his opponent a pummeling. The second round was a closer affair, Guiden working Seán's vulnerable left cheekbone, but even with his eye swelling up by the end of the round, the TV commentators agreed that Mannion still had the upper hand.

Things soon changed, however. Once Mannion got off his stool at the start of the third round, he knew he was in trouble. His arms felt heavy. His heels seemed glued to the floor. Suddenly, it felt as if his bounce and his strength and his speed had been spirited from him into the Nevada night. Mannion quickly realized that the only way he was going to leave Las Vegas with the U.S. title belt was to hit Guiden early and to hit him big. And so, at the start of that third round, he threw an uncharacteristic haymaker. It never made hay, however.

"If I had hit him with it, I would have knocked him clean out," said Seán.

If. But he didn't. Guiden took his opportunity when he saw Seán's defense wide open after throwing the big punch and caught him under the right eye. To make matters worse, the lacing on Guiden's glove tore the skin on Seán's face. When the bell went, the Nevada boxing commission doctor came rushing up to Mannion's corner to have a look at the cut. It was deep. Too deep. He wasn't allowed out for round four. Guiden was awarded the win and kept his belt.

Disaster. For Seán, it was as if a sudden darkness had fallen over him. This wasn't what was supposed to happen. He was to leave Vegas as champion, the next contender, not as a loser with a cut under his eye. After being bandaged by the doctor, he went back to the dressing room with Pat Quelly, Jimmy and Billy Connolly, without speaking a word. He showered, dressed, left his entourage behind, and headed to the Caesars Palace blackjack tables with a bottle of Budweiser in hand. By the time he sat down, the bandage had turned red from the blood seeping through. His left eye had closed up almost entirely.

Seán wasn't looking for conversation. All he wanted was the solace and silence of a beer and blackjack. He was no sooner sitting, however, when he felt a tap on his shoulder.

"You fighting tonight?" Seán recalled the stranger asking.

"No, I just woke up like this."

Mannion was in a foul mood but instantly regretted his rudeness. "Yeah, I was fighting."

The two began talking. The stranger asked Seán where he was from.

"Ireland, but I'm living in Boston."

"Yeah? Where in Boston?"

"Dorchester."

"Get outta here! My boss comes from Dorchester. You wanna come down and meet her?"

Curious, Seán followed his new friend down to the back of the casino. On the way down, the stranger introduced himself. He was a musician, part of Donna Summer's disco ensemble. Seán had never heard of her. The boxer was introduced to the disco diva. Gary Guiden was forgotten. Instead, they celebrated Dorchester and Boston. A big night. The man from Ros Muc and Donna Summer.

Despite the disco distraction, Seán didn't enjoy his trip to Las Vegas. As he left the hotel the next day, he noticed workmen in the Caesars Palace parking lot preparing for the world heavyweight title fight between Gerry Cooney and

Larry Holmes. Mannion knew Cooney well and was glad that his friend was getting a title shot, but the work in the parking lot only served to remind him that he was as far now from his own crack at the title as he ever was.

Seán's misery would only get worse when changed circumstances meant that the next shot at the WBA light middleweight title was to go to the winner of the Mannion vs. Guiden fight, although neither of them had realized it at the time of their fight.

WBA champion Davey Moore was to face a young boxer from the Lou Duva camp, Tony Ayala. Ayala had no fear of Moore, despite the fact that the champion had successfully defended his title three times after winning it against Tadashi Mihara in Tokyo. Indeed, Tony "El Torito" Ayala didn't seem afraid of anyone or anything. As a boxer, his merciless style would leave both audience and opponent gasping for air by the time the fight was over. Ayala wasn't the type to take pity on his adversary. He was the kind of man who would spit on a boxer after knocking him to the ground. And he did.

Ayala was only 17 when he started to box professionally, and it was evident early on that he had more than just malice about him. He was also skillful and managed to combine the two with devastating results in the ring. In his first four fights, he stopped his opponent in the first round. By the end of 1982, he had a record of 22 fights, 22 wins, and 19 KOs. The renowned trainer, Angelo Dundee, said of Ayala that he could go on to be the greatest boxer of all time. Michael Katz of the *New York Times* wrote that Ayala was the best young boxer he had ever seen. An inevitable world title challenge against Davey Moore was secured when he beat Carlos Herrera in 1982. Ayala's fans presumed that this would be the start of an "El Torito" golden era, that he would beat Moore easily, and that he would take on the big guns then. That's how the media saw it too.

"Ayala would be the favorite to stop Moore," wrote Vince Murray of Florida's *Ocala Star-Banner*. "After that he could fatten his purse with pretenders like Tony Braxton, Boston's Sean Mannion, Rocky Fratto, or Clint Jackson.

"Then Ayala would be ready for big-money tests against Benitez, Hearns, Leonard, and Hagler."

But that's not how things turned out. Tony Ayala was an extremely dangerous man in the ring, and even more so outside of it. At 4:30 a.m. on the first morning of 1983, four weeks before his scheduled fight with Davey Moore, Ayala told his wife that he was heading out for cigarettes. Drunk and on heroin (Ayala had been using heroin since he was 12 years old), he didn't go looking for cigarettes. Instead, he walked across the street and broke into the apartment of a 30-year-old school teacher. After threatening to kill her with a knife he found in her kitchen, he tied her to her bed with stockings and raped her. Tony Ayala was sentenced to 35 years in prison. "El Torito's" next journey would not be to Bally's Park Place Hotel Casino in Atlantic City to face Davey Moore, but to nearby Bayside State Prison.

The U.S. light middleweight champion was the second choice for the world title fight against Moore. Gary Guiden. Not Seán Mannion. Moore stopped Guiden in the second minute of the fourth round.

～

Seán Mannion's boxing career had begun to develop a worrying pattern. Win after win after win, resulting in a high-profile fight that he would then lose. For Seán, the fights that he won were no more than stepping-stones. But the fights he lost were devastating. Not just to his boxing record, to his confidence, to his love of the sport, but more significantly to his chances of a world title shot.

The huge gains he made by winning against the likes of the high-ranking Nino Gonzalez were wiped out by his loss to Gary Guiden, sliding back down again to the bottom rungs of the boxing ladder. Back again to small-money bouts in small halls in front of small crowds. From Caesars Palace to the Memorial Hall in Plymouth, Massachusetts, in the space of two fights. Knowing after the Guiden fight that a cut to the eye was what had stood between him and a title shot only made matters worse.

By this stage of his career, it was becoming more and more of a challenge for Mannion to stay under the 147 pound limit of the welterweight division, and his next two fights would prove as much. He just about made weight to beat Argentina's Ricardo Camoranesi, but the following fight against Hector Figueroa, which would be his last at welterweight, wasn't quite as straightforward.

"Back in those days, you weighed in on the day of the fight," said Tony Cardinale, "and if Seán did what he was supposed to, he'd be fine. He would leave the gym on target but he had a problem keeping the weight off, and by the time the fight came around, he could be well over."

For Mannion, this particular fight was about unfinished business. Hector "Papo" Figueroa had been Seán's first and only drawn fight, with the Connemara man strongly of the opinion that he had been the better fighter on that night. Now he would have the opportunity to prove it.

Mannion and Figueroa had top billing that night, and two hours before the fight, Seán left his Plymouth hotel and headed for the weigh-in at the Memorial Hall. The cutoff for welterweights was 147 pounds, although for this fight, another pound had been written into the contract for some much-needed flexibility. When Figueroa stood on the scale, the needle eventually settled at 143 pounds. When it was Seán's turn, he took off his robe and handed it to Tony Cardinale. He stood on the scale. 156 pounds. A massive nine pounds overweight.

Willie Pep, Papo Figueroa's manager, chuckled. He had seen this often enough through the years to know that it meant only one thing.

"You guys forfeit. Now pay up," Tony Cardinale recalled him saying.

Willie Pep had been the greatest featherweight boxer the world had ever seen. So graceful, so light on his feet that he was christened "Will o' the Wisp." Boxing journalist Jimmy Cannon wrote of Pep: "Sometimes there seemed to be music playing for him and he danced to his private orchestra and the ring became a ballroom."

In 1946, Pep laid a bet with another writer that he could win a round against Jackie Graves without throwing a single punch.

"For three minutes Pep moved, taunted, twirled, tied up Graves—but never threw a punch," wrote Don Riley. "It was an outstanding display of defensive boxing so adroit, so cunning, so subtle, the 8,000 roaring fans did not notice Pep's tactics were completely without offense."

The judges didn't notice either, and Pep was awarded the round!

But the Willie Pep in the Memorial Hall in southern Massachusetts on August 20, 1982, was in no mood for dancing.

"The fight is off, guys. Give us the money."

Tony Cardinale looked over at the Massachusetts State Boxing Commission official. Tommy Rawson just shrugged his shoulders. There wasn't much he could do about the situation. Rawson was Harvard's boxing coach, and he and Cardinale knew each other well.

"Tommy, can we at least try to get the weight off?"

"Sure thing. I've never seen that kind of weight shifted before, but you can give it a shot"

Cardinale looked over at the guy who had just come down off the scales.

"Are you up for it, Seán?"

"Yeah, why not?"

"Great. Tommy, how long do we have?"

"Well, the fight is on at seven so that's a little under two hours from now. I'll give you up to half an hour before it starts. If the weight's not off by then, you have to forfeit."

Jimmy Connolly stayed in the hall to take care of his other fighters while Cardinale and Mannion headed back to the hotel. When they got to the room, Cardinale went into the bathroom and filled the bath and sink with hot water.

By the time Seán walked in, Cardinale was already perspiring heavily from the steam. Mannion had pulled on his heavy rubber suit, used for emergency weight loss, and had taken out his skipping rope. Between the rubber suit, the hot steam and the skipping, it wasn't long before Seán was soaked in sweat.

An hour later, exhausted from the skipping, Mannion headed back to the hall with Cardinale. Figueroa and Pep watched as he climbed up on the scale. 152 pounds, announced the needle. While he had managed to lose four pounds in an hour, it was still only half of what he needed to lose. Cardinale looked at him.

"You want to keep trying, Seán?"

Seán nodded.

By this time, with the first fight of the night about to start, the weighing scale had been moved to a corridor being used by fight fans who were heading in to the auditorium. None of them who saw Mannion get off the scale realized that the night's star attraction was four pounds overweight and too heavy to be allowed into the ring against his opponent.

With the fight about to start in an hour, it was too late to return to the hotel. Seán put his rubber suit back on and went looking for stairs. He found them in one of the back corridors. Three flights up, three flights down. And so he began. Up, down. The sweat spilling off him. Up, down. His breath rattling from his lungs. Up, down. After half an hour, he heard Cardinale call.

"Seán, it's time."

Seán took off the rubber suit and toweled down, standing up on the scale as curious fans walked by, wondering what the hell was going on half an hour out from the big fight. Seán Mannion, Tony Cardinale, Papo Figueroa, Willie Pep, and Tommy Rawson watched as the needle on the scales began to rise in seeming slow motion. Eventually, it began to settle. It stopped. 149 pounds.

"Great stuff," said Cardinale, "we have a fight."

"We certainly do not," retorted Pep. "The weight is 147, the contract says 148 max. You forfeit."

"For fuck sake, Willie, it's only one fuckin' pound."

"I don't care, you forfeit. Now pay up."

Cardinale was furious.

"This is fucking ridiculous. One fucking pound. Do us a favor, Willie. One pound, goddamn it."

Tommy Rawson called Cardinale over.

"Tony, I'm going to give you another 15 minutes. Take your guy into the changing rooms, give him a rough rubdown, no oil, no nothing, and come back here for one last try."

"A raw massage? You think that's going to make a difference?"

"Just give it a try. It's not going to be soothing but I've seen it work before."

Tony Cardinale went into the dressing room with Seán. For 15 minutes, he gave Mannion a rubdown, his dry hands burning skin and pulling hair. By the time they had finished, Seán's body looked as red as the lobsters being served in downtown Plymouth's seafood restaurants.

They walked out towards the weighing scales, a blanket draped around Seán's shoulders. Pep and Papo were waiting. Tommy Rawson looked at his watch. Dropping the blanket, Seán stood stark naked on the scales. In an effort to save every ounce of weight, he had left his underwear in the changing room. Mannion still remembers some women screaming as they walked by into the auditorium, witnessing the naked welterweight wannabe. Cardinale, Rawson, and Pep crowded around the scale. They looked down. 148.

Still on the scale, Mannion looked into Papo Figueroa's eyes. "Now you fuckin' Puerto Rican, I'm going to make you regret every single drop of sweat I've just poured."

They got into the ring shortly afterward. Seán Mannion had lost eight pounds in two hours in one of the most intense training sessions of his life. Still, he knew that this fight would only have the one result. Papo Figueroa seemed to know it too. Mannion destroyed Figueroa in the first round, but when he had the opportunity to finish him, he let him off. This is how the fight would play out for the next nine rounds. Seán beating Figueroa convincingly, but not dropping him. Like a playful cat refusing mercy to a mouse. When it came to the final round, Seán went out, fury still in his blood, and knocked out Papo. To show that he could.

Seán was back.

Three weeks later, he was back in the ring as a light middleweight, never to return to the constant struggle of making welterweight. The ring was in Scranton, Pennsylvania, and he was up against a local fighter named Steve Michalerya. Mannion had little to fear from Michalerya, a man who had lost 11 of his 27 pro fights. Although the bout was tougher than he had anticipated, Seán turned to his corner, confident of victory, when the ten rounds were in.

The crowd seemed to be of the same opinion, as were the newspapers the following day. Everyone, it seemed, but the judges. When the referee brought the two into the center of the ring, it was Michalerya's arm, not Mannion's, that he lifted into the air. For Seán, the blow was worse than any Michalerya had managed to land in the 10 rounds previous.

Tumbling down that ladder again. But this time, it was different. Seán didn't realize it at the time, but being beaten by Steve Michalerya was the best thing that could have happened to his boxing career.

11

RESURRECTION

There's a strange-looking building in Canastota, upstate New York, just down the road from the International Boxing Hall of Fame. From a distance, it looks like someone has built a blue-and-white castle on the side of the highway with the leftovers of a lumber yard sale. As you get closer, you notice the red neon writing on the side of the fake castle: "Graziano's World Famous Inn and Restaurant."

Tony Graziano opened his restaurant in Canastota shortly after returning from Europe at the end of World War II, where he parachuted into the Normandy invasion and fought in the Battle of the Bulge. Shortly after opening the restaurant, Graziano got involved in the local boxing scene, managing Carmen Basilio and later, Basilio's nephew, Billy Backus, both of whom would go on to win world titles. It was Graziano's legacy that brought the International Boxing Hall of Fame to Canastota, with locals looking to acknowledge the rich boxing heritage of the small town that produced two world champions.

By 1976, Tony Graziano had retired from boxing when a young man from nearby Geneva, New York, came to visit. Rocky Fratto was looking to turn pro, and he needed a manager. Graziano had never met Fratto before, but knew enough about his reputation to decide to get back in the corner again.

It was a measure of Rocky Fratto's boxing promise that the *Geneva Times* saw fit to report three years earlier, on April 2, 1973, that a 14-year-old Fratto was to temporarily quit boxing so that he could focus on strength work. The precocious Fratto announced as much after unanimously beating a 23-year-old Jose Navedo in his hometown.

Ralph (Rocky) Fratto, Geneva's sensational, thinking 14-year-old boxer, whose goal is to become a professional middleweight, is going to hang up his gloves for a while, it was learned Saturday night.

Fratto, who had his first boxing match at the age of 10, has had 28 fights in his amateur career and has posted 27 victories. He is probably the youngest boxer to have ever won the regional Golden Gloves Championships.

A further measure of Fratto's promise was that he had the greatest featherweight of all time, Willie Pep, advising him at the age of just 13. By the time Fratto came to Tony Graziano, he had won amateur All Army titles, Interservice titles, Golden Gloves titles, and the trajectory continued upward once he turned professional.

By April 1981, Fratto had put together an unbeaten pro record of 24 consecutive victories to win the U.S. light middleweight title. With that came the dream shot of a world title, along with a further offer of half a million dollars to defend the belt against Charlie Weir in Sun City, Botswana, if he managed to win. But Rocky Fratto would never see Botswana or Charlie Weir. Japan's Tadashi Mihara knocked him down in the fourth round of their WBA light middleweight title fight, and went on to win after 15 rounds. Particularly galling for Fratto was that his first-ever professional defeat took place in his own backyard in upstate New York, in front of family and friends.

Rocky Fratto was about to share Seán Mannion's experience after those destructive defeats, starting all over again from what felt like the bottom rung of a very slippery ladder. Fratto wasted no time climbing back up, however. He beat Chris Linson. He beat Jesus Castro. He beat Roberto Colon. Steady, undramatic wins that went the distance.

As manager, it was Tony Graziano's job to ensure that there were no stumbles or silly defeats greasing Fratto's ladder. The plan was to secure another title shot as quickly as possible, and Graziano wasn't going to take any chances along the way. He scoured the results pages of boxing matches in the Northeast, looking for opponents who could give his man a decent challenge without actually beating him. After Fratto's victory over Roberto Colon, Graziano noticed that a ranked Boston-based boxer had been beaten by Steve Michalerya three days earlier. Given that Fratto had already beaten Michalerya twice, this was a no-brainer. Tony Graziano had just discovered their next opponent.

Seán Mannion had only 19 days' notice for the Rocky Fratto fight, but this time, Jimmy Connolly had no cause for concern. Mannion was fit, on the dry, and in the gym. All he wanted was to put right his controversial loss to Michalerya.

It was Seán's birthday the day before the Fratto fight, and on his way down to the Sands Casino venue in Atlantic City, he stopped off in Delsomma's, the Cardinale family restaurant in Manhattan. Frankie Cardinale and his brothers welcomed the young boxer and, after some fight talk, Frankie went back in the kitchen and returned with a parcel for Mannion.

"Happy birthday, Seán."

Seán opened the parcel to find a pair of green shorts with a shamrock sewn on one leg, "Seán Mannion" on the other. With it was a green robe, again with a shamrock and his name embroidered in white on the back.

"Now just make sure you nail Fratto tomorrow, Seán."

As Mannion woke up in Atlantic City the following morning, a bus left Fields Corner in Dorchester, carrying more than just Seán's regular Boston following. The Na Piarsaigh Gaelic football team from his home parish of Ros Muc were on tour in the United States, and had decided to travel to Atlantic City when they heard that Mannion was to fight the recently ranked number two in the world. When Seán heard that friends and family from Ireland would be ringside, he knew he couldn't lose.

Rocky Fratto was thinking the exact same thing himself, however. He knew he couldn't lose if he was to recapture that world title shot, and an interview with his local newspaper shortly before the fight showed little doubt on his part.

"If this fight wasn't going to be televised, I probably wouldn't have taken it," he told the *Finger Lake Times* on October 5, 1982. "I'm taking it for exposure. It's a good opportunity to make a name for myself and show people that Rocky Fratto can fight . . ."

At 9:20 p.m. on the night of August 10, 1983, a day after his 26th birthday, Seán Mannion walked from his room, down through the passageways of the Sands Casino Hotel, and into the ring in the Copa Room. A large crowd had traveled from Massachusetts to support him, as had a crowd from New York to support Fratto.

Refereeing that night was Zack Clayton, famous not just for being the first black referee for a world title contest, but also for refereeing one of the most famous fights in boxing history when Muhammad Ali beat George Foreman in the Rumble in the Jungle in Zaire.

When the bell went in the Sands Casino, Seán Mannion was first into the center of the ring. Mannion, wearing Cardinale's green shorts, wobbled Fratto early in the first round with a left hook. Then another one. Two more. All to the head. By the time the first round finished, Rocky Fratto looked dangerously out of his depth.

Fratto was putting in a huge amount of work just to stay in the fight, but was struggling to come to terms with Mannion's left fist. Indeed, he was lucky to come out of the seventh round at all. Like the previous rounds, Mannion took ownership of the center of the ring. Again, he forced Fratto onto the ropes. Again, attacking with the left. When Fratto closed up his guard, Mannion caught him on the chin with a vicious uppercut. Clayton went to stop the fight but changed his mind, saying afterward that he let it continue as Fratto was still able to defend himself.

"Young kids who want to start boxing, take notes from Seán Mannion. That's how to box," said ESPN's Randy Gordon.

But it seemed that the big effort in the seventh round had exhausted Mannion, and a perked-up Fratto took note. He won the eighth, and Mannion was on the ropes himself for much of the ninth round.

"What's Mannion trying to do?" asked commentator Steve Albert.

The answer was the same thing that he had been doing since Mike Flaherty had taught him, as a kid, how to come off the ropes with a punch. Like many before him, the series of left and right hooks to the head was the last thing an attacking Fratto expected.

By the tenth and final round, tiredness became a leveler, with both Mannion and Fratto going toe to toe, both looking for the killer punch. Mannion lay on the ropes, inviting Fratto before hitting him with a right hook to the body that opened up his defense, following it with a nasty uppercut that threw Fratto's head back, blood pouring from both nostrils. The bell went. The crowd stood, roaring in appreciation. Mannion, Fratto, and Clayton embraced, acknowledging the battle they had just been through.

"They are on their feet here at the Sands Hotel," said Albert, "Seán Mannion, Rocky Fratto, a great battle, hugging each other.

"How could you not stand? That was just terrific."

Afterwards, it seemed that neither fighter seemed entirely sure who had just won "one of the best fights of the year," as one newspaper described it.

As ring announcer Ed Derian began giving the result, Fratto walked around the ring anxiously, holding his still-taped hands to his face. Mannion stood still in the center of the ring, head bowed, hands on waist, his new robe draped over his shoulders.

"We have a unanimous decision."

The announcer read out the scores. 6–3–1 from the first judge, or six rounds out of ten for one fighter, three for the other, and one drawn round. 6–4–0 from the next judge. The referee scored it 8–1–1.

"And the winner . . . Seán Mannion."

The U.S. light middleweight champion had just been defeated by the man from Ros Muc, Ireland.

Seán threw his arms up in celebration. Paddy Mannion lifted his brother into the air. The traveling football players of Na Piarsaigh jumped from their seats in celebration. Seán was back. Again.

The result, only his second-ever loss, broke Rocky Fratto. He went on to box three more fights, but his heart was no longer in it. The man once ranked the number one contender in the world would lose two of his next three fights before quitting for good.

For Seán Mannion, it was a glorious resurrection. The *Boston Herald* declared him Fighter of the Year for 1982. The Massachusetts House of Representatives presented him with a State honor. The Suffolk County Police Department bestowed on him Honorary Deputy Sheriff status (ironic considering only two years previously, it had taken seven of their police officers to arrest him).

The focus and dedication that had been so apparent in his training in the late seventies had returned. ESPN started to show all of his fights, live from Atlantic City. Bill Bradley, 20 wins, 2 defeats. Mannion beat him. Larry Byrd, 20 wins, 2 defeats. Mannion beat him.

The middleweight boxers of the United States began to take note.

"We're taking a gamble on this one," Dennis Horne's manager, Dana Davis, told the *Oklahoman* newspaper in the buildup to their fight on the day before St. Patrick's Day, 1983. "We weren't exactly overjoyed about fighting a southpaw the caliber of Mannion. But Dennis is in good shape, and he wanted this fight. It would mean a lot to his career if he could beat Mannion."

But he couldn't. Seán Mannion was given the win after 10 rounds. The WBA released their latest rankings shortly after that fight. Seán Mannion—number three light middleweight boxer in the world.

~

On November 13, 1982, Ray "Boom Boom" Mancini fought Duk Koo Kim in a 10,000-seat outdoor arena under the searing Las Vegas sun. The world title fight between the reigning WBA lightweight champion and the number one contender from South Korea would become one of the most tragic moments in a sport not short on tragedy.

From the moment the bell was struck, neither Ray Mancini nor Duk Koo Kim took a backward step in a fight defined by its ferocity. It was always going to be as much. Shortly before leaving South Korea for Las Vegas, Kim, whose wife was expecting their first child, gave an unflinching press conference.

"He [Mancini] is going to die or I'm going to die."

Boxers often make over-the-top statements in an attempt to either sell tickets or scare their opponents. No one for a second thought that Duk Koo Kim was actually prophesizing truth.

Kim was the first to inflict damage during the fight, opening a cut under Mancini's left ear in the third round that had Mancini's legendary cutman, Paul Percifield, struggling to stop the spouting blood. The fight entered a pattern of Mancini starting rounds strongly, with Kim consistently coming back with unlikely recovery after unlikely recovery. The theme was distilled in the eighth, with Mancini pummeling Kim until the Korean caught him with a barrage at the end, rocking the champion and catching him with a punch that would swell and shut his left eye.

By the end of the 12th round, both boxers were clearly tired, with Kim seemingly approaching exhaustion. Recognizing as much, Ray Mancini came out of his corner at the start of the 13th, looking to finish off something that had become much more than just a boxing contest. From the moment the bell rang, he caught Kim with 44 unanswered punches. On the verge of collapsing, Kim finally managed to wrap his arms around his opponent and cling on. Mancini escaped the grip and threw another 17 successful consecutive punches. But, just as it looked as if it was all over, and not for the first time, Kim seemed to recover. It was Mancini looking for shelter from the storm as Kim rained down punches for the remainder of the round.

The fight was set for 15 rounds, but the bell that marked the start of round 14 wouldn't be struck again. Mancini flew out of his corner once again and caught Kim with a cruel right-hander with only nine seconds gone on the clock. Kim fell backwards so heavily, so completely, that his feet lifted off the ground when his head hit the canvas.

In a photo accompanying an article on the fight in *Sports Illustrated*, Mancini can be seen celebrating his win in the center of the ring, lifted into the Las Vegas sky by one of his trainers. In the background, the referee, Richard Green, is clutching onto Kim, trying to keep him upright, Green's arm in the air desperately calling for help.

Duk Koo Kim was taken out of the ring on a stretcher and brought by ambulance to Desert Springs hospital. That's where they noticed the blood clot on the right side of his brain. Kim died four days later, his mother, who flew in from South Korea to be with her only child, at his deathbed. Three months later, unable to tolerate the pain of her son's death, she took her own life by drinking a bottle of pesticide. A fortnight after her death, Duk Koo Kim's wife gave birth to their one and only child, Chi Wan, who was nine years old before he found out what happened to his father.

A year after the tragic fight, torn by the regret of not having stopped it in time, Richard Green, the referee, also committed suicide. As for Ray "Boom Boom" Mancini, he confessed to never being the same again after that fight in Las Vegas. He became depressed, losing his passion for a sport that had defined his life.

The sport would also never be the same again. The WBC decided that 15-round championship fights were too dangerous, and capped fights at a 12-round maximum. By 1988, all other sanctioning bodies had put the same rule in place. There would be no fight longer than 12 rounds from then on.

Other than one bout in the Philippines, the fight against Ray Mancini had been Duk Koo Kim's first outside South Korea. Boxing was big in Korea, but Bob Arum and Top Rank, who had promoted Mancini vs. Kim, would never again risk throwing a South Korean boxer straight into a world title fight without having tested him out first.

That's not to say that Arum didn't want to bring another Korean boxer over to the States. He had just discovered a fighter who had never been beaten, who had knocked out every professional opponent he had ever faced, had won and defended the Oriental and Pacific Boxing Federation title five times. World championship material if there ever was. His name was In-Chul Baek.

But after the Kim tragedy, Arum wasn't going to throw Baek immediately into a world title bout. Baek was told that if he won his first U.S.-based fight, he would then get the world title shot right away.

~

Seán Mannion was in the corner of the gym, mutilating a punch bag, when Jimmy Connolly walked over.

"Sean, I got a fight for you," Mannion recalled him saying.

"Fair play to you, Jimmy, still doing your job now and again, I see."

The tension between the two wasn't improving.

"Well, you wanna know who you're fighting? Who would you like to fight?"

"That's your job, Jimmy. You get me the fights, I'll do the fighting."

"He's from Korea. Know much about Korean boxers?"

"How the hell am I supposed to know any boxer from Korea?" erupted Mannion. "I follow boxing but I don't see any Korean results in the *Boston Herald*."

"In-Chul Baek. Number one contender in the world. Southpaw. You're fighting in Atlantic City in six weeks' time."

Seán laid off the bag.

"Ok. That's good, that's good. Thanks Jimmy. Let's get some southpaw sparring partners and let's get to work."

The first thing Seán did was quit his construction job for six weeks. He was working for his brother Tommy at the time, and both of them understood that long days on a building site weren't ideal preparation for taking on the number one contender in the world. Without the distraction of work, Seán took to training full time.

A friend would pick him up at 6:00 a.m. to bring him down to the running routes of Carson Beach and Castle Island in South Boston. He sparred with Danny Cronin, Paul "Polecat" Moore, Greg Joseph, and Billy Smith, who could switch from orthodox to southpaw effortlessly. By that time, Seán's old friend and regular sparring partner, Danny Long, had fallen out with Jimmy Connolly and had left the gym.

Training went well. It had to. In-Chul Baek's ranking was no accident. He had 26 fights before meeting Seán Mannion. He had won all 26. Not only that, he had knocked out all 26 of his opponents. Not one single pro fight involving In-Chul Baek had gone the distance. Until he met Seán Mannion.

The fight took place in the Resorts International Hotel in Atlantic City, live on ESPN. For the fight against Rocky Fratto, it was difficult to distinguish the two sets of supporters from each other. It was all Mannion fans for this fight, however. Not many had traveled from South Korea. Seán walked into the ring in his green robe and green shorts to a huge welcome. Baek wore a pair of red-trimmed white shorts, covered in the Korean script of Hangul. The first thing Mannion noticed after the bell went was that In-Chul Baek was no southpaw, despite what Jimmy Connolly had told him.

It didn't matter. Seán took a few hard punches to the body early in the fight while he was getting his head around the orthodox style in front of him, but it wasn't long before he had the measure of Baek. Having never suffered defeat before, it took until the end of the fifth round for Baek to understand as much. At the start of the sixth, and for every round afterwards, the Korean came out of his corner with the fury of a man looking for that punch that had knocked out 26 consecutive men. He couldn't find it. To make matters worse, he suffered the indignity of being stripped of the seventh round for hitting below the belt.

By the tenth round, the crowd was getting worked up.

"Go Seán, go. Go Seán, go."

The chant grew louder as the round went on.

"Go Seán, go. Go Seán, go."

A woman in the crowd held up a handwritten sign that said, "Boston Loves Sean Mannion and ESPN!"

In-Chul Baek knew that he had only one option left. The two came out of their corners for the tenth round, tapping gloves before commencing battle. Baek looked heavy on his feet, planting a foundation from where the killer punch would come. Mannion, despite having gone nine rounds, was still bouncing, still dancing. After what felt like an eternity of looking at each other, of sizing each other up, Baek came forward. He hit Mannion with a left. Another left. The Irishman was on the ropes. Another left to the head, a right to the kidneys.

Then, Seán pounced off the ropes, countering with a left before catching Baek with a left hook that almost put the Korean through the ropes. That was it. Baek had no more to give after that. Mannion kept hunting with the left hook, all Baek could do was try to avoid it.

"Go Seán, go. Go Seán, go."

When the final bell went, there was no tension, no waiting this time. Seán lifted his two arms towards the heavens. He then walked over and embraced his opponent.

"You've got to give Seán Mannion credit for being a superb boxer tonight," said the ESPN commentator. "This has been the fight of his life. He has been clever and he's beaten the number one contender."

"In-Chul Baek was the most important fight in Seán Mannion's life," said Jimmy Connolly in an interview with TG4 years later. "He couldn't have been any more important.

"It was beautiful. It was just like music. He did a hell of a job, and this guy [Baek] after the fight was amazed. He couldn't believe it [that] Seán Mannion beat him and he wanted to kill me and Mannion together."

In-Chul Baek made the long journey back to Cheonan in South Korea. He would go on to win his next 15 fights. He would win the world light middle-weight and super middleweight titles. But he would refuse to ever fight the man from Ros Muc again.

It didn't matter. Because after his win against Baek in 1983, Seán Mannion was the new number one contender.

Seán Mannion, age nine, at school in Ros Muc (front row, far right). *From the collection of Seán Mannion*

The Mannion family home in Ros Muc, Ireland. *Photograph by the Mannion family*

Seán, age 13, and his brother Colm (far right), with their father, Peaitín, and uncle Cóilín, showing off their first boxing trophies. *From the collection of Seán Mannion*

Seán Mannion's first boxing publicity photo for Na Piarsaigh Boxing Club, Ros Muc, age 17. *From the collection of RTÉ Raidió na Gaeltachta*

Seán, with his then boxing coach, Mike Flaherty, directly behind him, and members of Na Piarsaigh Boxing Club, after winning the Golden Shamrock title in 1976. *From the collection of Seán Mannion*

A young Seán Mannion, having just moved to Boston, posing with his new coach, Jimmy Connolly, in 1977. *From the collection of Seán Mannion*

Seán celebrating a 1981 win over Tony Taylor with his sisters in Dorchester, Boston. *From the collection of Seán Mannion*

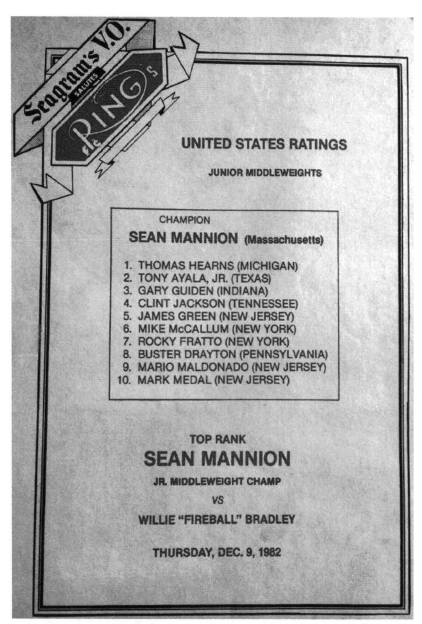

UNITED STATES RATINGS

JUNIOR MIDDLEWEIGHTS

CHAMPION

SEAN MANNION (Massachusetts)

1. THOMAS HEARNS (MICHIGAN)
2. TONY AYALA, JR. (TEXAS)
3. GARY GUIDEN (INDIANA)
4. CLINT JACKSON (TENNESSEE)
5. JAMES GREEN (NEW JERSEY)
6. MIKE McCALLUM (NEW YORK)
7. ROCKY FRATTO (NEW YORK)
8. BUSTER DRAYTON (PENNSYLVANIA)
9. MARIO MALDONADO (NEW JERSEY)
10. MARK MEDAL (NEW JERSEY)

TOP RANK

SEAN MANNION

JR. MIDDLEWEIGHT CHAMP

vs

WILLIE "FIREBALL" BRADLEY

THURSDAY, DEC. 9, 1982

Seán Mannion ranked Light Middleweight U.S. champion by *Ring Magazine* in 1982. *From the collection of the author*

Seán's 1982 publicity poster as U.S. champion. *From the collection of Seán Mannion*

Seán, in Connolly's Gym, with his nephew Patrick, along with his brother and trainer, Paddy, in the background, and Paddy's wife, Nellie. *From the collection of Seán Mannion*

From left, Peter Kerr, Paddy Mannion, Speaker of the Massachusetts House of Representatives Thomas McGee, Seán Mannion, and Jimmy Connolly, at a presentation of a state honor to Seán in 1982. *From the collection of Seán Mannion*

Seán beating Roosevelt Green by KO in Atlantic City, February 1984, in his last fight before the WBA world title fight against Mike McCallum. Photograph by Angie Carlino. *From the collection of Seán Mannion*

Seán relaxing during his pre-world title fight training camp at the Stevensville Country Club in upstate New York. *From the collection of Seán Mannion*

Seán (right) meeting a childhood hero, Rocky Graziano (center) along with Jimmy Connolly (left) at the world title fight press conference in Madison Square Garden. *From the collection of Seán Mannion*

The first round of the WBA light middleweight world title fight against Mike McCallum. *Photograph by the Mannion family*

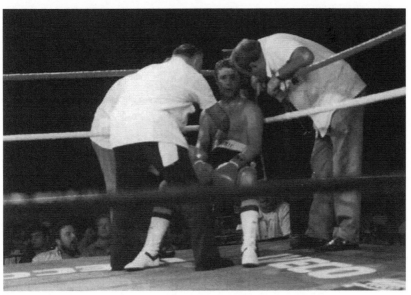

An exhausted and despondent Mannion late into the 15-round title fight against Mike McCallum. *Photograph by the Mannion family*

Returning to Ireland after the world title fight, to a hero's welcome on Eyre Square, Galway. *Connacht Tribune*

The author (age nine) with Seán at his homecoming celebration in Ros Muc. *Tomás Mac Con Iomaire*

Mannion beating WAA light middleweight champion, Bert Lee, in California in 1985. *Peter Kerr*

Training with then WBC heavyweight world champion, Pinklon Thomas (left) and coach, Angelo Dundee (right) at Dundee's 5th Street Gym in Miami. *Peter Kerr*

Celebrating with friends in San Francisco after a contentious fight against Billy Robertson in 1985. *From the collection of Seán Mannion*

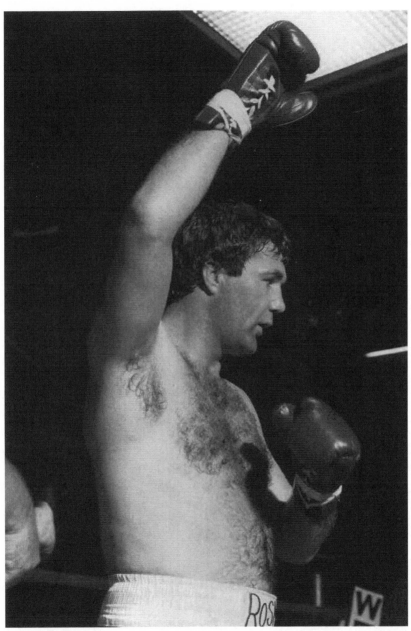

Seán being welcomed into the ring in May 1986 for his first of two fights against Fred Hutchings. *From the collection of Seán Mannion*

Seán Mannion and Mike McCallum at a 2004 event in Birmingham, UK, to celebrate the 20th anniversary of their world title fight. *From the collection of Seán Mannion*

Seán Mannion today, in the Grealish Boxing Club, Dorchester, Boston. *Photograph by Ronan Fox*

THE FOUR KINGS

Cape Cod Coliseum has an Aug. 11 show with Sean Mannion on top against Roberto Colon. Mannion, of Dorchester, has been told he may get the first shot at [Roberto] Duran's 154-pound title after the Hagler bout.

—Boston Globe, July 17, 1983

Boxing isn't like other sports when it comes to arranging contests. Fights are planned. Opponents are matched up. Bouts are publicized. And then they never happen. It doesn't happen in football, it doesn't happen in tennis, it doesn't happen in basketball. But in boxing, no one bats an eyelid when a seemingly set fight disappears into the ether.

Fights kept disappearing on Seán Mannion once he beat In-Chul Baek. According to the newspapers, he was to fight Roberto Duran. It never happened. He was to fight Thomas Hearns. It too never happened. He was to fight Sugar Ray Leonard. That never happened either.

His first high-profile opponent after beating Baek and becoming the WBA number three light middleweight was to be Thomas Hearns. Hitman Hearns was boxing royalty, one of the Four Kings along with Roberto Duran, Marvin Hagler, and Sugar Ray Leonard. At the time, Hearns, with the legendary Emanuel Steward in his corner, was the WBC light middleweight champion. He would go on to become the first man ever to win world titles in five different weight classes. *Ring Magazine* ranked him as the greatest light middleweight boxer of all time. Seán Mannion was living in a different world when he was being mentioned in the same breath as Hitman Hearns.

Any potential matchup wasn't to be a world title fight, however, because despite his WBA ranking, Mannion wasn't ranked among the WBC top ten. It didn't matter. This was an opportunity. It would add to Seán's profile, a man who somehow managed to become the highest WBA-ranked Irishman in 35 years without almost anyone in his home country noticing. It would also add to his bank balance. Mannion received $3,000 for beating In-Chul Baek. Fighting the Hitman would be worth $30,000.

Jimmy Connolly was busy telling the newspapers that he wasn't sure if $30,000 was enough, but he knew well that they had just hit the big time. He also knew that if there was ever a time to take on Tommy Hearns, this was it. Hearns hadn't been in the ring for seven months; he was returning from a hand injury, and was known to struggle with southpaws.

"Sean Mannion, Ireland's gift to Dorchester, is a slick lefthander who has a chance to fight Thomas Hearns, the WBC 154-pound champ . . . Mannion could be the second best fighter in the Boston area," wrote Steve Marantz of the *Boston Globe* under the headline, "Mannion's Big Chance" (there was no question but that Marvin Hagler was number one). Marantz continued:

> Such a distinction qualifies Mannion for the American Express commercial, where somebody says "Do you know me?"
>
> The fact is that Mannion is unknown hereabouts because he never fights here. Most of his bouts have been in Atlantic City, for ESPN. Connolly, the veteran South Boston fight man, says Mannion has been blackballed from any local cards of note because of Goody and Pat Petronelli, who handle Hagler, Sims and several others.

But despite getting so far as to set a date for the fight, Seán Mannion vs. Thomas Hearns never happened, and like everything else in boxing, there were two very different sides to the tale.

Ferdie Pacheco was Muhammad Ali's former doctor and NBC's boxing consultant, and when NBC was set to broadcast the Mannion/Hearns fight, it was Pacheco who vetoed it when he found out who Hearns's opponent was. Not because of Mannion, but because of his manager, Jimmy Connolly.

Prior to joining NBC's boxing team, Pacheco had spent 17 years as Ali's doctor. When he first noticed in 1977 that Ali's reflexes were beginning to slow, he became worried about long-term brain damage and advised the heavyweight champion to retire. Ali refused. Pacheco quit as his doctor on the basis that he could never take a chance with the health and safety of a boxer in the ring. Which is also why he opposed a Connolly boxer taking on Tommy Hearns.

When Seán Mannion's regular sparring partner, Danny Long, was sent to Liguria, Italy, in May 1981, Long reckoned he had hit the jackpot—an all-expenses-paid trip to a sun-dappled San Remo, fighting on Top Rank's "Tomorrow's Champions" card with the likes of Tony Ayala and Davey Moore. But the trip didn't go well for Long. His opponent, Alex Ramos, gave him such a beating at the end of that fight that it was reported afterward that "Long's face looked as if a baseball bat had been applied to it."

Incredibly, despite the nasty beating, Long was back in the ring 10 days later, this time in the Royal Albert Hall in London. Seán Mannion was supposed to fight former European welterweight champion, Davey "Boy" Green, but Mannion told Jimmy Connolly that he couldn't go to London as he was to attend a friend's wedding in the United States.

With Mannion refusing to travel, and with Connolly having accepted the bout, the manager put out a story that Seán had hurt his hand in training. Instead, he put Danny Long in the ring against Davey Green, seeing as Long was already on the other side of the Atlantic. Green pounded a tired Long and beat him in four rounds.

Ferdie Pacheco, who had signed off on broadcasting the Italian fight between Long and Ramos on NBC, was furious when he heard that Connolly had put his man back in the ring so soon after taking a heavy beating.

"This is the way fighters get killed," said Pacheco in a *Boston Globe* feature on the incident titled "Tale of South Boston's Long Shows What's Wrong with Sport." "Long had no business fighting Green. I saw him after the Ramos fight. His face was full of little hematomas, contusions, puffiness, cuts and abrasions. He should not have been allowed to fight for at least 30 days."

"I took the fight to save face for my manager," said Danny Long. "I didn't see any problem in going over there."

"What was I to do?" asked Jimmy Connolly. "Long begged me. He said he wasn't hurt. I felt he could hold his own. I didn't see anything wrong with it. The kid is a clean liver, no drinking or smoking. I knew he was okay.

"I have a reputation of always delivering a fighter. When the other kid [Seán Mannion] took a powder, I had to fulfill my commitment. I care about promoters and matchmakers. I know how tough it is because I was a promoter myself."

Pacheco dismissed his argument. "The direct fault lies with the manager and the fighter. The blame also falls on the lack of a system to adequately police fighters. You'll never be able to police boxing entirely, but you should be able to in the United States and certain civilized parts of Europe, of which I would include England. This may have been a borderline case, but why take the chance?"

Two years later, when a Seán Mannion vs. Thomas Hearns fight was set to be shown live on NBC on July 10, 1983, Ferdie Pacheco asked who Mannion's manager was. When he heard it was Jimmy Connolly, Pacheco just shook his head.

"I'm not putting any Jimmy Connolly fighters on NBC," he said.

That was the end of Mannion's shot at the Hitman.

Jimmy Connolly refused to lose face over Pacheco's decision, however. He denied that the NBC boxing doctor had anything to do with blocking the fight, claiming that he stopped it himself on the basis that Mannion wasn't ready for Hearns, and because the money wasn't right. In that order.

The negotiations with the Hearns camp had been led by a new Massachusetts-based promotions company called Titan Sports, but with Mannion paying for Jimmy Connolly's sins, they had little choice but to start trying to arrange a fight with another of the Four Kings, Roberto Duran of Panama.

Titan Sports would go on to become World Wrestling Entertainment (WWE) and turn its founder, Vince McMahon Jr., into a billionaire. McMahon set up Titan Sports, along with former ice hockey player Jim Troy, by buying the Cape Cod Coliseum, a 7,200 seat arena in Yarmouth, Massachusetts, with plans to host boxing and wrestling matches, along with ice hockey games.

"Our concept is to take top regional attractions like Robbie Sims or Sean Mannion or Dick Eklund, and put them on a card with young developing talent from local gyms," said Troy to the *Boston Globe* in May 1982. "We'd like to build a reputation for putting on strong cards. We'd also like to create regional rivalries. There's no reason somebody shouldn't challenge Herb Darity (the New England junior welterweight champion from Hartford) or Papo Figueroa (New England welterweight champion) or Sims or Dennis. We want to stimulate the local fighters and put some intensity into them."

Seán Mannion was waiting for Titan Sports to fix him up with Roberto Duran, but was becoming unfit and ring-rusty meanwhile. He needed a fight. Finally, three months after beating In-Chul Baek, Mannion appeared on a card of local heroes designed to attract a local crowd to the Cape Cod Coliseum.

On the card with Seán that night was Dicky Eklund, "the Pride of Lowell," who was up against Terry Crawley. Eklund had a big reputation in Massachusetts as the three-times winner of the Golden Gloves, a man who claimed to have knocked down Sugar Ray Leonard live on TV (although he would admit years later that Leonard actually slipped). Eklund developed a less attractive reputation a few years later following his appearance in a documentary on heroin abuse. After time in prison, however, he quit the drugs and began training his brother, Micky Ward, who would go on to win the light welterweight world championship.

Mannion, a sparring and drinking partner of Eklund's, was set to top the card that night against Roberto Colon, with a lot of media interest in his first fight since beating In-Chul Baek.

The *Patriot Ledger* reported on July 22, 1983:

> The fight is a big one for Mannion, who must win to earn a big payday against Roberto Duran—provided Duran is still in once piece and willing to resume his career after fighting Hagler in November.
>
> Titan Sports promoter Jim Troy is negotiating with Bob Arum of Top Rank for a Mannion-Duran title match. According to Troy, the fight will be signed within the next couple of weeks.
>
> "We're looking at Boston or New York City as possible sites," Troy said. "Even if Duran should lose to Hagler, he still must defend his junior middleweight title if he intends to continue boxing, and the feeling here is he will."
>
> Colon recently defeated Rocky Fratto in a fifth-round TKO. Mannion has also beaten Fratto, who was formerly the U.S. junior middleweight champion, the title Mannion now holds.
>
> "Sean has to be careful in this fight," Troy said. "Colon is a good boxer-puncher. We need Sean to be active, which is why we took this fight. The reason we didn't fight Hearns was because the money offered us was ridiculous. It wouldn't have been beneficial to Sean at this time."

But despite the careful buildup, no fight against Duran ever took place. Roberto Duran went 15 rounds with Marvin Hagler that November in a WBC, WBA, and IBF (International Boxing Federation) middleweight unification bout, with Hagler scoring a unanimous win. Duran skipped home to Panama afterward, where he began to eat, drink, and balloon in weight as he often did. He had earned about $5 million for the Hagler fight and wasn't long burning his way through the money, renting out an entire orchestra to accompany him with Latino music as he traveled around Central America. In the end, Duran didn't return to the United States until the following summer. No more than Tommy Hearns, there would be no fight between Roberto Duran and Seán Mannion.

There wasn't even a fight with Roberto Colon, as it happened. A family funeral saw Colon withdraw at the last minute and Danny "Thunderhand" Chapman from New York stepping in. Chapman was a young boxer whose record didn't reflect his nickname, having lost 8 of his 19 fights by the time he met Mannion.

Coming into the fight, Seán was in a state of readiness that left him uncon-
cerned about either Chapman or Colon. Having put on some weight during the
three-month layoff since fighting Baek, he had a $100 bet with both Peter Kerr
and Tony Cardinale that he would make the 154-pound weight limit, which he
made comfortably, coming in two pounds under the cutoff. On the way to the
fight, he stopped off at his sister's house in the verdant suburb of Milton to visit
his mother, who had traveled to Boston on vacation. Nan, Seán's sister, was
taken aback by the amount of weight her brother had lost.

"Are you sick?" she asked.

Seán wasn't sick. Seán was ready. The fight against Danny Chapman was his
first fight in Massachusetts in almost a year, and a large group of his supporters, including his mother and six of his siblings, had made the trip down from
Boston to the Cape.

The fight started as expected, Mannion with the upper hand, Chapman with
the hands up, defending himself. Conscious of the dangers of overcommitting so
close to a potential world title shot, Mannion kept prodding away while staying
out of trouble. But as the fight went on, Chapman started to advance. Suddenly,
in the tenth round, Danny Chapman caught Seán with a punch to the ribs. Bang.
The legs almost buckled under Mannion. Thunderhand had just struck.

Chapman's fist broke two of Mannion's ribs and left him with a 60 percent
collapsed lung.

"I'd never been in pain like that in the ring before," Seán said.

Mannion was in trouble. He couldn't breathe. He dropped his left arm to
protect the ribs and lung, leaving the rest of his body open to attack. Chapman
kept up the attack and Mannion could barely stand, let alone fend him off. The
dream was as good as over—his shot at the world title blown away by a stray
punch from a New York boxer no one had ever heard of. In the audience, fear-
ing for her son, tears rolled down Teresa Mannion's cheeks.

That's when the Cape Cod Coliseum dropped into darkness.

"Whoa, the lights have gone out, folks," said the ESPN's Al Bernstein. "Well
fans, in the tenth round somebody pulled the plug."

Across America, fight fans stared at a black screen. The referee steered the
boxers to their corners, Seán stumbling back, still barely able to draw a breath.
The doctor came to Seán's corner, fixing him up temporarily with a painkiller.
After 20 minutes of darkness and recuperation for Mannion, the lights came
back on.

What was behind "The Night the Lights Went Out" as renowned boxing
writer George Kimball called it? After the fight, the rumor started that Paddy
Mannion had turned off the lights in order to save his brother.

"It wasn't Paddy," said Peter Kerr. "He was beside me all night in the corner."

Kimball wrote that it was Mannion's Irish fans that cut the power in order to give their hero an opportunity to recover.

"Definitely not," insisted Seán. "I used to spar regularly down at the Cape Cod Coliseum and I didn't know where the plug was, let alone the guys who had just arrived down for the night."

Mannion himself was of the view that lightning saved him from Thunderhand Chapman. "There was definitely thunder in the air that night," he said.

ESPN's Al Bernstein disputed this theory in his memoir, *Al Bernstein: 30 Years, 30 Undeniable Truths about Boxing, Sports, and TV*:

Chapman's manager/trainer Bob Miller smelled a rat. The timing of the blackout was, well, let's say too perfect. The conflicting answer about the blackout suggested that it might have been caused by ingenuity, not electrical failure. Wouldn't you know, we found out days later that there was no power outage reported in that area that night, so somehow the lights had gone out only in the arena. Curious.

Seán's lawyer, Tony Cardinale, had the closest thing to a plausible explanation. Cardinale had spent the night sitting beside Vince McMahon Jr., the owner of the Cape Cod Coliseum.

"Vince and I were sitting there and Seán was winning the fight early on," said Cardinale. "All of a sudden, this kid hits Seán a body punch from a very weird angle and from where we were sitting, it looked like he broke a rib or pinched a lung because all of a sudden, Seán couldn't breathe. It really looked bad."

Cardinale knew that if the referee stopped the fight, Seán's shot at the world title would vanish.

"I'm watching what's going on and it's getting scary. I'm afraid that the referee might jump in and stop the fight because he can't breathe when all of a sudden, the lights go out. I look to my right and Vince wasn't there. I'm not saying anything happened but he wasn't there anymore!

"When the lights came back, Vince came walking back over and resumed his seat. The fight restarted and Seán got through."

Despite the pain, Seán continued to box after the lights came back on and was awarded a split decision win by the judges. Some of the audience, convinced of a Chapman win, received the decision by whistling and throwing cups of beer into the ring.

Mannion didn't agree with any perception of injustice. "I won it, if just about."

By that stage, Seán couldn't have cared less about the whistling or about cups being thrown at him. He was in agony. All he wanted to do was get out of that ring and get back to the dressing room. When he finally made it, he started to vomit. He had never been in so much pain.

His mother, Teresa, came into the room. She was furious. "Didn't I tell you to give this up ages ago," she shouted at her son. "Look at you, the state you're in."

"For the love of God, stop and leave me alone," Mannion groaned back.

Seán was brought to the hospital and kept overnight. He was given a choice: an injection down through the shoulder to freeze the side of the body in pain, or to wait three months and let the injury heal itself. He was uneasy about the freezing. It didn't feel natural. He chose to quit boxing for three months.

Meanwhile, Al Bernstein's surreal night in the Cape Cod Coliseum kept getting stranger, as he recounted in his memoir.

After the show, I had to go to the bathroom, having gone through a two-and-a-half-hour show on the air without a break. As I was standing at the urinal a man dressed completely in black leather came in and stood at the urinal right next to me, even though others were available. Before unzipping to urinate, he reached in his back pocket and took out a very big handgun and placed it on the urinal.

I was wide-eyed at that point, wishing very much that I had concluded my business, but alas I had not. He looked at me and said, "What do you think about the fight?" I looked down at the gun, thought for a moment, then looked at him and said, "What would you like me to think?" He just chuckled and didn't say a word. A few moments later we were both ready to leave. As he was putting the very big gun inside the back of his pants, he turned and said to me, "Be careful. A lot of people were drinking tonight. You might run into somebody who's crazy." Well, well, a little too late for that warning.

That was August 1983, by which time Jamaica's Mike McCallum had climbed up the WBA rankings and had become the number one contender, with Mannion as number two. Seán's injury meant that he wasn't in the ring again until February 1984, but he certainly wasn't lying dormant in the meantime.

The attempts to organize a fight between Seán Mannion and Roberto Duran failed, as had the attempts to get him in a ring with Tommy Hearns. With Marvin Hagler fighting a weight division above him, that left only one member of the Four Kings. Sugar Ray Leonard.

Sugar Ray was the Golden Emperor among the Four Kings. After winning a gold medal at the 1976 Montreal Olympics, he announced his retirement before almost immediately changing his mind. Having hired Muhammad Ali's corner man, Angelo Dundee, as his trainer and lawyer Mike Trainer, as his manager,

Leonard would go on to win a world title in five different weight divisions and become the first boxer to earn over $100 million in the sport.

But in November 1982, having beaten the likes of Roberto Duran, Wilfred Benitez, and Tommy Hearns to win welterweight and light middleweight titles, Sugar Ray Leonard announced once again that he was retiring from boxing. Ten months earlier, while defending his WBA and WBC welterweight belts against Bruce Finch, Leonard's eye was seriously damaged, with the retina becoming detached from the tissue around it. That was enough for Leonard to call it quits. Even if the eye healed, he said, he wasn't getting back in the ring.

But just like his last boxing retirement after winning Olympic gold, Sugar Ray soon changed his mind. He missed the ring. More than that, he wanted a shot at Marvin Hagler, the only great of his era whom he hadn't fought. In December 1983, Sugar Ray announced his second coming. The decision wasn't universally welcomed, especially after the doctor who had performed the operation on his eye said that his former patient should never fight again. But Leonard wasn't listening. He was back, and his first fight in over two years was going to attract huge interest.

Sugar Ray needed an opponent for his comeback, and there was one name mentioned from the start. Seán Mannion. The logic was pretty clear: use a Massachusetts-based southpaw to prepare for Marvin Hagler, another Massachusetts-based southpaw. Sugar Ray's manager, Mike Trainer, contacted Jimmy Connolly, and Seán Mannion was offered over $100,000 to take on Leonard, more money than every fight he had ever fought previously, combined.

Connolly told Trainer that he'd get back to him.

"The only stipulation was that the guy had to be free of promotional entanglements and in a position to make a deal," said Trainer, according to George Kimball in his book, Four Kings. "We didn't want to be wrangling with any outside promoters over this thing, and I told Jimmy Connolly that more than once."

As it happened, Seán's contract with Top Rank had just finished up with the Danny Chapman fight, leaving him free of any ties. But Jimmy Connolly was short on cash. He disregarded Mike Trainer's warning and called Bob Arum, using Trainer's offer to leverage more money out of Top Rank. Arum reminded Connolly of the work he and Top Rank had put into Seán Mannion in order to get him a shot at the world title, and told Connolly that Seán's WBA ranking would be in jeopardy if he lost to Sugar Ray Leonard.

That night, Jimmy Connolly drove Mannion to New York to sign a new contract with Top Rank. Teddy Brenner drafted the contract, and both Seán and Jimmy received a $10,000 bonus for signing up. Brenner was Top Rank's

man on the East Coast, the man who picked the fighters and put the fights together. It was Brenner who arranged the first fight between Muhammad Ali and
Joe Frazier in Madison Square Garden. It was Brenner who arranged fights for
Sugar Ray Robinson and for Jake LaMotta. When Teddy Brenner asked you to
sign something, you listened. The contract was signed.

Dear Mr. Mannion,
　　You hereby acknowledge your receipt of the sum of $10,000 by the check of
Top Rank, Inc. delivered to you today.
　　This payment shall constitute a loan payable to you and your manager, jointly
and severally; such loan to be repaid only from your purse for the bout described
herein.
　　In consideration for this loan and our mutual promises you hereby grant to
Top Rank, Inc. the exclusive, irrevocable right and option to promote a 10-round
or 15-round bout (at Top Rank's selection) at any time during the period of January 1 through April 15, 1984, against either of the following opponents for the
indicated purses:

Opponent	Purse
Nino LaRocca or an equivalent opponent	$75,000 OR
Sugar Ray Leonard	$150,000

Jimmy Connolly had just signed the contract that Mike Trainer had told
him not to. There would be no fight between Mannion and Nino LaRocca, an
Italian boxer with a big reputation and a 54–0 record. Nor would there be a
fight between Mannion and Sugar Ray Leonard because, regardless of what arrangement Top Rank tried to come to, neither Leonard nor Mike Trainer were
willing to cooperate.

Signing the Top Rank contract was a huge mistake by Mannion's management, according to Trainer, for a number of reasons.

"It was a pretty stupid move on their part," Trainer said in George Kimball's
Four Kings. "Mannion would have gotten more money for fighting Ray—
$100,000—than he would end up getting to fight Mike McCallum for the title,
and even if he'd lost to Ray but looked good, his career wouldn't have suffered.
And when you look at what happened in the two fights, Mannion probably had
a better chance of beating Ray, who was coming off the layoff, than he did Mc-
Callum, which was zero."

Mike Trainer despised Bob Arum, and the feeling was mutual. The two had
fallen out over the 1981 Leonard/Hearns world title fight, and there was no
way Trainer was going to get involved with Seán Mannion now that Mannion

had signed a contract with the man who said, "Mike Trainer is an absolute, despicable liar."

Jimmy Connolly said at the time that he was of the view that the contract was open enough to ensure that Trainer wouldn't have to deal with Arum. But that's not how Mike Trainer saw it. Once again, Seán Mannion was denied a huge fight and payday because of his manager.

"Arum has helped me," said Connolly in a *Boston Globe* piece called "Money in Way of Big Fight." "I couldn't kiss him off."

In the end, Sugar Ray Leonard fought little-known Kevin Howard in Worcester, Massachusetts. Howard managed to do something no boxer had done previously when he knocked down Sugar Ray in the fourth. Leonard got up again and took the win after a controversial ninth-round stoppage, but was so disappointed with his comeback performance that he announced once again that he was quitting boxing. If there had ever been an opportunity to beat Sugar Ray Leonard, it was that night.

For Mannion, it was a huge opportunity lost, but the regret of not having fought the legendary Sugar Ray Leonard and losing out on the $105,000 purse was offset by his world title dreams finally becoming reality.

Roberto Duran was the holder of the WBA light middleweight title, but wasn't particularly keen on taking on the number one contender, Mike Mc-Callum. Mike Trainer put his finger on it when he told the *Boston Globe*, in an article titled "Mannion May Get Shot at Leonard," that Duran would sooner give the belt up than get in the ring with the Jamaican.

"There's no money in that fight. McCallum is a big, strong kid. Duran's people aren't stupid." "I can understand their position," said McCallum's then-trainer, Emanuel Steward, in an interview with the *New York Times* on February 22, 1984. "Why fight a McCallum who can be just as tough as a Hearns? Duran doesn't care about titles. He's interested only in money. He wants only two more fights."

In the end, Duran surrendered his WBA belt and challenged Tommy Hearns for the WBC title instead. The vacant WBA title would be contested by the number one and number two contenders. Seán Mannion would take on Mike McCallum in Madison Square Garden on October 19, 1984. All Seán had to do was win one more fight.

The fight was set for February 17, 1984, live once again on ESPN from Atlantic City, and Teddy Brenner chose Roosevelt Green as Seán Mannion's opponent. Brenner wasn't in the habit of putting easy fights together. Roosevelt Green was a bronze medal winner at the 1978 World Amateur Boxing Championships, having won the Chicago Golden Gloves the previous year, and had scored 12 KOs in his 19–5–0 pro record.

Mannion, after the enforced break following the Chapman fight, had only once been heavier going into the ring, and that was against Ralph Doucette three years earlier. He felt good, though, and he felt ready. But just as he was about to leave the dressing room, Seán felt something snap in his lower back, followed by a rush of pain. Whatever had happened meant that he could only move forward. No moving back. Not even a slow shuffle.

Mannion managed to leave the dressing room but was in a bad way by the time he got to the ring. Without being able to move backwards, he knew that he had no choice but to go on the attack from the outset, something he wasn't entirely comfortable with. It meant spending the fight inside Roosevelt Green's reach and hoping his opponent wouldn't catch him cleanly. Losing a fight this close to the world title would be more than a little careless.

Green climbed into the ring wearing white shorts with a black band. Seán Mannion wore new shorts with the by now familiar shamrock embroidered on one leg, "Sean Mannion" stitched above it. On the waist, "Rosmuc."

With no other choice open to him, Mannion came at Green from the moment the bell struck. Green's corner didn't understand what was happening. They had prepared their man for a different Seán Mannion. The skillful, measured Mannion. The Mannion that danced in and out of his opponent's reach. Where the hell was that Seán Mannion?

He certainly wasn't the guy in the ring with Roosevelt Green. Without the option of backing away, Seán spent the entire fight on the attack. It worked. By the second round, Green was bleeding from the mouth. By the sixth, he had to assure the referee, Joe Cortez, that he was able to continue.

He didn't get past the seventh, however. Roosevelt Green threw a left jab. Mannion ducked. Green threw another, followed by a huge right hook that caught nothing but the humid, clammy air of the Resorts International Hotel, leaving him wide open. Seán attacked with a right hook, catching Green on the jaw. The legs almost went from under the Chicago man. Mannion followed him in on the ropes. Left. Right. Cortez jumped in before Mannion could do any more damage. The fight was stopped. Seán turned around. He walked back to his corner, lifting his arms in the air. He had done it. Seán Mannion's next fight would be for the world title, and no one could stop him now.

Only one man stood between him and the greatest accolade in boxing. Mike McCallum.

⓭

THE DEAL

A dull sleep hung over Kingston. Lying in the dust under a palm tree, a dog scratched out a bed, looking to escape from a sun that could bore holes in a wall. The thin ridges of her ribs heaved slowly under fur as she drew a languorous breath. Nothing stirred in this heat. Another day in Jamaica.

On the street, two young boys escaped the pall of sleep cast by the sun on the rest of the population. Two fighting cousins, throwing punches at each other. As they fought, Errol Corinthian, a former pro boxer, happened to walk by. Drawn by the style of the taller cousin, Corinthian stopped to speak to him, according to Austin Killeen's online profile, titled "Mike McCallum: The Body Snatcher."

"Son, you're a natural."

The young boy looked up. "What the hell does that mean?" he asked in his heavy Jamaican accent.

Mike McCallum was 15 years old.

What Errol Corinthian saw in Kingston that day in 1970 would soon become apparent to the rest of the world as Mike McCallum took his place among the greats of boxing history. He won world championships at three different weights, successfully defending his titles 11 times. He was inducted into the International Boxing Hall of Fame in 2003. *Ring Magazine* ranked him as the second greatest light middleweight boxer of all time. Thomas Hearns, who refused to get in the ring with McCallum despite many invitations to do so, was ranked number one.

But despite his incredible achievements, few have heard of Mike McCallum, certainly when compared to the other great boxers of his era and weight. It didn't help his profile that not one of the Four Kings was willing to get into the ring with him, despite many promises to the contrary. Indeed, McCallum didn't get his first title shot until Roberto Duran refused to fight him, with Duran sooner relinquishing his WBA belt than taking on the Jamaican.

"I wanted to fight these guys in the '80s and they just laughed," said McCallum. "I say 'why ain't you ever fight me' and they look at me and smile. The only shot of Hearns I got was a picture.

"You can't call yourself the best if you pick and choose who you fight. They always made out that it was the money but they were afraid of getting in the ring with me."

Eddie Futch, who trained the likes of Joe Frazier and Larry Holmes, was in no doubt about the Jamaican's ability, as he recalled in an interview with the *Baltimore Sun* in 1991. "Quite simply," he said, "McCallum is the best fighter nobody knows."

~

Mike McCallum was 16 years old when he first won the Jamaican senior boxing championship. The following year, he won it again. All of a sudden, a young boy who never set foot in a ring until he was 15 was boxing for his country. McCallum was sent to Cuba to represent Jamaica in the 1974 World Championships where he was beaten in the quarterfinals by Clint Jackson, the U.S. representative, who went on to win silver. The following year, he met Jackson again in the North American Championships and again, the American won.

Despite Jackson having twice beaten him, the two became friends after getting to know each other at the 1976 Montreal Olympics. The following year, McCallum moved to Jackson's hometown of Nashville, Tennessee, where his friend worked as a deputy sheriff. Jackson found him a job cleaning out prison cells, and at night, McCallum would sleep in one of the empty cells.

Although neither of them managed a medal in Montreal, they both had extremely successful amateur careers. McCallum won both the Golden Gloves and Amateur Athletic Union U.S. titles, as well as a gold medal for Jamaica at the 1978 Commonwealth Games. Clint Jackson won national Golden Gloves and AAU welterweight titles, along with his silver world championship medal. Jackson, however, never managed to succeed in the professional world as McCallum did. After six years of pro boxing, he quit in 1985. Four years later, police arrested Jackson after he kidnapped a banker in southern Alabama in an attempt to extort $9,000. He was given a life sentence.

Mike McCallum had initially decided to turn pro after failing to win a medal in Montreal, but was stopped by two things. First, the only manager who was willing to give him a contract lived in Jamaica, and McCallum was in no mood to return to his native country. The second reason was more significant. McCallum received a phone call from Michael Manley, then prime minister of Jamaica. Manley told him that he had seen him fight, that he had a great style and a great future, and that he wanted him to stay amateur in an attempt to win a medal for Jamaica at the 1980 Moscow Olympics.

Mike McCallum wasn't going to say no to his prime minister, but received criticism from his home country for remaining in the United States to train rather than returning to Jamaica. But with the boxing facilities and opportunities in the United States considerably better than those at home, young McCallum wasn't going to let nationalism scupper his personal ambition.

Despite the fact that no Jamaican had ever won an Olympic medal in any sport that didn't involve running, Mike McCallum traveled with an air of confidence to the Soviet Union in the summer of 1980. There was more than a place in history at stake if he managed to win a medal. There was fame, there was wealth, and there was the greatest springboard available into the world of professional boxing. It worked for Sugar Ray Leonard after the Montreal Olympics, and it had worked out well for other Olympic gold medalists such as Cassius Clay, Floyd Patterson, and George Foreman.

A week before the start of the Games, McCallum was training in the Olympic Village, about half an hour west of the center of Moscow, when a pain in his stomach began to bother him. He ignored it initially, but when the pain got worse, he had little choice but to go to the doctor. Appendicitis. It was disastrous news for Jamaica's golden hope. McCallum had to pack up and leave for home, without having thrown a single competitive punch. He was devastated.

"I couldn't believe it," he said, "all I wanted to do was represent my country."

Mike McCallum was 24 years old. He had put in 250 fights as an amateur, 240 of which he had won. With another four years before the next Olympic Games, Mike decided that it was finally time to fight for money. He initially signed a pro boxing contract with a Florida-based music promoter, but by 1982 he had abandoned the Sunshine State to travel north to Detroit.

Detroit was known for cars, music, and the Kronk Gym, and that's where McCallum signed up with the legendary Emanuel Steward. The Kronk is among those few fabled boxing gyms, such as Angelo Dundee's 5th Street Gym in Miami or Joe Frazier's Gym in Philadelphia or Gleason's Gym in New York, that have shaped the legends of world boxing. But among these temples, the

Kronk was a cathedral. In the 30 years that Emanuel Steward ran the place, almost 40 world champions came out of the Kronk Gym, along with three Olympic gold medalists.

Mike McCallum took to professional boxing with the intensity he displayed as an amateur. He stopped every one of his first 14 opponents within the distance. In his 15th fight, his opponent, Kevin Perry—trained by Joe Frazier—started well with a strong first round, but suffered McCallum's long left arm for the remaining nine. A unanimous decision for McCallum, it was his first pro fight to go the distance.

Despite the great start to his career, McCallum managed to stay under the radar of the general public until his fight with former world champion Ayub Kalule in 1982. Kalule had won the light welterweight world title three years earlier, which he successfully defended four times until Sugar Ray Leonard beat him in front of 30,000 people in Houston, Texas.

For Ayub Kalule, taking on Mike McCallum was about beating a genuinely good young boxer, where victory would tee him up for another shot at the title. For McCallum, it was all about the kudos of fighting a former world champion, and despite Kalule being the first southpaw he encountered as a pro, he took it in his stride. Having spent years sparring with leftie amateurs such as Clint Jackson and Johnny Bumphus, he felt as comfortable against a left-hander as he did an orthodox boxer, something Kalule, and later Seán Mannion, would find out.

Ayub Kalule never stood a chance against Mike McCallum. An uppercut left him on the floor in the first round, and although he got back up, he continued to suffer for the next six rounds.

"A one-way beating," was how the NBC commentator described the fight.

In the seventh round, McCallum began an all-out assault. Left. Right. Unrelenting. Left. Right. Over and over again. Kalule, overwhelmed, just couldn't cope. When the bell went, the referee, Joe Cortez, followed the Ugandan back to his corner.

"Get the doctor in here," shouted Cortez, "I want him checked out. I want to protect the man."

The fight was stopped once the doctor had inspected Kalule, who seemed almost glad of the decision. Shortly after the fight, he announced that he was retiring from boxing for good, only to change his mind a year later.

"I seen Sugar Ray Leonard fight Kalule and I said to myself I can beat him better than Sugar Ray because Sugar Ray can't punch to the body like I can" said McCallum. "That fight broke me into the top 10 and gave me a title shot eventually.

"That was the biggest test of my professional career at that point. I had to win. To be champion, I had to get through Kalule."

By the time McCallum faced Seán Mannion for the world title four fights later, the Jamaican had put together a formidable 21-0-0 record. He had also picked up a nickname. Tommy Hearns had taken to calling him "The Body-snatcher" because of how hard and how often McCallum would punch to the body during their sparring sessions in the Kronk Gym.

"People don't know that even though Tommy was the star at the Kronk, Mike was the one I was the closest with," said Emanuel Steward in an interview with the online CBZ Journal.

> He was my close buddy. I mean almost every night I went out to eat, wherever I went, Mike was with me. We got to be that close. Not Tommy. Mike and I were much closer. I've watched his career as it went on, and I was right there in the front row when he knocked out Donald Curry with a beautiful, picture-perfect left hook.
>
> The main thing that I remember about Mike is he's the most naturally gifted fighter that ever walked into my gym. He did everything effortlessly. I mean he was just so smooth, so automatic. You would show him a little trick, and well, here's a good example. One day he was boxing with Tommy, and I said to him, "I'm gonna show you a little trick. Tommy jabs with his left hand down, so I want you to parry it and step over real smooth, and shoot a little one, two and hit him on the chin." He hit him three consecutive times, and finally Tommy stopped and said, "How come I can't stop him from hitting me?" And everyone laughed!
>
> He did it so smooth, and I've shown that to a lot of fighters but no one was ever able to do it, and he could hit anybody to the body! The workouts between Mike and Tommy were just unbelievable. They were better than most fights. They were just phenomenal!

But no one else, other than those who witnessed their training sessions, ever got to see Mike McCallum fight Tommy Hearns, or any of the other Four Kings for that matter. By the time McCallum had earned his number one contender status, Roberto Duran was the WBA light middleweight champion, having given Davey Moore an unrelenting beating that left the referee with no choice but to stop the fight in the eighth round. Duran looked like he was back to his ferocious best for the first time since uttering "no más" against Sugar Ray Leonard three years earlier.

Roberto Duran returned home to Panama for the first time since the Leonard fight, this time as champion but still unsure about what awaited him. His last homecoming had been a poisonous, hostile affair, as if Panama had been ashamed of the man who quit a fight for no reason. But now, champion once more, all was forgiven. Over 300,000 people lined the streets from the airport to Panama City to welcome him home.

A month later, about 1,500 of Duran's supporters attended a press conference in New York, where it was announced that Duran was to go up to middleweight, so as to take a shot at Marvin Hagler's WBA, WBC, and IBF titles, and at the pot of gold that came with it.

"Here's a fight worth $50 million that wouldn't have been worth 50 cents six months ago," Budd Schulberg of *Sports Illustrated* wrote. The fight went 15 rounds and, although there was little between them, Marvelous Marvin Hagler was awarded a unanimous victory. There would be no middleweight titles for Duran, but he still had his WBA light middleweight belt.

But with the WBA looking for a mandatory defense against Mike McCallum, there was no way Duran was going to take the Jamaican on. McCallum had limited box office value as an opponent when compared to any of the Four Kings, and there just wasn't enough money in it for Duran, especially given the real risk of defeat.

Maybe Duran wasn't keen on McCallum, but McCallum was plenty keen on Duran. "In his day, Roberto Duran was a great, great fighter," McCallum told the *New York Times* in July 1982. "But I'd love to fight him now. I'd knock him out."

In the end, with the WBA threatening to strip the Panamanian of his title unless he agreed to take on McCallum, Duran forfeited his belt and declared that he would instead fight Tommy Hearns for the WBC title.

Emanuel Steward was delighted. Now he had a world title fight for both of his light middleweight boxers. Tommy Hearns would fight Roberto Duran, and Mike McCallum would fight the WBA's number two contender, Seán Mannion.

"To wait for Duran to be stripped of his title might take until November or December," Steward told Thomas Rogers of the *New York Times* at the time. "So the agreement I reached has Duran vacating his title to fight Hearns, which will give Mike a shot at the vacant championship."

But Mike McCallum was furious. Not only was he the number one WBA contender, he was also the number one WBC contender. Yet his manager had arranged that he would fight neither of those two title holders. He criticized Steward, his own manager and trainer, at the press conference announcing the fights.

"I did everything in my power to get him a fight with Roberto," replied an exasperated Steward in an interview with the *Washington Post* in March 1984. "You cannot make a man fight someone if he doesn't want to."

Emanuel Steward and Thomas Hearns and Roberto Duran all had the same reason for going with the Hearns vs. Duran option, as opposed to Hearns vs. McCallum or Duran vs. McCallum. It was called money. Pitting the two better-known boxers against each other was always going to be a bigger draw than going up against the new guy. It was agreed that the WBA and the WBC title fights would take place on the same card in a new, 17,000-seat venue in Nassau in the Bahamas. Hearns vs. Duran. McCallum vs. Mannion.

But it never came to pass.

McCallum fell out with Emanuel Steward and pulled out of the card. Years later, Steward explained what happened in a 2003 interview with the CBZ Journal.

I signed Mike and moved him into the number-one spot, and we were supposed to fight Roberto Duran. Then Duran's people told me [they weren't] going to fight Mike McCallum. I said, "What do you mean, we have a contract, he's the number-one contender!"

Duran just had a good fight with Hagler and lost a close decision, and they wanted to make a rematch. With McCallum, they would only make $500,000, but with a rematch with Hagler, they would make $5 million. So, I made a deal that Duran would fight Tommy Hearns, but Duran would have to give up his WBA title. I allowed Duran to fight Tommy and make more money than Tommy, but the bout would only be for Tommy's title.

I made him give up the belt so Mike could fight for that vacant title. So, Mike was gonna fight Seán Mannion for the title on the undercard of Duran/Hearns. I was using Tommy to get him his title shot because they were not gonna let him have it. It was advertised as being a double-header with Hearns/Duran for the WBC title and McCallum/Mannion for the WBA title, and I told him that under these conditions if Duran won, he would have to give McCallum a shot.

Anyway, we all agreed. Mike was getting $250,000 and keeping all of it—as his manager I wasn't taking anything—and then suddenly he gets a phone call from [boxing promoter] Shelly Finkel telling him that I was screwing him and so on. I explained to him that I thought I was doing the safest thing for him that would guarantee him a title shot. We had an argument, and he ends up pulling out of the card.

That's why when you saw the Hearns/Duran fight it was only for Tommy's title even though they were both champions. It should have been a title unification, but that's what we sacrificed to get Mike his shot. He didn't want to fight on the card, so later on the fight takes place, and he ends up fighting for about $30,000. He won the title, but shortly after that we severed our relationship because I got to realize that he always talked to everyone. He was always looking for advice, and when you do that you stay confused.

Years later, Seán Mannion bumped into Emanuel Steward and was told the same story, but with an additional galling detail. "He told me McCallum and I would have been on the undercard for Hearns and Duran," said Mannion, "and that McCallum would get $250,000 and that I would get $200,000, but that McCallum withdrew from the deal."

"The bastard," was Seán's reaction after listening to Emanuel Steward, realizing for the first time how close he had come to the biggest payday of his life.

Mike McCallum lost out on a big payday himself, but there was no way he was going to fight on the same card as Duran and Hearns.

"It was a conflict of interest," said McCallum. "I realized that he was giving the title shot to Tommy [Hearns] and that Tommy was the one going to make the money. At that stage, I said to Emanuel that he could go fuck himself. I wasn't fighting on any Duran/Hearns undercard."

Without Hearns or Duran on the card, a world title bout between Mike McCallum and Seán Mannion was never going to attract big money. The fight was put out to contract by way of sealed bid, and Bob Arum's Top Rank made the highest offer, $75,000. Fighting for the WBA light middleweight world title, Mike McCallum and Seán Mannion would only receive $30,000 each.

The contract was signed live on Channel 7 three months beforehand, Mannion in Boston and McCallum in New York. Bob Arum arranged for the bout to take place in Madison Square Garden on October 19, 1984, on the same card as Marvin Hagler's mandatory defense of the middleweight titles against Mustafa Hamsho.

There might have been relatively little money for the fight itself, but at least the winner had the promise of riches. He would get $185,000 for the first defense of the belt, against Luigi Minchillo in Milan, Italy, the following December. Both boxers were also given the choice of signing an additional $30,000 contract giving Top Rank the rights to the first three defenses of the title. Mannion signed on Jimmy Connolly's advice. McCallum refused.

Connolly took his training and management cut from that second $30,000, as well as the money for the title fight itself, despite the fact that he wasn't entitled to do so because the second payment wasn't a fight fee. It would take hindsight for Seán to realize this, by which stage he was left with little over half of the $60,000 he received from Top Rank.

As for Hearns and Duran, the Bahamas deal fell apart and the fight was held instead at Caesars Palace in Las Vegas. The match was christened "Malice at the Palace," and it turned out that Hitman Hearns was way too malicious for Roberto Duran. Prior to the fight, Duran had only been knocked down twice in his career. Tommy Hearns had him on the canvas twice in the first round, and knocked him out cold with a right-hand punch 67 seconds into the second round.

Meanwhile, McCallum and Mannion, the two of them born within a month of each other, would finally get their coveted shot at the world title. But for McCallum, it was a time tinged with sadness. His partner, Yvonne Ladely, died during a heart operation at the start of year, leaving Mike without the love of his life and leaving his daughter, Michelle, without a mother. He was heartbroken. His final conversation with her was a phone call to New York from Detroit, telling her how he was going to beat Roberto Duran and take the world title. Him in the Kronk, training for a fight that would never happen.

It didn't help either that the relationship between McCallum and Emanuel Steward, bound together by a management contract, hadn't improved. About a month before the big fight, Steward arranged a training camp for McCallum at Grossinger's Resort in the Catskill Mountains in upstate New York. Steward sent only one sparring partner, Donald Bowers, with McCallum. Bowers was short, slow, and right-handed. Definitely not Seán Mannion.

Renowned trainer Lou Duva happened to be in Grossinger's at the same time as McCallum, where he was running a training camp for his own boxers. When Duva saw what McCallum was left to work with, he brought three southpaws up to the Catskills from New Jersey. Maybe McCallum still had a management contract with Steward, but he was finished with him as a trainer. As far as he was concerned, he was now a Lou Duva fighter.

"I was messed over," McCallum told Michael Katz of the *New York Times* at the time. "Emanuel is a great trainer and even a great man. I've never said anything derogatory about my managers. They knock me. But the thing is, all my problems with managers, I'm always right." Emanuel Steward was Mike McCallum's third manager in three years of professional boxing. He was now on the lookout for yet another new manager.

"If all his managers and trainers come to the fight," the *New York Times* reported Lou Duva as saying three days before the world title fight, "we'll have a sell-out."

14

BORSCHT

R usting sun loungers float on beds of soft green moss. Paper birch trees pro-
trude from the floors of once grand hotel lobbies. Silence echoes around
crumbling walls still clinging to the laughter and joy of another era. One hundred miles north of New York City, concrete ruins covering hundreds of acres
are slowly being reclaimed by the ground ivy and sugar maples of the Catskill
Mountains.

This is the Borscht Belt, where Irish and Italian immigrants vacationed at the
end of the nineteenth century as an escape from the steamy, sticky summer city.
By the 1950s, the Catskills had become a giant resort, hidden among trees and
hills, for Jewish American families looking to get away from the damned heat
of New York City. The area took its name from borscht soup, popular among
eastern European Jewish immigrants, and featured on the menus of giant resort
hotels such as Grossinger's, Kutcher's, and the Concord.

When the Borscht Belt was in its heyday, over 500 hotels catered for up to a
million visitors every summer. Each large hotel had its own golf course. Hotels
were built on lakesides so that guests could swim, but as competition increased,
swimming pools began to appear. When every hotel had an outdoor swimming
pool, they started building them indoors in order to gain an edge over their
rivals. Ice-skating rinks appeared in the middle of July. Large-scale outdoor
games were organized. Jewish comedians such as Jackie Mason, Joan Rivers,
and Mel Brooks provided entertainment for the crowds. Every night, 3,000
guests would sit down together in super-sized hotels for a super-sized kosher
dinner. Returning home from the Catskills having gained weight was a matter
of pride.

But by the mid-1970s, things began to change. As their children grew up in the United States, the Jewish immigrants of eastern Europe became more rooted in American culture, and the desire to vacation among their own diminished. Casinos began to draw visitors away to the hotels of Atlantic City. The advent of cheap flights meant that vacations in Europe or Hawaii were no longer outlandish dreams.

One by one, the large hotels began to close. The Young's Gap Hotel first, followed soon by the likes of the Ambassador and the Laurels. The closure of the enormous Grossinger's Resort, with its own airport and post office, confirmed the end of an era. The last of these once-great temples to vacation-making, Kutcher's, closed in 2013 and was demolished a year later. Nearby, the once mighty Tamarack Lodge is a mess of scorched corridors and gutted bedrooms. A shattered chandelier hangs over the reception of the Pines, mourning another era. Nothing remains of the Concord but a few concrete stumps pushing up from the soil and blue craters where swimming pools once laughed and lapped through summer.

But back in 1984, the larger Borscht Belt hotels were still clinging on, and part of the reason was boxing. No one knew that better than Jennie Grossinger, who convinced her parents to sell their Catskills farm in 1919 and buy a hotel on 63 acres of land in nearby Liberty. When her father died during the Great Depression, Jennie took over but struggled to keep Grossinger's hotel doors open in the face of the biggest economic depression in U.S. history.

In the end, Jennie Grossinger's salvation came in the form of a sport she despised. When Orthodox Jew and boxer Barney Ross started winning fights, he needed a training venue that would accommodate his religious practices. Jennie invited him to Grossinger's, ensuring that he had access to kosher food and to a rabbi. In 1933, Ross won both the world lightweight and light welterweight titles in one night, and word soon spread in the boxing world of his "home away from home" at Grossinger's. Seeking to replicate Ross's success, managers began organizing training camps for their boxers in the Catskills. The larger resorts started offering free accommodation to the more famous fighters preparing for world title fights. Soon, people started flocking to Grossinger's just to see the likes of Sugar Ray Robinson and Rocky Marciano train. By 1984, Mike McCallum was yet another world title fighter shadowboxing his way around Grossinger's.

~

Ten minutes' drive from Grossinger's, past the town of Liberty, through the forests along Ferndale Road to the shores of Swan Lake, was the Stevensville

Country Club. The Stevensville didn't have a boxing history, no photos of Sonny Liston running along its golf course, no Ezzard Charles sweating in its gym. But in 1984, with the whole Catskills tourism industry on the brink of collapse, the hotel management decided that salvation might be found in some boxing publicity. And so Seán Mannion and his entourage were invited to spend six weeks at the Stevensville Country Club in order to prepare for the WBA light middleweight world title fight.

The indoor tennis court at the Stevensville was cleared out and turned into a boxing gym, with a ring erected to the side of the room. Punch bags and speed balls were hung off the ceiling, weight machines trundled into place. At the back of the hotel, Seán Mannion had acreages of running trails all to himself. Green golf pastures sculpted out of forest, narrow tracks running between trees as golden leaves announced autumn in the Catskills. A world away from Boston, as Seán suggested in an interview with Leigh Montville of the *Boston Globe*, four days after moving to the shores of Swan Lake:

> The place is the Stevensville Country Club in Stevensville, N.Y., a small town plunked into the middle of the Catskills. Open a window and the mountain air invades the room. Clean air. Fresh air, pure as bottled mineral water. Air that can make a man dizzy about the possibilities of things to come.
>
> The fighter and the trainer breathe deeply every day.
>
> "Takes a while getting used to this air," junior middleweight Sean Mannion of Dorchester reported yesterday. "Maybe I should be doing my roadwork behind a taxi. Just to feel at home."
>
> "It's beautiful," trainer Jimmy Connolly said. "Just beautiful."
>
> Through the mountains, down the roads, ran the champions of the mind. Rocky ran here. Right across the lake at Grossinger's. Rocky. The real Rocky. Joe Louis ran here. Roberto Duran. Emile Griffith. Sugar Ray. The real Sugar Ray. Through the mountains, down the roads, runs Sean Mannion with Jimmy Connolly in charge. Every morning. Reality merges with memory and possibility. This is the fringe of the luxurious red carpet that is spread for champions.
>
> "I've never gone away to train," Sean Mannion said. "This is a first. Usually, I'll take two or three weeks off work to prepare for the big fights in the gym. That's it. Then back to work . . ."
>
> This is the shot. Capitalize the letters. This is The Shot. On Oct. 19 in Madison Square Garden in New York, five weeks from tonight, Sean Mannion will fight Mike McCallum for the junior middleweight championship of the world. The rule of boxing is that if you wait long enough and do well enough, a night will come along in which you can change your life with a single well-placed uppercut. There will be one grand spin of the roulette wheel. One shot. Win or lose.

This is it.

"I always knew it would happen," Jimmy Connolly said. "I knew it would come sometime. Why? I can't say for sure. You just have the feeling . . ."

The word "professional" has been used to describe the kid's career, but in a lot of ways Sean Mannion has been much more an amateur than your average Edwin Moses or Carl Lewis, athletes who do nothing but practice for their events and go home to rest. The kid has worked a regular job, for his brother's construction business, during the days. He has worked a part-time job for Jimmy Connolly's boxing business, running along Carson Beach and around Castle Island in the morning, punching the big bag at night in the gym.

The luxury of simply working at boxing alone has never existed. Not for the fighter. Not for the trainer. Not until now.

"If I can win this fight, that's it," Sean Mannion said at the end of his fourth day at the Stevensville Country Club training camp. "I'm a fighter. I'm not doing anything else. Fighting's my job. I'm a 3–1 underdog, but if I can win this fight, if I can show people, if I can win this title and bring it to Ireland . . . "

"Any trainer or manager looks for this moment all his life," Jimmy Connolly said. "It's the culmination of a long, hard road."

The window is open. The air enters and the fighter and the trainer breathe deeply. The view is without limits.

Little did Seán Mannion realize that there was about to be a wall erected around that view without limits. The day after the man from the *Boston Globe* headed back home, Mannion started the morning as usual, getting up at 6:30 a.m. to go for a run. With a chill in the air, he pulled on a pair of training pants under his green shorts and pulled a black woollen hat down over his ears. His sweatshirt bore a call for a united Ireland. "Ireland 32." At 7:00, he shut the door of his chalet behind him and ran through the trees at the back of the hotel until they faded into the open expanse of the golf course, shadowboxing his way down doglegs and around bunkers. After six miles of running, he returned to the gym for some more shadowboxing before taking a shower.

The entire crew got together around the breakfast table at 9:30. Manager. Trainers. Bodyguards. Sparring partners. Jimmy Connolly had brought three sparring partners to Stevensville for Mannion: Billy Smith, Hector Jaiman, and Darnell Knox. Jaiman and Smith both sparred regularly with Seán and were from Boston. Knox, from Detroit, was perhaps the most valuable of the three for this gig, having trained under Emanuel Steward in the Kronk. He had gotten to know Mike McCallum so well that he could actually imitate the Jamaican's style.

At the table next to the Boston crew sat another boxing entourage.

Mustafa Hamsho and Seán Mannion had been on the same card for Seán's first-ever pro fight in Rhode Island in 1978. Now, they were sitting a table apart, in the same training camp, the two of them preparing to appear on the same card once again. This time, however, Mannion and Hamsho were both contending for a world title, with Hamsho taking on Marvin Hagler for the WBA, WBC, and IBF middleweight titles.

A few days earlier, Hamsho's manager, Al Certo, had asked Jimmy Connolly if their man could spar with Seán, given that Mannion, like Hagler, was a southpaw and given that Mannion knew Hagler's style well from sparring with him in the past.

"Sure you can spar with him," Mannion recalls Connolly telling him, but Mannion was furious when he heard the news.

"What the fuck would I be doing sparring with a southpaw when I'm fighting an orthodox?" he asked his manager. The sparring arrangement was duly cancelled.

This hadn't been the first time Mustafa Hamsho had fought Marvin Hagler for the world title. Three years earlier, Brockton's champion gave Hamsho a bad beating over 11 rounds in Chicago. Hamsho felt more prepared this time, however, having put together six consecutive wins since that horrible fight against Marvelous Marvin, beating the likes of Bobby Czyz and Wilfred Benitez on his way to Madison Square Garden. He had also brought a new trainer, Al Silvani, to his camp.

Al Silvani was 74 years old when he traveled to Stevensville Country Club, and had the experience to show for it. He had trained Rocky Graziano. He had trained Jake La Motta. He had even trained Rocky Balboa in the Rocky movies! Silvani was actually a prolific actor (he had 15 separate roles in one movie alone, *The Greatest Story Ever Told*), but boxing was his world. For Seán Mannion, being able to sit down with Al Silvani felt like an indulgent privilege. Mannion loved the history of boxing and boxers, and in the Catskills he was in the company of a man who had trained some of the best of them.

"Al, who was better, Jake La Motta or Rocky Graziano?" he recalls asking Silvani one evening.

"You talkin' as a person or a boxer?" asked Silvani back. "As a person, Graziano was a way, way better person. As a boxer, Jake La Motta would have beaten him with one hand."

But Seán's time with Silvani was cut short when Hamsho and his camp pulled out suddenly from the training camp and moved to Miami. The official story was that he had a bad cold and wasn't able to deal with the chilly Catskills. Given that Hamsho was living just 100 miles away in New York City since arriving from Syria in 1975, it seemed unlikely that he was unable to cope with a climate two hours up the road. The story around the Stevensville Country Club was that an underlying tension between the Arab boxer and the Jewish hotel owners had led Hamsho to depart.

After breakfast, Seán returned to his room. By his bed was an old copy of "Ó Pheann an Phiarsaigh," writings by the Irish revolutionary, Patrick Pearse, along with a few boxing biographies and a copy of *Ring Magazine*. He flicked through the magazine, a photo of Livingstone Bramble, one of McCallum's sparring partners in nearby Grossinger's, on the cover. A new album by a Connemara singer, John Beag Ó Flatharta, played songs in Irish in the background.

This was the slowest part of the day, with no training again until evening time. Seán loved the training camp, wallowing in the almost decadent focus on his own boxing needs, but if there was a downside, this was it. Trying to kill time between sessions. A few days earlier, his brother, Paddy, had stumbled across an Atari 2600 games console in one of the recreation rooms, sparking brotherly competitiveness over games of Pong and Video Olympics.

Finally, a few hours after lunch, it was time for Seán to return to where he really wanted to be. In the ring. He warmed up first with a skipping session before slipping in under the red, white, and blue ropes. Above him hung two banners. One from the hotel, "Welcome to the Stevensville Country Club," and one from the TV station broadcasting the world title fight, "HBO Sports."

Seán was wearing the same shorts from the morning session, along with a blue t-shirt with white sleeves, "Sean Mannion" written across the back. In the ring, Paddy wore boxing pads, his brother dancing, jabbing, flickering around him.

"Keep up your arms after throwing that left," his brother shouted.

Right. Right. Right. Left. Right. In the background, John Beag sang songs of love and emigration. The only other sounds in the hall came from Paddy's occasional advice and the dull thud every time Seán hit the pads. Right. Right. Right. Left. Right.

After a while, Paddy stepped out of the ring to let Darnell Knox get in under the ropes. Seán, looking forward to 10 rounds of sparring, felt good.

"I was boxing well at the time," said Seán, "too well if anything, that far out from the fight. But I could definitely feel that I was in tip-top shape."

Knox went four rounds with Seán, after which Billy Smith stepped in for another four rounds. Hector Jaiman wasn't feeling well, choked up with a cold, but offered to put in two rounds. The two boxers decided to take those two rounds nice and easy, given Jaiman's cold.

The ninth round, Jaiman's first, had just started when he threw a left hook that caught Seán on the right eye. The eye split. Blood spilt.

"Oh. Fuck," was Paddy's instant response from the ringside.

"Jesus Christ," screamed Jimmy Connolly, "watch your elbow," thinking Jaiman had caught Seán dirtily.

The sparring stopped immediately. Connolly ran into the ring and looked at the eye.

"You'll be alright, Seán," he said, "it'll be alright."

But there was more doubt than conviction in Jimmy Connolly's voice, and for good reason. The cut was on the eyelid, and it was a nasty one. Jaiman, hovering on the periphery of the ring, began to feel nauseous when the implications of his errant punch hit him. The world title was at risk.

"Seán, man, I'm sorry, man. Damn, I'm sorry Seán. I'm really, really sorry."

Seán stood in the ring, gloves off, hands bandaged, a crowd around him yet absolutely alone. Above him, the HBO banner seemed to taunt him. Flashes of the journey that had brought him here popped in and out of his head. From Ros Muc to Rhode Island. From Johnny Thornton to Danny Torres. A tumbling roller coaster of Gonzalez and Guiden crescendoing with In-Chul Baek. And now, on the verge of fighting for the world title, on the verge of fighting in the Garden itself, on HBO, on RTÉ showing the people of Ireland what he had achieved since leaving home as yet another Connemara emigrant of the seventies. And now, this had happened. What should have been an insignificant left hook had just jeopardized everything.

Seán returned to his chalet and changed out of his training clothes before driving to New York with Paddy and Jimmy. In a clinic under the grandeur of the Brooklyn Bridge, a doctor who specialized in boxing injuries examined the damaged eye, recalls Paddy Mannion.

"This doesn't look great," he said shaking his head slowly. "This is going to take a few weeks to heal and even then, it'll be vulnerable.

"To be perfectly honest, guys, I can't see how you can spar again before the fight."

The date was September 15. Thirty-three days before the fight for the world title. Thirty-three days of running around Catskill forests while Mike McCallum worked his way through a queue of quality sparring partners at Grossinger's. For the second time that day, Seán Mannion felt a weight of lead in his chest. He hung his head.

The doctor put eight stitches in the cut without using painkiller. It stung like hell but Seán didn't care, given that the doctor's logic was that the cut would heal quicker if he didn't use Novocaine. It didn't.

The two-hour drive back to Stevensville was as long a journey as Seán Mannion had ever made. All three in the car knew how bad things looked, but no one was going to admit it openly. By the time they had reached the hotel, the cut eye had swelled up and turned oxblood red. Seán phoned Peter Kerr, who had gone home to Boston for the weekend, and told him the story. Kerr could barely believe what he was hearing.

"We can postpone the fight," he said. "You'd be crazy to get in the ring with a guy like McCallum without any sparring. You'll get crucified."

Peter Kerr's logic was that Mike McCallum was the world number one contender, that Seán Mannion was number two, and that the belt was theirs to decide between them as Roberto Duran had conceded it. Given that no one else could be handed a shot at the title other than McCallum and Mannion, it would be easy to postpone, especially with the fight still five weeks away.

Paddy agreed with Peter Kerr.

"There was no way on this earth that Seán should have gone into a ring to fight for the world title against Mike McCallum without having done some sparring," said his brother.

Jimmy Connolly didn't agree, however. Connolly was afraid that Seán would somehow lose his title shot if the fight was postponed. This being the first time he had his own man fighting for a world title after 20 years in boxing, Jimmy Connolly wasn't about to let it slip away now that he was so close to Madison Square Garden. Seán agreed. They couldn't take the chance. They couldn't put back the fight. Seán and Jimmy agreed to keep on keeping on.

With hindsight's inconvenient clarity, Seán regretted afterward not going with Paddy and Peter's opinion.

"I was on Connolly's side at the time as I was afraid of losing my shot at the world title, but looking back, I would have had to be given the shot. I don't know if it was that Connolly was beholden to Top Rank and that he didn't want to leave them without a fight, I just don't know.

"What I do know is that my being young and foolish made sure that I didn't want the fight put back. Today, I wouldn't send a child into the county championships without having any sparring done, let alone a world title fight. It was insane."

Jimmy Connolly ordered everyone in the camp to keep quiet about the cut. McCallum couldn't find out that Seán wasn't sparring. But at an event in England years later, Mike McCallum told Seán that he had known all along.

"Yeah, I knew about the cut," he laughed, "and I knew that you didn't get much sparring in either."

"Much?" answered Seán. "I didn't get any sparring in for those last five weeks."

"Serious?" was McCallum's response. "Thank God you didn't or my life could have been very different!"

McCallum found out through one of Mustafa Hamsho's sparring partners, a Jamaican boxer named Noel Tucker. Someone in the Mannion camp had noticed that Tucker seemed to have more interest in Seán than in Hamsho, and when they found out that he was Jamaican, he was asked to leave the Stevensville Country Club. Unsurprisingly, Tucker strolled up the road to Grossinger's to join McCallum's camp.

Things changed in the training camp after Hector Jaiman's left hook. Confidence evaporated. In a desperate effort to compensate for the lack of sparring, Seán loaded on more training. During the evening sessions, he worked the punch bag ("that bag suffered," he joked), skipped, shadowboxed, and went eight rounds on the pads. Ten rounds sometimes. He was fitter than he had ever been in his life, the skin on his face taut around his cheekbones.

Meanwhile, Seán's sparring partners were redundant. Jimmy Connolly had received $10,000 from Top Rank to cover training costs, and it made little sense to Mannion that he still had sparring partners when he couldn't actually spar.

"You might as well send them home," he said to Connolly about Smith, Jaiman, and Knox.

"Why would I?"

"Because we're not bloody using them, that's why."

"They weren't sent home," said Mannion, "and I never saw a penny of that $10,000 either."

But despite the lack of sparring, Seán still enjoyed the training camp. Certain things annoyed him, however. Like the sparring partners who weren't sparring. And the bodyguards. Connolly had brought a few heavies from South Boston to act as Seán's bodyguards, Kevin "Andre the Giant" McDonald among them, who was later imprisoned for drug dealing and for possession of a loaded weapon. Seán told Jimmy that he didn't want any bodyguards around him.

"Seán, you have to have bodyguards."

"I don't friggin' need bodyguards," Seán shot back. "If I need bodyguards, what the fuck am I doing fighting for the world title?"

The bodyguards stayed.

After six weeks in the training camp, it was time to leave the Catskills. Removed from the rest of the world for a month and a half, with nothing to do other than train, Mannion's team was happy to move on. Yet, Seán himself felt a sadness leaving the Stevensville Country Club, the first time in his life where everything was geared toward fulfilling his needs. He had gotten on great with the staff. Despite the occasional argument, he had gotten on great with Jimmy Connolly and the rest of the entourage. But it was time to go.

Seán and the team pulled out of Sullivan County on Wednesday evening, October 17. It was dark by the time they reached the Penta Hotel on 7th Avenue in Manhattan. Waiting for them outside the hotel was an Irish television crew, filming a documentary about the man who was seeking to become the first Irish world champion since Rinty Monaghan won the flyweight title in 1947.

In the documentary, Seán can be seen walking into the Penta, Peter Kerr by his side, Paddy behind him, both wearing green jackets with "Sean Mannion" written on the back, white shamrocks on either side of the name. By Seán's right shoulder is Andre the Giant, who gives a thumbs-up to the camera as they walk by. At the front desk, Jimmy Connolly is busy arranging rooms.

Outside, on the other side of the street, looms Madison Square Garden.

15

THE FIGHT

There was something different about South Station that morning. Tommy Mellett wasn't quite sure what it was, but something felt off. Once the world's busiest train station, Boston's South Station, with its annual torrent of 20 million commuters, isn't the sort of place to reflect on atmospheric nuances.

But on the Friday morning of October 19, 1984, there was something different about the place. Tommy stood in the center of the station's Grand Concourse, 17 years old and on his way to watch his uncle Seán fight for the WBA world light middleweight title in New York City.

He was walking out toward the train platform with his father when it finally dawned on him what it was about South Station that morning. Everyone there seemed to be speaking Irish.

"When I looked around, I realized I knew everyone in South Station," said Tommy. "There was singing, there was drinking. People just walking from car to car meeting people they hadn't seen in years. There was tremendous excitement there."

Amtrak had put on five trains for those traveling to New York for the fight. Tommy's train, which seemed to carry half of Connemara, pulled out at 11:00 a.m. They hadn't left Massachusetts by the time the bar had dried out.

~

Seán Mannion woke up in the Penta Hotel that Friday morning. He was in no hurry to get out of bed. The weigh-in wasn't scheduled until midday, and there was nothing else to do before then. He lay back in bed, thinking of the day ahead. Thinking of Mike McCallum.

Mannion had met Mike McCallum for the first time a day earlier, while choosing fight gloves in Madison Square Garden. Despite knowing what to expect, he was still taken aback when he met the Jamaican. McCallum was tall. He had long arms. Seán knew immediately that he was going to have problems with Mike McCallum. And whatever chance he would ordinarily have had against him had been considerably diminished by the lack of sparring.

"We're gonna beat your ass tomorrow," Jimmy Connolly said to McCallum when they met. "Shut the fuck up," muttered Seán underneath his breath. He shook hands with McCallum. Nice man. Long arms.

Seán closed his eyes and fell back to sleep.

~

Around that same time, Bab Sullivan stood in her kitchen in Pembroke, about an hour south of Boston. Bab used to live in Dorchester, among her brothers and sisters from Ros Muc, but as her family grew older, she craved space and peace, neither of which existed around Fields Corner.

Bab had visitors. Sitting at the head of the kitchen table was Mike Flaherty, drinking tea with Bab's mother, Teresa.

Teresa had been over and back regularly from Ireland to visit her family, but this was Mike Flaherty's first time in the States since settling down in Ros Muc. The first time to see Seán fight since he left home as All-Ireland champion in 1979. Mike and Teresa laughed, joked, spoke of times past, of the big fight that lay ahead. Bab didn't utter a word.

Bab was nervous. Seán had asked her to sing the Irish national anthem, Amhrán na bhFiann, before the fight. She could hardly refuse him. She would have to stand in the center of the ring in Madison Square Garden in front of 20,000 people, mindful of the millions watching live on HBO and on RTÉ back home in Ireland. But it wasn't the singing that had her on edge. If Seán had asked her to stand in the middle of Times Square and sing, she would have said yes.

Bab was nervous about the fight. She didn't enjoy boxing. In fact, she hated it. She had been to the Danny Chapman fight. She had seen her brother badly injured in the ring. As a nurse, she knew only too well the damage one man could inflict on another using no more than his fists.

Bab put the Aran sweater she had chosen to wear for the national anthem in her suitcase and zipped it shut. She told Teresa and Mike to head out to the car. It was time to leave for New York.

Seán woke again. He sat up in bed, rubbed his eyes. His right eye. Under his index finger, he felt the raised ridge of skin, puckered by the stitches on his eyelid, that had taunted him every morning for the past five weeks. It was time to get up.

He had spent the night before in the Gramercy Gym on 14th Street, putting in his final training session before the fight. The Gramercy was a monument to boxing history, owned by Cus D'Amato until he escaped New York City to the Catskill Mountains and ended up training a 14-year-old kid named Mike Tyson.

Thirty-one years earlier, another 14-year-old had walked into the Gramercy Gym looking for a trainer. Under Cus D'Amato's tutelage, Floyd Patterson won Olympic gold and went on to become the youngest man ever to win the world heavyweight title. Patterson fought ten times in Madison Square Garden, winning every one of those fights until Muhammad Ali beat him in his final outing. All Seán Mannion wanted was one win in the Garden. That's all. One fight, one win.

When Seán had finished with the heavy bag, finished with the speed ball, finished with the pads, finished with the history of the Gramercy looking down at him from the old boxing posters pasted on the walls, he changed his clothes and headed back to the Penta.

Alone in the room, he started to think of McCallum. Again. Of the McCallum fights he had seen on tape. Of what he had read about him. He thought of himself. Of how fit he was. Fitter than any moment previously in his life. He thought of how little sparring he had put in. The least he had ever put in before a fight. And not just any fight. The world title fight.

Suddenly, he thought of his friend, his old fighting buddy, drinking buddy, Michael Newell. He hadn't spoken to Michael in a while, as Newell had enlisted in the Marines and was stationed in Camp Pendleton in California. Seán phoned him. Michael gave him confidence. Enough confidence to come up with a plan.

Before falling asleep that night, Seán figured out what his strategy needed to be. He knew that his lack of sparring meant that he had zero chance of beating Mike McCallum in a straight fight. He had to try something else. It was a pretty basic plan, as plans went, but he had seen it work before.

"I knew in my heart of hearts that I was going to have problems with him, and I knew that the lack of sparring would mean that I would now have twice as many problems," said Seán.

The plan was to stay in the fight, stay standing until the two men were deep into the last of the 15 rounds, and then, when McCallum tired, to take his chance. If McCallum grew tired.

~

Mike McCallum walked into the front hall of Madison Square Garden at noon on fight day. Waiting for him beside an old brass-and-wood weighing scale was Seán Mannion. McCallum was accompanied by Lou Duva, with no sign of McCallum's manager, Emanuel Steward, following their falling out in the fight buildup.

Seán was the first up on the Fairbanks scale. The same scale had been in use for years, having recorded the weights of Muhammad Ali and Joe Frazier before the "Fight of the Century" in 1971, Joe Louis and Rocky Marciano for Louis's last ever fight in 1951, and Roberto Duran before his controversial first world title win against Ken Buchanan.

On that October Friday, the scale recorded Seán Mannion's weight at exactly 154 pounds, the maximum allowable weight. McCallum came in a fraction lighter at 153 3/4 pounds. All was in order. The last potential obstacle to the fight going ahead was out of the way. There would be no late drama like there was on the night against Hector Figueroa in Plymouth, Massachusetts.

As they left the Garden, Seán bumped into Marvin Hagler, his old Brockton sparring partner.

"Good luck Seán," said Hagler, "you can do it. You can beat him."

Speaking on TV about Mannion's chances, without having heard about his cut eye, the world middleweight champion believed that Mannion had a more than decent shot.

"I have to go with my man," said Hagler. "He's a very tough kid, and I've worked with him sometimes myself."

Marvin Hagler would earn $1.4 million for his night's work against Mustafa Hamsho, 23 times what Mannion and McCallum would receive between them. Even a journeyman like Hamsho earned $450,000 that night. The value of catching a fight against one of the Four Kings was clear.

Hagler was defending the WBA, WBC, and IBF belts, and few gave Hamsho any chance whatsoever. In an attempt to drum up interest in the potentially one-sided bout, the New York State Athletic Commission announced that three women would judge Hagler vs. Hamsho, the first time ever for a world title fight. The Hagler camp was furious, with the Petronelli brothers hitting back with a reaction that didn't augur well for the future of female participation in boxing.

"This is a man's sport and a man's game," said Pat Petronelli in an interview with *New York Times* reporter Michael Katz. "There's going to be a lot of blood and I don't want the three judges throwing up."

"We don't want to be laboratory mice," added his brother, Goody. "We're upset and we won't put up with this. This is something that requires experience."

Jimmy Connolly wasn't too pleased about his judges, either, namely Harold Lederman of New York. "We think he's too close to McCallum [who also lived in New York]," Connolly told Steve Marantz of the *Boston Globe*. "We'd trade him for one of the women."

And so the trading began. Eventually, only one woman ended up judging Hagler's fight, with the halo of history falling instead on Mannion vs. McCallum. That became the first-ever world title fight to feature two female judges: Carol Polis and Carol Castellano. Polis was already immersed in boxing history, having become the first woman ever to judge a professional boxing match. The third judge was Johnny LoBianco, who had refereed the controversial Roberto Duran vs. Ken Buchanan fight, where Duran won his first world title after seemingly kneeing Buchanan in the testicles. LoBianco saw nothing.

Tony Perez, who was chosen as referee, was another man who attracted controversy, almost invariably involving Muhammad Ali. During Ali's second fight with Joe Frazier, with Frazier in trouble on the ropes, Perez came between the boxers thinking that he had heard the bell. This despite the fact that there were another 20 seconds to go in the round.

The following year, Perez refereed another Ali fight, this time against Chuck Wepner. Perez stopped the fight in the 15th round and gave Ali the win, but the champion was livid. He believed that the referee had allowed Wepner to throw illegal punches all night, and started off a tirade of insults by calling Perez "a dirty dog."

"He's not black and he's not white—he's Puerto Rican," said Ali, according to Joe Valerio of *People* magazine. "He is more black than white, but he is trying to be white.

"He was paid probably by some gangsters or somebody, or he had some money bet on Frazier," he continued, referring to Perez's premature intervention in the Ali/Frazier fight.

An outraged Perez announced that he was filing a $20 million lawsuit against Muhammad Ali. The jury sided with the world champion.

⌒

Seán Mannion had returned to his room in the Penta after the weigh-in when he heard a commotion outside his door. A woman screaming. A man shouting. He opened the door to find his sister, Nan, dwarfed by his bodyguard.

"Are you telling me I can't see my own brother?"

Jimmy Connolly had ordered Kevin "Andre the Giant" McDonald not to let anyone into Mannion's room, but no one, not even one of the most intimidating members of the Boston Irish mob, was going to stop Nan. Seán told his body-guards to let her in. The Giant conceded. Connolly had tried to ensure that his fighter had total rest before the fight, but Seán, as usual, put the considerations of family and friends ahead of his own.

"Seán was very family orientated and we had a problem keeping his family away from him," said Peter Kerr. "We were constantly battling with trying to keep people away from him in New York."

"He shouldn't have seen anyone before the fight," said Paddy Mannion. "He had come down from a training camp after six weeks, where he was locked away in a box as it were, separated from the rest of the world, and he should have stayed in that box.

"When you start seeing people you haven't seen in a long time, you lose the focus you had developed for the fight. But thunder and lightning wouldn't have kept him from talking to the people who had gathered in the lobby of the Penta Hotel."

Paddy joined Nan in Seán's room, the boxer asking them if many had trav-eled from Boston for the fight.

"There isn't an Irishman left in Boston, they're all downstairs," answered his brother.

He was only half-joking. Twenty stories down, it was bedlam. Seán's sup-porters had set up camp in the Penta lobby in the hope of spotting their star. On the stairs, Bab practiced the Irish national anthem with Jim McCann and Brian McCormick. McCann was a former member of the legendary Irish folk group, the Dubliners, and McCormick was lead singer of the Barleycorn, whose pro-test song about British internment in Northern Ireland, "The Men Behind the Wire," was the biggest selling song in Ireland at the time of its release in 1971.

Rehearsals weren't going well, however. McCann and McCormick were to sing the English version of the anthem, "Soldier's Song," and not the Irish ver-sion, "Amhrán na bhFiann." When Bab said that she didn't know the words in English, she was told that it was okay, that the other two could do the singing instead. Seán was furious when he found out that not only would Bab not be performing, but that his national anthem would be sung in English. He gave the fight organizers an ultimatum.

"Barbara is singing and she's singing in Irish, or else there's no fight."

In the end, Jim McCann and Brian McCormick were relegated to guitar ac-companiment. Bab put on her white woollen jumper and climbed into the ring to sing "Amhrán na bhFiann" to 20,000 people in Madison Square Garden and millions more worldwide.

~

At 5:30 p.m., Seán Mannion left his room for Madison Square Garden. Despite his constant complaints about Jimmy Connolly's bodyguards, he needed them by the time his elevator reached the ground floor of the Penta Hotel. The lobby was heaving with a raucous Irish party in the middle of Manhattan. Drinking. Singing. Looking for tickets. Looking for Seán Mannion.

The entourage pushed its way through the crowd. A limousine waited outside the front door. Seán looked at the long black car. He looked at Madison Square Garden on the opposite side of the street.

"Are we friggin' crazy?" he asked Paddy. The notion of taking a limo to cross the street seemed ludicrous to two men from Ros Muc, and so they stepped out into the traffic of 7th Avenue and made their way across on foot.

Once in the Garden, Seán and his crew headed to the dressing room after meeting with the fight doctor, with nothing to do until fight time but get ready and relax. Mannion rarely had an issue with relaxing before fights, having once fallen asleep in a dressing room shortly before representing Connacht in the Irish interprovincial championships.

This time, it was different. There was a tension in the air. For the first time since coming together six weeks earlier, there was no noise, no talking, no singing, no shouting. Just quiet. Jimmy, Billy, Paddy, Peter. All quiet. All thinking the same thing. No one was going to say it out loud, but they all had a hunch as to what lay ahead. They knew what was in store for Seán.

On a small wooden table to the side of the dressing room was a photo of Peaitín Tom Mannion. It had been eight years to the day since Seán's father was buried, his son's All-Ireland boxing medal placed in his coffin with him. After having his hands taped, Seán said a small prayer in memory of his father.

"Alright, Seán, we might as well get ready."

Seán looked at his brother.

"Do you remember, Paddy, when we were kids and you asked me one day when we were in the field if I thought that I would fight in Madison Square Garden someday?"

Paddy shook his head.

"Christ, Seán, stop. I can't remember anything right now, I'm too bloody nervous."

Someone knocked on the door. It was time. Seán pulled on his green robe and walked out into the crowd. Outside the dressing room, traditional Irish music began to blare from the speakers. The roar from the stands became a deafening boom the moment Seán stepped into the arena. With an estimated 50 percent of the 20,000 crowd supporting the Irishman, the noise in the auditorium was incredible. Seán had expected a big crowd. But not this. He tried to block it out but failed. He looked around him, his eyes and mind wandering. Familiar faces he hadn't seen in years popped out of the crowd. He thought of the lack of sparring. Of the people back home in Ireland who would see him box for the first time ever. He thought of the cut to the eye. Would it open? Would the fight be stopped?

Just before stepping into the ring, Seán said another quick prayer, this time praying that Mike McCallum wouldn't come out to the ring. But he did. Of course he did. Seán glanced over. There he was. Resplendent in the gold, green, and black of Jamaica. And those arms. So long. So tall.

Despite the earlier concerns, the fight was a sellout. Madison Square Garden was full. And despite Mike McCallum living next door in Brooklyn, it was a Seán Mannion crowd, his fans and Marvin Hagler's fans backing Massachusetts all night long.

~

Back in Boston, Joe Mulkerrins manned the bar in the Twelve Bens, batting away Guinness orders coming at him from a never-ending stream of customers. The owner, Gabriel Mannion from Connemara, along with most of the regular bar staff, had headed to New York for the fight, and Joe, who had just arrived from Ireland, had been left to run the packed Dorchester pub.

On the other side of the Atlantic, Máirtín Khate Conroy stood in Clarke's bar in Ros Muc, a pint of Guinness in one hand, a cigarette in the other, and an anxious, agitated crowd around him. Máirtín had immigrated to England in 1983, but when his friend ended up fighting for the world title the following year, there was nowhere he wanted to be other than among his own people. Where else could he watch a man from Ros Muc fight for the world title but in Ros Muc? Like the Twelve Bens, many of Clarke's usual crowd had traveled to New York for the fight, but like the Twelve Bens, the place was packed.

If you couldn't be at Seán Mannion's fight, you could at least watch it from Seán Mannion's world.

~

"Welcome to Madison Square Garden, the temple of big-time professional boxing."

Michael Buffer stood in the center of the ring, microphone in hand, his rolling inflections defining his status as the most recognizable fight announcer in the world.

"Ladies and gentlemen, man your battle stations, this is for the vacant World Boxing Association junior middleweight championship of the world."

He introduced the man in the red corner.

"Originally from Ros Muc, County Galway, Ireland."

A roar filled the Garden.

"Now out of Dorchester, Massachusetts, ladies and gentlemen, the number two contender in the world, Irish Seán Mannion."

Seán briefly lifted his arms in the air, throwing punches at the ghosts of his training camp as he bounced back to his corner. He wore the same shorts he wore for the Roosevelt Green fight, but with the Irish tricolor now emblazoned on the right leg. Mannion had been presented with the shorts at an event shortly before the Green fight, and had brought them to a Boston tailor to have the name of his home village embroidered across the waist. It turned out that "Rosmuc" occupied valuable real estate, at least in the boxing world if not the real world.

Shortly before the title fight, Seán received an offer from a sports company called Aqua-Leisure Industries, who were looking to develop a new boxing brand. Aqua-Leisure was, and still is, known for its swim clothing and equipment, but in 1982 the company attempted to cash in on the boxing boom with a new brand called Wear-Hard.

Based just outside of Boston, backing a local world title fighter to put their new Wear-Hard boxing equipment on the map seemed a no-brainer for Aqua-Leisure. The company offered Seán $5,000 to wear a pair of shorts with "Wear-Hard" written across the waist. Seán refused. Aqua-Leisure offered $10,000. Seán refused again. In the end, mistaking Seán's refusals for a negotiating strategy, they offered $25,000. Almost as much as he earned for the fight itself.

"Look, you can offer me a million dollars but it's not going to make a difference," Seán told them.

That night in Madison Square Garden, Peter Kerr, Paddy Mannion, and Jimmy Connolly wore Wear-Hard shirts. One word was embroidered on Seán Mannion's waist. "Rosmuc."

"If they had offered me 100 million dollars, I wouldn't have changed my mind," said Seán. "Nothing was going to change the fact that Ros Muc was to be written on my waist that night."

Michael Buffer introduced Mike McCallum. The Bodysnatcher walked confidently into the center of the ring, his right arm in the air, acknowledging his fans.

Tony Perez brought the two men together. McCallum looked at Mannion. Mannion didn't look back.

"Shake hands and good luck to the both of you."

Seán lifted his gaze from the canvas, winked at McCallum and tapped gloves with his opponent. As they walked back to their corners, Paddy shoved the mouthguard into Seán's mouth, giving his brother one final piece of instruction: "Keep your arms up and don't get hurt."

Seán gave him a dirty look.

"I haven't come here to stay out of the way. I'm here to win."

The bell struck.

Mike McCallum was three inches taller than Seán Mannion, his reach two inches longer, and the difference between the two was immediately obvious. Like a carpenter measuring up before starting a job, McCallum began by throwing long, light, left-handed jabs. Measure twice, cut once. And once he had the distance down, those jabs began to cut.

Ringside, Sugar Ray Leonard thought both boxers looked stiff.

"I wouldn't be surprised if something dramatic happened, like a knockdown," he said.

But Mike McCallum didn't start off looking like a man chasing knockdowns. Instead, he kept with that long left arm. It was clear that the Bodysnatcher had changed tactics for this fight, aiming for the head and not the torso. Aiming for the right eye. He knew about the right eye.

Sugar Ray was quick to notice the jab. "It's very straight, it's accurate. This left jab is going to do a lot for him against a southpaw like Seán Mannion. It will keep Mannion off balance and also, it will enable McCallum to deliver a right hand, a left hook."

The crowd in the Garden noticed only one thing, however.

"Mannion, Mannion, Mannion."

The same chant over and over again.

"Mannion, Mannion, Mannion."

McCallum cut through the noise with that long arm, while Mannion attempted to break through his opponent's guard and attack the body. He wasn't succeeding, however.

"He needs to make a brawl of this, he can't stand back and try to box a guy like Mike McCallum," said Leonard.

By the end of the first three minutes, McCallum's work was already showing results.

"So we come down to the end of the first round," said HBO's Barry Tompkins, "a round which has already seen a bit of redness, just the slightest bit of puffiness on the right side of Seán Mannion's face."

In the Irish TV commentary position, Shawn O'Sullivan, who had won a silver medal for Canada at the Los Angeles Olympics three months earlier, analyzed the fight with commentator Noel Andrews.

"The pattern being formed here is basically Mike McCallum scoring time and time again with his left hand, Seán Mannion receiving left hands on his face and body," said O'Sullivan. "I think Seán Mannion needs to be a little more aggressive in these next few rounds to catch up."

It was the same advice being given to Mannion by Sugar Ray Leonard on HBO, but trying to get around that long left arm after five weeks of non-contact training was proving difficult.

In the third round, Mike McCallum switched his focus from the head to the body. Nasty punches to the ribs, to the kidneys. You could feel the snap in the Bodysnatcher's punches every time Mannion took one of those body hits. Afterwards, Seán insisted that McCallum never hurt him, but he certainly didn't look like he was enjoying it.

The fight wasn't entirely one-sided. Two minutes into the third round, Mannion caught McCallum with a left, but couldn't build on it. It was as if the lack of sparring had led him to forget how to give off punches while taking them.

But even if Seán had managed to put together six weeks of quality sparring in the crisp autumn air of the Catskill Mountains, he would have found it near impossible to develop a rhythm in the face of those long raking arms of McCallum. Coming near the end of the third round, blood appeared around the right eye. This is what Seán feared most. Anything but having the fight stopped due to a cut.

Larry Merchant gave an unsparing analysis of Seán Mannion at the start of the fourth round. "He's overmatched right now. He's brave, he's a spirited fighter, and he'll hang in there as long as he can but he appears to be overmatched."

But just as Seán was being written off, there was a slight shift in round four. Mannion's attacks in the third had put McCallum on his guard, staying out of reach as the man from Ros Muc led the attack for the first two minutes. But Mike McCallum ensured that his opponent never cornered him, and soon regained control of the ring. For the first time in the fight, with less than a minute left in the round, he caught Seán on the ropes. A right to the stomach. Another. A big hook from Mannion that failed to connect. A right to the kidneys from McCallum. An uppercut that threw back Seán's head. The bell rang. The cheers in Clarke's bar in Ros Muc were becoming hushed murmurs.

By the end of the fifth round, Seán's right eye had shut almost entirely. Billy Connolly used his toolbox of ice and Vaseline to try and keep it open and to stop the cut from widening. That fifth round had been a furious three minutes, huge punches being thrown by both men but with McCallum again inflicting most of the damage.

For the sixth round, McCallum put away the hammer and returned with the tape measure, using the long left jab to pick at the right eye. But when Mannion threw his own left, he caught the Jamaican by surprise. He came forward again. Another left. Another one. Sugar Ray sprung to life ringside.

"Mannion does not come alive until he's hurt. That's when he starts throwing punches and starts becoming aggressive."

But this wasn't the same Seán Mannion that upset the odds and the rankings when he beat Nino Gonzalez. Or the Seán Mannion who broke Rocky Fratto's boxing will. Or the Seán Mannion who sent In-Chul Baek back home to South Korea nursing his first-ever defeat. That Seán Mannion, the patient craftsman, wasn't in the Garden that night.

Seán Mannion never had a reputation for a big punch. A TV commentator once described him as having "no crunch in his punch," but his ring skills more than compensated. He was a keen student of other boxers and of other styles, and practised mastery of the ring. But against Mike McCallum in Madison Square Garden, that mastery was missing. It seemed like Seán didn't know what he wanted to do. Stay away from that long left arm? Come inside? It was as if he wanted to try everything while succeeding at nothing.

The eye had gotten to him. The lack of sparring had gotten to him. Without even realizing it, the pressure had gotten to him. For the first time, Ireland was looking at him. Looking to him. The man from Ros Muc who went his own way and reached the top of the boxing ladder on his own terms. He wanted to win a world title for Ireland. That added pressure.

"This is a chance to fight for my country," he said at the pre-fight press conference. "If I win, I'd like to make my first defense there."

"This is the biggest moment of my career. This is everything I've worked for."

When Seán Mannion came out of that red corner for round nine, it was clear that he had just had a conversation with himself.

"This is my last chance."

From the moment the bell went, Seán started throwing punches, leaving himself open regardless of whether he hit the mark or not. But a little over a minute into the round, he finally found his mark with a clipped left uppercut followed by another left. McCallum wobbled. The unflinching, immovable Mike McCallum actually wobbled. Seán kept coming forward, McCallum's arms up in an effort to push the Irishman away. With the Jamaican rattled, Mannion threw a huge right uppercut to finish the fight in unforeseen glory. Instead, he connected with nothing more than the empty echo of his own name coming from the fans.

But Mannion wasn't finished. He caught McCallum again, and again he hurt him. Another left hook. Momentarily, the Jamaican's legs buckled. He grabbed onto Mannion, suffocating the attack.

"It wasn't too terribly long ago when it looked like Mannion's legs were gone and just like that, he turned the thing around here," said the HBO commentator.

"It's somewhat unpredictable, the outcome," said Sugar Ray, but really, there was nothing unpredictable about it.

Mannion had had his chance in the ninth round, but failed to knock McCallum out. Seán was too tired. There was no way he could continue with the intensity of attack needed to finish off his opponent. McCallum escaped, regained his rhythm. The chance had gone.

That was the last time in the fight that Seán managed to shake Mike McCallum. By the time the 12th round was over, he was bleeding from cuts around both eyes. There was no power left in the arms, a hollow noise in his head. His pre-fight doubts were being converted into facts, and Mannion knew then that there was no way he was going to win the world title that night. All he wanted at that stage was to finish the fight with dignity, with honor. In the red corner, Jimmy Connolly was witnessing his dream of training a world champion being smashed away by every McCallum jab. But Connolly wasn't letting go easily.

"Hit him, kick him, bite him, do anything Seán. This is it."

Through the squinting eyes, through the ringing ears, Mannion answered dolefully.

"I've never fought dirty in my life and I'm not about to start now."

The bell went again.

Mike McCallum came out for round 13 like a man who had had enough. He was looking to finish things there and then. There seemed to be no fight left in Seán, blood seeping from his nose. Yet, he continued. He wasn't about to surrender to anyone.

"He's fighting from the heart," said Sugar Ray. "I have to take my hat off to him."

Mannion went inside McCallum's guard, trying to get some sort of shot at the body. He never did. Instead, McCallum let off six uppercuts to the head. Six clean uppercuts without reply. Mannion couldn't even defend himself anymore.

Mike McCallum kept attacking, Seán Mannion held on with the desperate grip of a drowning man. By this time, the right eye had shut entirely. Yet, whenever Tony Perez broke the two fighters apart, Seán kept marching forward, trying to find the punch he had been looking for all night.

He never found it. It wasn't there to be found. By this stage of the fight, Mike McCallum could do whatever he wanted with Seán Mannion. There were no long left jabs anymore, only uppercuts to the chin or huge hooks to the liver and ribs. Mannion was in serious trouble. He could no longer hold his arms up. His body sagged, knees bent under the combination of McCallum's attacks and the weight of Irish expectation. The Jamaican threw out that long left arm once more, as if to measure the big punch he needed to finish the fight once and for all. Seán looked out at him through what remained open of his left eye.

"Come on and fight," he screamed across at McCallum, punching his fists together, almost feral by this stage. "Come on!"

McCallum didn't decline the invite. By the time the round was over, Sugar Ray was telling the American viewing public that the fight should be stopped. Tony Perez went over to Seán's corner to examine him, asking for the doctor to check if Mannion could continue. Perez asked Seán if he wanted the fight stopped.

"No way," Seán answered, "the only chance I have is by going the distance."

Seán Mannion was still sticking to the plan, the only plan he could possibly have had. That McCallum would eventually tire as the rounds went on. But it never happened. McCallum didn't tire. Being in total control of the center of the ring and of the fight itself, Mike McCallum was able to rest in some rounds when he needed to, and put in a big effort in other rounds. Without that option, Mannion was exhausted by the end of the fight.

The 14th round finished. Seán turned back to the red corner one last time. Connolly was still screaming at him.

"This is an alley fight, you understand?" he asked, finger jabbing in the air. "Go after him."

Paddy rubbed his brother's face, replaced his mouthguard, wishing it was over.

"You'll be alright."

The bell struck for the 15th round. The two went out into the center of the ring one last time. They touched gloves. They began to fight.

Every single punch that Mike McCallum threw at Seán Mannion in that 15th round found its mark. Seán had neither the strength nor the energy to defend himself. The legs had gone. The arms had fallen. The eyes had shut. But he remained standing.

When the bell rang for the last time after those horrendous final three minutes, Mike McCallum threw his arms up in victory. Seán Mannion, crestfallen, made his way back to his corner, head bowed. For the first time ever, a Jamaican had won a boxing world title. There would be no WBA belt making its way across the Atlantic to worm its way up the small, stonewall-lined roads of Ros Muc.

After recovering his composure, Seán went to embrace the man who had just given him the biggest beating he had ever experienced. He returned to his corner and turned to face the crowd, thanking the wall of Irish people who came to the Garden to support him. McCallum walked over and lifted Seán's arm into the air. Two exhausted heroes acknowledging each other after the longest fight either of them ever had.

"The heart of a lion" was how Sugar Ray Leonard described Mannion, but courage meant nothing in the end. "Seán Mannion showed a great deal of pride but just couldn't get inside."

In the post-fight interview, HBO's Larry Merchant asked McCallum why he couldn't knock Mannion out.

"Seán is a durable fighter, very tough," replied McCallum. "I knew before the fight going in there that Seán would be tough to fight."

Looking back, Seán didn't doubt for a second that the best man won. "People have hit me harder than he did, but no one has ever hit me as much."

"He never quit," said McCallum, reminiscing about that night in Manhattan. "Seán is a bad boy. You can't go to sleep against Seán Mannion, he kept coming forward all night.

"Other guys, they would have quit. Guys like Seán don't quit. He kept trying to win, trying to find that space, trying every angle. That was one tough fight, and I was glad it was over."

After the press conference, Seán walked across 7th Avenue, back to the Penta. His brothers, Paddy, Tommy, and Colm went up to the room with him, along with his brother-in-law, Tommy Mellett, and Tommy junior.

"He went in to the bathroom to get washed," said young Tommy. "Looking at him, it looked like it was no big deal, he put on a brave face. But he was devastated. You could tell."

Seán closed the door behind him once he got into the bathroom. Under the shower, he could barely feel the tears rolling from his torn eyes.

~

It seemed like half of Connemara had somehow managed to make their way into the Glocca Morra on 3rd Avenue, with the other half in the queue outside. Manhattan's the Gloc, described by the *New York Times* as "a long, dark, narrow, endearingly seedy establishment," was owned by a Ros Muc man called Mike Keane. Seán Mannion stood outside in the queue to his own after-party until someone spotted him, told him to cop on, and ushered him in.

When Seán walked into the Glocca Morra, both face and heart torn to pieces, everyone stood and applauded. On stage, his old trainer, Mike Flaherty, spoke to the crowd after singing a song in his honor.

"I know that you're fed up that Seán lost tonight, but don't be, because he went 15 rounds and it'll be a long time again before any man goes 15 rounds with Mike McCallum. If it ever happens. If it does, I won't be around to see it."

Mike Flaherty was right. No one ever did go 15 rounds again with Mike McCallum. After the Mannion fight, McCallum stopped every opponent before time until the WBA's decision in 1987 to cap world title fights at 12 rounds.

Mike McCallum returned to Jamaica a hero. Thousands thronged the streets of Kingston for his homecoming, in what was only the beginning of a glorious pro boxing career. He successfully defended his WBA light middleweight title six times. In 1989, he beat Herol Graham to win the WBA middleweight title, and by 1994 had won world titles in three different weight divisions when he took the WBC light heavyweight title. He lost his last-ever fight in 1997, over 40 years old at that stage, yet still challenging for a world title and still able to go the distance.

After Mike Flaherty finished speaking, Seán was brought up on stage and handed a microphone. He looked down at his friends, relatives, countrymen. He didn't have much to say.

"I'm sorry, lads, but I'll be back."

The city that never sleeps was just waking up by the time Seán left the Glocca Morra the following morning. Some friends and family headed to his hotel room for some more drinks until Seán finally asked them to leave. He couldn't fall asleep, however, and within half an hour, had tracked down the gang to a local bar where the party was in full swing again. All Seán wanted, however, was someplace where no one would recognize him.

By midday, they decided to head back up to Boston. Seán's nephew, Colm, drove and after visiting his sisters' kids in Dorchester, they headed down to Fields Corner. The Blarney Stone was wedged. On stage, Margaret Dalton and Erin's Melody played songs from 3000 miles away. Seán was asked up on stage. Again, he was given a microphone. Again, he had little to say.

"I'm sorry, lads."

16

ROCKY ROS MUC

The conveyer belt juddered into stumbling mechanical life. Seán's head throbbed as bags spilled out from the bowels of the airport. He was tired. All he wanted to do was pick up his suitcase and get the hell out of there.

Someone placed a hand on his shoulder.

"Hello sir. If you don't mind coming with me, we'll take care of your bags."

Seán looked back at the voice. A policeman. He had just gotten off the plane at Shannon airport and was already in trouble. He followed the officer.

"What the fuck have I done now?" he mumbled to himself.

A fortnight had passed since Mike McCallum gave Seán Mannion a one-way beating for the WBA light middleweight title. For Mannion, it had been two weeks of insanity. Nonstop invites to events all over Boston. Phone calls of job offers from around the United States. One woman started calling and writing from Texas, accusing him of having taken a bribe, alleging that he had lost the title fight intentionally.

"I seen you fight often on TV and I knew you could beat that guy."

"Well, you knew wrong," Seán answered, hanging up the phone for the umpteenth time.

Seán hadn't planned on returning to Ireland. The truth was that he was embarrassed. He had been badly beaten and he knew it, and while his fight against Mc-Callum wasn't an accurate reflection of his boxing abilities, what good was that? No one at home knew otherwise. He was fighting on U.S. television regularly, but they hadn't seen any fight of his at home other than the one in which a man from Jamaica beat the crap out of him over 15 rounds.

He had no problem in admitting his shame. "I let you all down: Mannion" was the headline in Ireland's Sunday *Tribune*. The *Tribune* reported a bust-up between Seán and his manager after the fight, Jimmy Connolly shouting at him that part of boxing was accepting your defeats, Mannion shouting back that the last thing he needed was another Connolly lecture. Losing wasn't a novel experience for Seán; he had lost five pro fights before meeting McCallum. But he had never lost a fight in that manner. And he had never lost a fight with all of Ireland looking on. He was in little mood to return home to the people he had let down. That he thought he had let down.

Yet, when Seán was invited to the Galway People of the Year awards, he felt he couldn't refuse. On November 7, 1984, he boarded a Northwest Orient Boeing 747 to return to Ireland for the first time since 1979. And the first person to greet him was the policeman leading him out the arrivals door.

Seán stood out among those waiting for bags in Shannon airport's baggage hall. He was wearing a new duck-eggshell blue suit. Inside his waist-jacket, a once-crisp white shirt with the top three buttons undone. His handsome, angular face healed since Mike McCallum's pounding. Not the sort of man to walk by unnoticed.

Peter Kerr, who had also traveled from the States, followed Seán and the policeman out of the baggage hall. The first thing they noticed were the cameras. The second was the people. It was then that the noise hit him.

The noise was like a punch to the gut. He hadn't expected this. The plan had been straightforward. Land in Shannon. Hire a car. Drive quietly to Ros Muc. But instead, Ros Muc had come to him. Friends. Family. Faces he recognized leaping from the crowd. Faces he had never seen before. Old mates from school. Media. Musicians. Shannon Town Council presented him with an award. Shannon Boxing Club had organized an official welcome. He felt dizzy, overwhelmed.

"Lift him up," someone shouted.

Seán Mannion made his way out of Shannon airport on the shoulders of Connemara men.

He definitely hadn't expected this. Outside the door were two buses. Behind them, a long line of cars. He was put on the first bus. The caravan of vehicles headed for Galway, the first bonfires appearing 30 miles up the road from the airport. The town of Gort had come out in his honor, led by a local teacher called Paddy Grealish, originally from Ros Muc, who had been at Seán's first-ever boxing session back in 1968. Gort Boxing Club led a parade through the town, the first stop in a 100-mile journey that would take 15 hours to complete.

When they arrived at the outskirts of Galway, the buses stopped and Seán was asked to get off and walk into the city behind the Irish flag. A huge crowd had gathered in Eyre Square in the center of the city, where the mayor hosted an official welcome. Seán was reeling. He couldn't believe what was happening. Two months earlier, in the lulls between training in the Stevensville Country Resort, he sometimes fantasized about what kind of welcome he would be afforded if he won the world title. He had never imagined this. Having lost, he had never even considered a homecoming welcome.

"By the time we got to Galway, I was numb," he said. "I was embarrassed, more than any other feeling, I just felt embarrassed."

Once the cavalcade got back on the road and passed west of Galway city, Seán felt like he was among his own people for the first time. Back in the Irish-speaking Gaeltacht of Connemara where a crowd had gathered around bonfires at the top of every road. He stopped at each fire. Máirtín Thornton's home village of An Spidéal put on a big welcome. In the townland of Mine, he stopped in to see an old friend of Mike Flaherty's who couldn't come out to the road. At the crossroads of Doire Né, Connemara gathered to catch a glimpse of their new hero before he turned home for Ros Muc. Hundreds of people illuminated by the dancing light of a bonfire, bellowing their appreciation when their hero arrived.

Once Seán got back on the bus again, the convoy headed west. As they came closer to Ros Muc, a quietness descended. The songs, the laughter, the stories on board stopped as they came closer to their destination. In front of them, the flicker of fire marked the way through the darkness. The hero was home. On the side of the road, someone had painted "Rocky Ros Muc" onto a large rock.

They drove into Ros Muc. The bus stopped in Cill Bhriocáin, where Seán's family had gathered at the bottom of the road. At that moment, all he wanted to do was make the short trip to his father's grave, but there was no derailing the convoy. They kept on before the final stop at An Crannóg, the community hall built on the site of the school where Seán had first started boxing 16 years earlier. There, Seán Mannion was given his official welcome home to Ros Muc.

It was four in the morning by the time Seán could make his way home. But before going to bed, he hopped the stone wall into the graveyard next door. At his father's grave, the grave in which his All-Ireland medal rested, he said a prayer to the man who set him off on what had turned out to be an incredible boxing journey.

∿

The following morning, a friend of Seán's who had traveled on the bus from Shannon knocked on his door.

"Come on, we're going down to tí Mhicó."

They headed to the local pub where the lounge had been renamed in Seán's honor, a "Seán Mannion Room" sign erected above the fireplace. A small group had already gathered in the bar, the gentle, lilting hum of an early-morning drinking session permeating the room. Among them were two who had traveled from Gort to meet Ireland's newest hero, having missed Seán the day before. They each bought the boxer a drink.

That was the start of it. Seán spent almost three months at home after his world title fight, liberated from training, liberated from Mike McCallum, liberated among his own people. Well, almost liberated. Every day, every night of the week, he was invited to some event. On his first week home, for example, he was special guest at an occasion organized by the *Connacht Tribune* newspaper on Wednesday, he was at the Galway People of the Year awards on Thursday, at a presentation by the Galway Boxing Club on Friday, and at another occasion in his honor in An Cheathrú Rua the following night. During the day, he would fulfill invitations to visit schools.

Seán's reception in Ireland had him in a state of perpetual surprise. People would come up to him on the street to shake his hand. Children wanted their photo taken with him. Coming out of a TV studio in Dublin, he found a crowd waiting for him, breaking into applause.

On a visit to Cork city, the mayor welcomed him before Seán was presented with a car by Ford. The Escort Cabriolet was the only one of its kind in the country at the time.

"I had it for six weeks and I think I might have driven it twice," Seán said. "Every man in Ros Muc took her out for a spin. It was said that the car was badly battered by the time it was given back to Ford, but that's the way of the Irish, exaggerating all the time. She was in good nick going back, although I'd have to admit that she had a few scratches alright!"

On the weekends, he traveled around the country attending events as a special guest. Nightclub openings. Football club dinners. Award ceremonies. Every night, drinking. Every night, eating. The peak athleticism achieved for the McCallum fight was a distant memory.

One morning shortly before Christmas, Seán was to travel to Mayo to shoot a TV commercial. All he had to do was drink a glass of milk, look into the camera and say "Ah, milk . . . it's good for you." For this, he would receive £2000.

When Colm Ó Mainnín of the local boxing club, who had organized the deal, went looking for Seán that morning, he didn't find him at home. Seán was already in Clarke's pub with Máirtín Khate Conroy, and neither were drinking milk.

"Come on, lads, let's go," Colm recalled saying.

"We'll have one more," said Máirtín, "and we'll hit the road then."

One more followed another. Colm, worried, looked at his watch.

"Lads, if we leave now, we can stop for one in Peacock's and in Keane's on the way, but we'd want to leave soon if we're going to make it."

Someone ordered another round. Colm sighed quietly. Finally, Seán put down his pint, licked the Guinness head off his upper lip and looked across at his two friends.

"Do you know what, lads, I don't even like milk."

That was the end of it. No one left Clarke's for the rest of the day.

Seán didn't make any money from his newfound fame other than what was given to him locally. A Connemara publican organized a dance in his honor, and presented him with £500. When new owners took over the same pub, the Poitín Stil, a few weeks later, they invited Seán back for another party, and again gave him £500.

Eventually, even Seán realized that it was time to escape the madness. This wasn't the Ireland he left in 1979. He was being stopped everywhere he went. Every time he opened a newspaper, there was some reference to him. "He will be received like a reigning monarch," wrote the *Connacht Tribune*, previewing yet another Seán Mannion ceremony. It was time to get back to Boston, but getting back to Boston wasn't easy.

Three times Mannion left Ros Muc to head across the Atlantic. Twice he turned back before reaching the airport, such was his loneliness at leaving home, family, and friends. Finally, in February 1985, he made it to Shannon, and headed back to Boston.

"It was some welcome given to me," said Seán, thinking back of the time. "I don't think I could have been given a bigger welcome even if I had won.

"But the truth was I was really embarrassed by it all, I was ashamed. I didn't think that I had deserved it after the beating I had been given. If anything, I thought that people were being nice to me out of pity."

But it wasn't pity. Connemara had found a new hero, a welcome distraction from the depression of 1980s unemployment and emigration. Even if he hadn't won the world title, Seán Mannion had achieved more in the boxing ring than any man from Connemara had ever done, and he had been given the respect and acknowledgment he deserved. But in the back of Seán's mind festered a doubt. A doubt that it had been all about pity rather than respect.

Twenty-one years after that world title fight, another Irish boxer called Kevin McBride became famous overnight after knocking down Mike Tyson. When he returned to Ireland from the United States, he was invited to an event in Carna near Ros Muc. Hundreds filled the specially erected marquee to see the man who had defeated one of the greatest heavyweights in history. McBride went on stage to a huge welcome. Seán Mannion, who had also been invited, was then brought on stage. The roar of appreciation, two decades on from his fight with Mike McCallum, shook the marquee.

It was then, finally, that Seán understood that it wasn't pity in the hearts of his people. But pride.

THE SPLIT

The first thing Seán Mannion did when he arrived back in Boston was to head down to the Twelve Bens and order a bottle of Budweiser. And then another. No remnant of the McCallum fight remained on his face, but he was still badly cut up inside.

"I was really depressed after the fight with Mike McCallum. Really, really, depressed. I put everything into that fight and it still wasn't good enough. All I could think of since I was 11 years of age was winning the world title and then, when I was given the chance, I failed.

"After the fight, my mind-set was that I just wasn't good enough to win and that I would never get the opportunity again. And even if I did get another chance, I felt that I could never call myself a champion until I had beaten Mc-Callum himself.

"I don't think people realized how good Mike McCallum was. I fought and sparred with a lot of world champions, and knew that there was little between us. But there was a big gap between me and McCallum. I felt that I had let down my country and let down those around me."

After returning to Boston, Seán could get neither head nor heart back into boxing. The need, the hunger, had gone. Instead of returning to the gym to lose the weight he had gained in Ireland, Seán headed to Washington, D.C., for a march protesting Ronald Reagan's decision to refuse Sinn Féin president Gerry Adams an entry visa. Adams had planned on coming to the United States to object to British prime minister Margaret Thatcher's visit to Washington. While Thatcher addressed Congress, 1,500 people protested on Capitol Hill, and afterward, Seán and his friends sought out a bar on Capitol Hill. That's where he was approached by a senator, he says, with an interesting offer.

"Mr. Mannion, how would you like to meet the president of the United States?"

Ronald Reagan was a big sports fan. A sports commentator before becoming a Hollywood actor, it wasn't unusual for him to invite boxers to the White House. According to Mannion, the senator told him that Reagan knew who he was, that he had seen his fight against Mike McCallum, and that Seán could meet the president the following day.

Seán refused. He was in Washington to protest Reagan's visa decision. There would definitely be no photo of him shaking hands with the most powerful man on earth. Principles. Again.

~

It was March before Seán got into the ring again, six months after his last fight and almost 20 pounds heavier. Mannion had put on so much weight boozing in Boston and Ireland that even after a week's fasting, he was still two weight divisions heavier than before. Taking on Doug Kaluza in Troy, upstate New York, he fought as a light heavyweight for the first time ever.

One thing hadn't changed, however. Despite taking his place on the world stage, despite now being ranked among the top middleweight boxers of his time, Seán was back fighting anonymous young boxers in the middle of nowhere, punching for scraps, something even the local newspaper found bizarre.

"While Troy might seem an odd spot to launch a comeback," wrote the *Schenectady Gazette*, "Mannion says he had planned to fight in the area, no matter the outcome of his title fight. 'I had promised that I would fight up here, whether I won or not,' said Mannion. 'And it's good for me, too. The more places you fight, the more exposure you get and the more people see you fight.'"

Like most of Seán's stranger decisions, this one was based on principles, sticking by his word. As a reward, Mannion, ranked sixth in the world, earned a grand total of $1,500 for the fight, $855 when his costs were taken into consideration.

Doug Kaluza wasn't a bad boxer. A young man from Lincoln, Nebraska, he had won all six of his previous fights. But this was his first fight away from home, his first fight against a ranked opponent, and his first loss, as it turned out. He didn't get past the fifth of eight rounds.

Making his pro debut that night was John "Red" Shea, a young man from South Boston who, five years later, would be sentenced to 12 years in prison for his role as a drug dealer in Whitey Bulger's Southie empire. Shea had three

pro fights before retiring to take up crime on a full-time basis. All three were on
Seán Mannion undercards, and he won all of them.

"I looked up to Seán, watching his skills and all that," said Shea. "As a fighter,
I always tried to not be so stuck to what I had learned. I wanted to advance myself,
so I took a little bit from any fighter that I thought could help advance me.

"So I look at Seán and I say to myself, the reason I was getting so good was
because of him, watching him and how good he was and inspiring me to be
absolutely the best that I could be."

Things didn't improve, glamour-wise, for Mannion's next fight. Seán Mannion vs. Ricky Burgess took place in the Spinoff Roller Disco, across the street
from the Boston Red Sox's Fenway Park and a long way from the prestige of
Madison Square Garden. But at least Seán was back in Boston, his first fight in
the city since beating Tony Taylor in 1981.

Seán had lost some weight for the fight, not much, but enough to bring
him down to middleweight. Despite that, one newspaper reported some of the
crowd laughing when he took his robe off in the ring and revealed his expanded
midriff. The laughter didn't last long, however. Burgess was on the floor inside
the first minute after a vicious left from Mannion. Seán knocked him down a further three times in that first round before the referee, Dick Flaherty, reluctantly
stopped the competition.

In his report to the Massachusetts boxing commissioner, Flaherty wrote that
"the first time Burgess went down he was dazed, but after that he wasn't hit that
hard."

"He hit me and I was groggy," was Burgess's answer. "What do they want
me to do, stagger around in there? Am I supposed to let him hurt me?"

The commissioner, Tommy Rawson, announced that Burgess's $650 purse
was to be held back pending an investigation, but he never did get his money.
By the time the inquest had finished, it was discovered that Burgess didn't
even have a boxing license from his home state of Maine, and despite having
informed the Massachusetts Boxing Commission that he had knocked out Jose
Rivera in Fairfield, Maine, six months earlier, Maine's commission had no
record of the fight ever happening. Or indeed, of Burgess having fought at all
in Maine since 1980. Ricky Burgess never fought again after that night against
Mannion in the Spinoff Roller Disco.

After the glory and recognition of fighting for the world title, Seán had
quickly fallen back into a depressingly familiar pattern. Small fights for small
money. The *Irish Independent* reported that Mannion was being offered a fight
in Denmark against former world champion Ayub Kalule, but that Kalule's
agent never received a reply from Jimmy Connolly. Business as usual.

"If I had heard about that fight, I would have taken it straight away because Kalule had an open style that I could beat," said Seán, "but I never heard about the offer.

"I know that Connolly was getting offers from Europe but for whatever reason, I wasn't getting any fights out of them. I think that he had his own deals and commitments in the States and that he had kind of lost interest after I failed to give him a world title."

But in July 1985, it looked as if things were about to get a whole lot better. Until the early eighties, there had been only two recognized international boxing sanctioning bodies, the World Boxing Association (WBA) and the World Boxing Council (WBC). But during the 1980s, new bodies such as the International Boxing Federation (IBF) and the World Boxing Organization (WBO) began to pop up. Suddenly, it was a hell of a lot easier to get a world title fight.

Among the new sanctioning bodies was the World Athletic Association (WAA), established by Pat O'Grady in 1981. O'Grady was a trainer and promoter whose son, Sean, was a world-class boxer inaugurated into the World Boxing Hall of Fame in 1992. But when the WBA stripped O'Grady junior of his light middleweight title following a dispute with his father, Pat O'Grady set up his own sanctioning body. The WAA was one of the smaller sanctioning bodies at the time but, crucially, was recognized by many national bodies, the Boxing Union of Ireland included.

Bert Lee was the WAA light middleweight champion in 1985, and a fight between Lee and Mannion was set for Irvine, California, on July 22. The purse was an underwhelming $2,500 for the top-billed Mannion, and when Pat O'Grady said that he was looking for half of that in order to sanction the fight as a title bout, Jimmy Connolly told him to go to hell. The promoter, Don Fraser, told O'Grady that he wasn't going to fork up the cash either.

With no sanctioning fee paid, Pat O'Grady kept the oversized world title belt in the changing room, and the two boxers were sent out for 10 rounds. Lee couldn't cope with Mannion, who had come down under 160 pounds and was in good shape for the first time since losing to McCallum. Seán's confidence in his conditioning was obvious, pacing himself carefully through the first six rounds, pushing Bert Lee's effort to one side. Once Lee began to tire, Mannion went on the attack for the last four rounds, using his left fist to inflict the damage. Lee was stunned.

"Who shot me?" the *Los Angeles Times* reported Lee as having asked after the fight, deciding, like many before him, that he would never go back into a ring after fighting Seán Mannion.

"Bert Lee fought the best fight of his life and still lost," was how the *Los Angeles Times* fight report began. Mannion had beaten the champion easily, but left without a belt.

Two months later, Seán Mannion was back in the same ring in the same hotel with the same referee. Lou Filippo was well-known for refereeing world title fights, but also for his role as a referee in the Rocky movies, along with TV roles in series such as *The A-Team* and *Moonlighting*.

Fights in Los Angeles were different from fights on the East Coast. The referee was an actor. Ringside, Donny Osmond sat with his wife, Debbie. The parking lot was full of BMWs and Mercedes Benzes. This was what they called yuppie boxing, and there weren't many places more yuppie in 1985 than Irvine in Southern California.

At a time when the Felt Forum in Madison Square Garden was struggling to fill a quarter of the seats, boxing was big business on the West Coast. This was a new market, with bouts being held in hotels, and the night pitched at a younger audience with a disposable income, the kind of audience that would leave $15,000 in the hotel tills after a night's wining and dining.

No less than the hotels, promoters were also cashing in on their wealthy new clientele. Both of Mannion's top-card fights in the Irvine Marriott had sold out, bringing in about $35,000 per night for the promoter, Don Fraser. It wasn't all profit, but the economics were sound. The ring cost $400 to rent for the night, the gloves another $220. The two young ladies parading around the ring between rounds were paid $75 each, but it was the boxers who absorbed most of the profit, particularly given that travel costs were paid along with fight fees. Still, it was a good earner for Fraser, who would clear $15,000 for the night.

Over 1,400 people filled the Irvine Marriott ballroom on September 26, 1985, to see Seán Mannion win over Billy Robertson in a fight in which Robertson seemed more inclined to use his head than his fists. After repeated warnings from Filippo, the fight was stopped in the seventh round and Mannion, ahead on points, was given the victory. Newspapers reported Donny Osmond placating his crying wife ringside, upset at the damage Robertson's head had caused Mannion. Seán's face was badly cut in several places, with a large fold of skin hanging off under his right eye.

After the fight, Jimmy Connolly looked to organize a rematch between the two.

"You can fuck off if you think I'm getting in the ring with him again," said Mannion. "What's to gain anyway? He fights dirty and he's going nowhere."

This was not how Seán had imagined his world after fighting for the world title. Meaningless fights for a couple of thousand dollars against the likes of Billy

Robertson. He remembered that after the Mike McCallum fight, NBC's boxing man, Ferdie Pacheco, came into the dressing room in Madison Square Garden.

"We're going to have a lot of boxing on NBC next year," he told Seán, "and I'm going to make sure you're going to get fights."

He never did hear again from NBC. In his head, he blamed Connolly. He had no idea if he had any basis for blame, but it didn't matter. The relationship between Seán Mannion and Jimmy Connolly was so broken by that stage that he was suspicious of everything Connolly did, or more importantly perhaps, everything he didn't do.

It was time for a change.

18

ANGELO

When Seán Mannion called to set up a meeting, Tony Cardinale knew straightaway what he wanted. The same thing he always wanted. Mannion was looking to leave Jimmy Connolly. Cardinale had been hearing the same refrain for a while now, but he never thought that Seán would take the big decision and actually follow through with it.

The following day, Seán, accompanied by Paddy Mannion and Peter Kerr, knocked on the lawyer's door. A delegation, no less. Cardinale sat up. They looked serious.

"Tony, I want out. The contract is finishing up soon and I'm not staying with Connolly anymore. I've had enough."

"Well, what do you want so?" asked Cardinale. "Are you finished with boxing or are you finished with Jimmy?"

Paddy's ears pricked up when he heard the question.

"Are you finished with boxing?"

Seán's brother only wanted one answer to that question, but he knew that it wasn't the answer he was going to hear. "I had almost finished up with Seán after the world title fight," said Paddy. "I thought that he should have quit afterwards because of the beating he took. Certainly, I wasn't as involved with him anymore."

But Seán was in no mood to quit.

"I'm definitely not finished with boxing," he told Cardinale. "I'm still training, and I want to keep training. To be honest, I don't care if I don't sign a new contract with anyone, I'm happy to manage myself."

Tony Cardinale arched his eyebrows when he heard Seán mention self-management.

"What about Angelo Dundee?" he asked his client.

Seán laughed, presuming that Cardinale was joking.

"Fuck off, like a good man," he said back to his lawyer. "I'm serious here. I'm finished with Connolly and I'm ready to look after myself."

"Well, I'm being serious too," said Cardinale. "Why don't we call Angelo?"

Seán was stunned. Angelo Dundee? He had always had one hero above all others in boxing, and that was Muhammad Ali. And now, Tony Cardinale was proposing that Ali's trainer would take him on.

Cardinale picked up the telephone and called the 5th Street Gym in Miami. Dundee was put on the phone. The four men in the well-appointed Boston legal office gathered around the speaker to hear what one of the biggest men in world boxing had to say.

"Seán Mannion? Yeah, of course, I'd be interested. Why doesn't Seán come down to Miami and see if we can set things up?"

Seán couldn't believe it.

"I was in heaven at the opportunity of talking with Angelo Dundee on the phone, let alone him being my trainer," he said. "It was something I never thought would happen, that the man who trained Muhammad Ali would train me."

~

Angelo Dundee was somewhat different from other trainers in the boxing world. With Dundee, the fighter came first, and he went out of his way to defend his men. According to the *Daily Telegraph*, boxing commentator Howard Cosell said of him: "Dundee is the only guy in boxing to whom I would entrust my own son." When a boxer of his was in trouble, Dundee had no problem with breaking the rules if needed. When Muhammad Ali was struggling against Henry Cooper in 1963, for example, Dundee tore a small hole in his glove between the fourth and fifth rounds, giving his man an extra few seconds to recover while the glove was being replaced.

But Ali wasn't the only boxer on the Angelo Dundee resumé. He had trained world champions such as Sugar Ray Leonard, George Foreman, Carmen Basilio, and Wilfredo Gómez, and yet, despite his huge successes, he wasn't a boastful man. Indeed, it seemed like he rarely spoke. But when he did, you listened to what Angelo Dundee had to say.

When he said, "You've got nine minutes. You're blowing it now, son. You're blowing it," to an exhausted Sugar Ray after the 12th round against Thomas

Hearns in 1981, he knew what he was doing. Leonard tapped into whatever reserves he had left, and went out to destroy Hearns in the 13th round. The referee stopped the fight 1:45 into the 14th round, and Leonard became the WBA and WBC welterweight champion.

"He couldn't have been more different to Jimmy Connolly," said Paddy Mannion. "Connolly would bawl and shout all the time but he would have nothing to say. Angelo would only say two words but you'd remember them for the rest of your life."

A gobsmacked Mannion listened as a deal was struck with Dundee over the phone. Angelo would train and manage Seán for 15 percent of his purses, a significant reduction on Jimmy Connolly's 33 per cent management cut, not to mention the other 10 percent for training. It was also agreed that Dundee would pay for Seán's flight to Miami, so that he could train in the 5th Street Gym. It was like starting anew for the man from Ros Muc.

The first thing that struck Seán Mannion when he got off the plane at Miami International Airport was the heat. It was early December, and up north in Boston, the weather had long given up any notion of trying to stay above freezing. Seán closed his eyes and felt the sun warm his bones, warm his core. This new life felt better already. But when he reached 5th Street, there was no sign of Angelo Dundee. Instead, he was introduced to his brother, Chris, who told him that Angelo was in California with another boxer called Michael Nunn.

Nunn was fighting none other than Billy Robertson, the same guy who had repeatedly planted his forehead in Seán's face a few months earlier. Nunn won on points and would go on to fame and glory, winning the world middleweight and light heavyweight titles. Mr. T became his bodyguard, and Gene Hackman, the actor, became his friend. But like many other boxing stories, Michael Nunn's didn't have a happy ending. The wealth disappeared. So did the friends, and a devastating downward spiral ended with a 24-year prison sentence in 2004 for dealing cocaine.

Back in Miami, Seán got to know Rick Mandris in Angelo Dundee's absence. Mandris was one of Dundee's trainers, and was tasked with taking care of Seán while Angelo was out of town.

"When we got him, Seán was in pretty good shape," said Mandris. "There wasn't much to do with him but to put him in the ring.

"I think we would have gone in a different direction with his career if we had him earlier. I thought that he had a lot of problems early on, taking fights at short notice and taking fights when he was sick. He was a consummate pro, a real gent and we really wished that we had him earlier on."

Years after that first visit to Miami, with Seán on the verge of quitting boxing, Angelo Dundee had much the same thing to say about him. "If only I had gotten him when he was 20 instead of 30," one of the greatest trainers in boxing history told the *Boston Herald*, "he'd have been a champion, no question about it."

Seán's first post–Jimmy Connolly fight was a top-of-the-card bout against Stacy McSwain in the Miami Beach Convention Center. McSwain was a decent boxer, the kind that could go 10 rounds with the likes of Wilfred Benitez and Iran Barkley. He went ten rounds with Seán Mannion too, but as the *Miami Herald* reported the following day, "Mannion dominated the fight, knocking down McSwain in the sixth and eighth rounds en route to capturing a 10-round unanimous decision."

Seán wasn't long settling down in Miami and in the 5th Street Gym. He was enjoying this new life. Sparring with Sugar Ray Leonard. Helping Pinklon Thomas prepare for his heavyweight title defense against Trevor Berbick. But it would be the guts of six months after the McSwain fight before he would finally have Angelo Dundee in his corner.

Meanwhile, Seán returned to Boston and to the Twelve Bens, the Blarney Stone, the Emerald Isle, to a boxing life that didn't have quite the same focus it once had. By this stage he had given up on trying to make light middleweight, and settled for the next weight grade up.

"The constant struggle with his weight during his entire boxing career was the real killer for Seán," said his brother and ex-trainer, Paddy. "You would see it coming up to a fight, having to eat salads for two months just trying to keep that weight down.

"We would all sit at the table together, Seán eating rabbit food and the rest of us eating a fine dinner. I used to feel so bad in the end that I began eating the salads with him and sneak out afterwards for a McDonald's.

"Trying to keep the weight down used to kill him. That was the main reason I didn't enjoy boxing anymore, having to watch him struggle against the weight. It was really tough, training while wearing a load of sweaters and plastic bags. I don't know why but it really bothered me looking at the work that had to go into keeping the weight off."

Seán had one fight in Boston after coming back up from Miami, beating Wesley Reid in Dorchester on St. Patrick's weekend, 1986. A month later, he got the call he was waiting for. It was time to head out to California and meet Angelo Dundee.

Dundee had arranged a fight against Fred Hutchings, a tall, strong boxer who had fought Tommy Hearns for the world light middleweight title two years previously, and who had traveled to South Korea in 1985 to challenge In-Chul Baek. Baek did the same thing to Hutchings that he had done to every boxer he ever faced up until that point, with the notable exception of Seán Mannion, and that was to finish the fight early by knocking him out.

Mannion and Dundee got on well from the start, Dundee telling jokes about the Irish, Mannion mocking his trainer's Italian lineage.

"Seán and I had a lot of kicks together," said Dundee in an interview with the Irish radio station, *Newstalk*. "He once came out and called me a dumb Guido. I tell him, hey you better be careful. My wife's Irish and she's gonna kick the hell outta you!"

Dundee's training style couldn't have been more different from Jimmy Connolly's. The focus was always on the fighter, on developing the man mentally as well as physically. There was none of the shouting, none of the threatening. "My guy" is how he referred to every fighter he ever had.

"It was like being back again with Mike Flaherty," said Seán. "He believed in me and he supported me from the start. I enjoyed training with him as opposed to hating it when I was with Connolly.

"The first time I met Angelo, he told me that he had 13 world champions. 'I know you're going to be number 14,' he said, 'because I don't like the number 13.' He thought a lot of me."

"Angelo really liked him," agreed Tony Cardinale. "He liked that he was such an incredible technician. Seán had a phenomenal style and that's what Angelo appreciated."

Seán had another reason to get on well with Angelo Dundee. In his last trip to California to fight Billy Robertson, Seán's purse was $2,500, but he would earn $10,000 to face Fred Hutchings. Not only that, the percentages he gave up to training and management fees were considerably lower. Life certainly seemed better around Angelo Dundee.

The fight was held in Stockton, about 80 miles east of San Francisco. John Verner, the promoter, had three fights on the card, and despite Hutchings being a local boy, he was concerned about breaking even. The auditorium held 4,300 people, and Irish boxers weren't usually on the card. But Verner had no cause for concern. San Francisco's Irish bars bussed the city's Irish community to Stockton for the night to see their man. In the end, Verner took $41,570 at the door. He was inclined to see more of Mannion after that.

Fred Hutchings was six foot two inches in height, almost six inches taller than his opponent, and while Mannion struggled to cope with Mike McCallum's height advantage, Hutchings couldn't make it count in the same way. In what was a tough encounter, Hutchings was on the canvas in the first round, but the referee ruled that Mannion had pushed him. After the fourth round, Seán went back to his corner complaining to Dundee of pain in his right hand.

"Do you want me to stop the fight?"

"Jesus, no," answered Seán, "but it hurts like hell."

"Just keep throwing it because whatever happens, it's still going to be painful in the morning."

Seán took his advice and, after 10 pounding rounds, he was given a win on points. When the doctor examined his hand afterwards, it was found that Seán had fought the last six rounds of the night with a broken thumb. His hand was in a cast for six weeks afterward.

The injury meant that Seán wouldn't fight again until August, this time considerably closer to home, in Lowell, Massachusetts. Lowell was home to future light welterweight world champion Micky Ward, who was also on the card that night.

"Sean had a good jab, good head movement, was really good on his legs, a great mover," remembered Ward. "He was awkward too, and to be in the mix with the likes of Hagler, Hearns, Leonard, that tells you how good he was."

After Ward beat John Rafuse in the Lowell Auditorium, Mannion and Jose Quinones of Puerto Rico took to the ring for the main attraction of the night. Quinones was a tough fighter who had won the WBC Continental Americas title the year before. The fight started slowly, but Seán started to get the upper hand as the rounds went on. In the final round, Mannion picked up the pace of attack, a stinging left to the jaw, another to the ribs. Quinones fell back on the ropes, trying to ward off the Irishman. Seán didn't manage to knock him down, but it didn't matter. His unanimous victory consolidated his position as number six in the world. As it turned out, it would be his last fight on ESPN. Almost the end of the Mannion era. Almost.

"He hit very hard tonight," said Mannion to reporters afterwards. "I was surprised he was on the defensive so much. I kept expecting him to tire out, but he didn't."

But the big news around Mannion that day wasn't the fight, but rather the story in the morning newspapers. It had been reported far and wide, from the *Times* of London to the *Toronto Star*, that Mannion was to take on his first pro fight outside of the United States. Angelo Dundee had arranged for Errol Christie as the opponent, the fight to be held in a circus tent on the grounds of Shendish Manor outside London, and to be promoted by Frank Warren.

But two days before Seán was to travel to Florida to pick up his training after the Quinones fight, he injured his back. The same injury that led to his change of tactics in the Roosevelt Green fight. He called Angelo Dundee.

"What do you want me to do, Seán?"

"Postpone the fight for a while," answered Mannion, "because I don't want to go over to England and lose to an Englishman. I want to be 100 percent for this one."

The fight was put back until October 29, 1986, and rescheduled for the Alexandra Palace in north London.

~

This was a big fight for Seán Mannion, his biggest since the McCallum fight. It was to be shown live on British TV and broadcast in Ireland on RTÉ Raidió na Gaeltachta. This was his chance to redeem himself among his home fans. Another shot at showing them what kind of boxer Seán Mannion really was. This was a fight he had to win.

But there was an added pressure for Seán. Immersed in the republican, anti-English sentiment so pervasive among the Boston Irish at the time, particularly given the trouble in the north of Ireland, Mannion felt that he couldn't lose to an Englishman. That would be really letting down the people of Ireland. But it wasn't going to happen. He was certain of that. Seán Mannion was feeling great. He had Muhammad Ali's trainer in his corner, for God's sake! He hadn't lost a fight since the McCallum debacle. And that was the only fight he had lost in the past four years. His last two defeated opponents had both been ranked in the world top ten. Seán Mannion was a sure thing.

Errol Christie was English boxing's princeling of promise during the 1980s. He won the Amateur Boxing Association of England title in 1981. The following year, he captained Britain to the European title. Indeed, he had such a prolific amateur career that he earned a place in the Guinness Book of Records for the number of amateur titles won. His early success transferred across to his professional career, winning 20 fights and losing only one before meeting Mark Kaylor for the British middleweight title in what was a nasty night. Christie, of Jamaican descent, walked into the Wembley Arena to a wall of racist abuse from Kaylor's fan base of young white men from the West Ham area of east London, and was knocked out in the eighth round to baying cheers. A year later, having won three fights since the Kaylor beating, Christie was set to take on Mannion.

Five days before the fight, Seán flew in from the United States with his brother Paddy and Peter Kerr. Waiting for them in London was Angelo Dundee. Frank Warren had booked training time for the entourage above the Thomas A Becket pub on the Old Kent Road in south London. The Thomas A Becket had an unusual history. Built in 1898, it was as famed for its gym upstairs as it was for its bar downstairs. Henry Cooper spent 14 years training there along with visiting boxers such as Muhammad Ali, Joe Frazier, and Sugar Ray Leonard.

Despite all the focus on the fight, Seán had one particular goal that had nothing to do with Errol Christie, and that was to visit a park called Clapham Common on a Sunday morning. Back home in Connemara at the time, a lonely emigration song titled "Pócaí Folamh is Cloigeann Tinn" [Empty Pockets and a Sore Head] was hugely popular. It described a Connemara man in London who sorely missed home, living a harsh life of drinking and sleeping on park benches.

But it was the chorus that seduced Seán Mannion.

> Maidin Domhnaigh i gClapham Common
> ó nár bhreá 'bheith dallta aríst
> sínte siar anseo le balla
> ar phócaí folamh is cloigeann tinn.

> [Sunday morning in Clapham Common
> Wouldn't it be great to be drunk again
> Lying here against the wall
> On empty pockets and a sore head]

Whatever about empty pockets and sore heads, Seán wanted to fulfill the Sunday morning in Clapham Common part of the song and so, three days before the fight, he left the Hotel Russell on Russell Square with three friends from Ros Muc and headed south to the Common. The three running with Seán through the park, singing, sweating, and laughing. "Maidin Domhnaigh i gClapham Common."

Seán's other two commitments before the fight were the press conference and the weigh-in. In front of the media, his confidence was apparent.

"I should have been European champion years ago but my former manager steered me away from that direction," he told the *Irish Press* in a pre-fight press conference. "Now I am coming after the title. Herol Graham refused to fight me in Las Vegas on the Barry McGuigan–Steve Cruz show in June, and people will see why tomorrow night."

Speaking in Irish, he told Raidió na Gaeltachta that his hope was that he wouldn't let down his home support.

"Seán is one real good fighter," Angelo Dundee told the *Irish Independent*. "When I joined him, I didn't try to change anything about his style—I tried instead to add little things on."

"I'm impressed at what Seán can do. He's a boxer, very strong, but very smart."

By fighting Christie, Mannion was aiming for a shot at Herol Graham's European middleweight title, and at the wealth within the thriving European boxing market. Christie's aim was to climb up the world rankings. A generous three pounds of flexibility had been written into the contracts, and Seán needed every ounce. He stood up on the scale. One hundred sixty-two and a half pounds. Half a pound over the maximum allowable. He glanced over at Dundee, at Frank Warren, and at Errol Christie's manager, Burt McCarthy. The extra half-pound wasn't contested.

Christie's turn next. "One hundred sixty-three and a half," shouted McCarthy as a muscular Christie jumped off almost immediately.

"When he got on the scale, his weight went up instantly and he was signaled out straight away," said Seán. "He was much, much bigger than me that day in every way, but still somehow lighter on the scales."

"Next thing, when Angelo went looking for him to put him back on the scales, he was nowhere to be seen. He was gone."

Christie had left with his manager and his new trainer, Jimmy Tibbs, and wouldn't be seen again until just before the fight. Tibbs had been brought in during the buildup to the Mannion fight, as Burt McCarthy had been worried about the effectiveness of Christie's boxing. And although they only had a month to work together, both Tibbs and McCarthy felt that their man was already more focused, more self-confident, more settled in the ring than before.

Paddy Mannion, on the other hand, was concerned that his brother didn't seem to have quite the same focus. Instead of being tucked away in his dressing room a few hours before the fight, Seán was in the lobby of the Alexandra Palace, surrounded by a crowd from Ros Muc and Connemara. No one looking on could have imagined that Seán was about to get into the ring for one of the most important fights of his career.

"Instead of being focused on the fight, he had a crowd around him and was asking about people back home," said Paddy. "I was trying to take him out of there, but it was like trying to pull a calf away from a cow. The focus was gone. The spirit he had before the fight had disappeared because his focus had gone elsewhere."

Inevitably, the fight against Errol Christie was a disaster. On paper, it seemed like there could only be one winner. The ranked Seán Mannion, whose only loss since 1982 had been a world title fight, taking on Errol Christie, a fighter who struggled in his last fight to beat someone competing four weight grades below him. Christie had achieved nothing in professional boxing that would indicate any result other than a win for Mannion.

Errol Christie destroyed Seán Mannion over 10 rounds in the Alexandra Palace. In front of his friends from Ros Muc. His friends from Connemara. On ITV. On Raidió na Gaeltachta. A full house in the Twelve Bens in Dorchester listening over the phone to Seán Bán Breathnach's radio commentary. Destroyed.

Christie gave Seán such a hiding that the referee, Mickey Vann, was brought in front of the British Boxing Commission to answer questions as to why he hadn't stopped the fight earlier. The only positive Seán could possibly take was that he wasn't knocked down. Christie, in his book *No Place to Hide*, recalls his own ferociousness:

> In one of the last displays of the classic Christie form, waves and waves of combination punches crashed down on the persistent southpaw as I delivered one of the most brutal beatings of my career. I couldn't allow him to win: this had to be a clear and uncompromising victory, with no room for question marks. But Mannion refused to lie compliantly on the canvas. Like a Terminator, he rose up, again and again. I had to fight like a lion for that victory.

Mannion had only one half-decent shot at Christie all night, when he wobbled him at the end of the fourth round, only for the bell to go before he had a chance to build on the damage done. By the end of the 10 rounds, Seán had taken so many punches that he struggled to make his way back to his own corner.

No one had an answer for Seán's failure. It was jokingly speculated that Mannion was somehow jinxed by Raidió na Gaeltachta, given that he had lost the only two fights they had commentated on. Others questioned whether, at 30 years of age and seven years older than Errol Christie, he was too old to fight at this level.

But it wasn't that. He had recently beaten better than Christie. He had unanimously defeated Jose Quinones, a boxer who stopped Christie in four rounds. But none of that mattered now. Errol Christie had beaten Seán Mannion, and had beaten him well.

"There was something different about me that night," said Seán. "When I went over to England, I thought that there might be a couple of Irishmen there, and that all the rest would be English. But when I went into the ring that night, it was as if the audience was 90 percent Irish. I hadn't expected that.

"I really didn't want to lose to an Englishman. I think I wanted to be even better than I already was, and that left me making a lot of mistakes. I didn't fight my own fight. A bad night in every way.

"The two fights I had that could be seen on TV in Ireland were by far the two worst fights I ever had, especially the Christie fight. That fight was different from the McCallum fight. Regardless of what happened in the buildup, it would have always been difficult to beat McCallum, but I was in good shape against Christie."

Seán's post-fight ringside interview for Raidió na Gaeltachta heard a quiet, lonely voice crackling over the airwaves.

"What happened to you tonight?" asked Seán Bán Breathnach.

"I don't know," Mannion answered, "he just boxed better than me, much better. He hurt me once or twice, that's all. I wasn't able to do anything. Anytime I'd go inside, he hit me."

"Why was that?"

There was a frankness in Seán's answer that seemed, for the first time, to signal an awareness of the end.

"I don't know, I think I'm getting old. I think it might be time for me to leave this to the young lads . . . I have no excuse. I tried my level best all my life. I think that's it now."

Seán Bán paused for a second, processing what he had just heard.

"That's it? Are you retiring?"

"I think I am," said Mannion. "It's been in my head for a while. I'm 30 since last month. If something else doesn't come up, I think that that's it . . . I've been boxing for 17 years, so I think that it's time to say goodbye. I had made up my mind that that was it if I got beaten. I was beaten easily. I was beaten in every round. That's it, unless something else happens."

When he left the ring, his old trainer, Mike Flaherty, was the first person to speak with him. "I wonder if you haven't done enough, Seán?" the old master asked the boxer. "Maybe it's best you retired now."

Sitting in the dressing room, heartbroken, embarrassed, Seán told Angelo Dundee of the advice he'd just received from Flaherty.

"Never make a decision like that right after a fight," Dundee said back to him.

19

FINISHING TOGETHER

Seán Mannion didn't quit boxing after the Errol Christie fight, but it soon became painfully obvious that he should have paid more attention to Mike Flaherty's advice.

Before the Christie fight, Mannion had lost six fights in a professional career spanning back to 1979. One loss in the four years between beating Rocky Fratto in 1982 and his arrival in London. But the fights he had after Errol Christie would stain his boxing record forever.

Despite losing, Seán returned to Boston $15,000 better off. The fight against Christie was his third and final decent payday of a five-figure purse.

"I've often been told that if I took care of the money I made during my boxing career, that I'd never have to do another day's work," said Seán. "The truth is I just didn't make that much money.

"When I think about it, Duran, Leonard, Hearns, Hagler, Benitez used to get more money in their training expenses for one fight than I earned over my entire career."

The fight against Errol Christie was the beginning of the end of Seán's boxing career. After spending a fortnight in Ireland, he returned to the States and beat Doug Mallett in the Strand Theatre in Boston five days before Christmas. Like many before him, Mallett never fought again after facing Mannion.

"I am glad to have that fight out of the way," said Seán after the fight. "I felt really depressed after the Christie fight but I know that it was a once-off bad night."

On the card that night were two young boxers who had come over to the United States as part of the Irish national team, Michael Lally from An Cheathrú

Rua in Connemara, who had just won the Irish national title, and Steve Collins from Dublin. They both won their fights.

Michael Lally's promising pro career was cut short by arthritis after just three fights, but Steve Collins was another story altogether. Collins failed in his first two attempts to win a world title, one of them against Mike McCallum, but eight years after that night in the Strand Theatre, he finally won the WBO middleweight title against Chris Pyatt in Sheffield, England.

Collins focused on the European market, and achieved both fame and fortune in a series of high-profile fights against Chris Eubank and Nigel Benn in both Ireland and England. The market that would have suited Mannion most, according to Tony Cardinale.

"Had he been marketed in Europe, it would have been very different," said Cardinale. "I tend to fantasize that Seán became very popular and wealthy fighting out of England.

"You can always look back, it's hard to say how things would have turned out if you did things differently. Seán had that very classic European style and he would have been a huge, huge hit in Europe, as big as Stevie Collins.

"I believe in his day that Seán would have beaten Collins easily. No disrespect to Stevie, but in my view, for whatever that's worth, he didn't have the skill-set that Seán did."

For his next fight, Seán turned west to California rather than to Europe, with John Verner looking for another big payday off the back of a Mannion/Hutchings rematch. For Seán, there was also the more significant prospect of a win leading to a shot at the IBF super middleweight title.

At the time, Angelo Dundee was cooped up in Sugar Ray Leonard's training camp for what was billed the Super Fight between Leonard and Marvin Hagler. Years had been spent trying to make this fight, and it finally happened in April 1987. Leonard beat Hagler by majority decision, but to this day, the result is disputed.

With Mannion fighting in February, Dundee left the Sugar Ray camp to come out to California. Few watching Leonard vs. Hagler realized Mannion's impact on the Super Fight.

"Angelo was constantly asking questions about Hagler, because he knew I used to spar with him," recalled Seán. "'Whatever you do,' I told him, 'don't get Ray to make him mad. If you get him mad, he'll kill you.' And that's what they did. Leonard boxed him but didn't provoke him, and won. That said," said Seán, laughing, "I still think Hagler won that fight!"

It was a reflection of Dundee's respect for Mannion that he would abandon a training camp for one of the biggest fights in boxing history so that he could help the Irishman. Looking on as Seán sparred in Stockton, Paddy Mannion recalls Dundee turning to him.

"You know, Paddy, I've only ever had two fighters that could take any sort of punch thrown at them, Muhammad Ali and Seán. And Seán's the only guy I've ever had that's never been knocked down. It's the way he goes with the punch, he doesn't stand there taking the force full on."

Dundee stopped and sighed. "Too bad I didn't have your brother 10 years ago."

"Too late now," was his brother's answer.

"I'm afraid so, Paddy," replied Dundee, "I'm afraid so."

When it came to fight night, Fred Hutchings put in a blistering start and, despite finishing strongly, Mannion lost.

"Hutching's just decisioned Sean Mannion," reported Jack Fiske in the *San Francisco Chronicle*.

"I spoke afterward to the referee, Terry Smith," said Seán. "He told me, 'I didn't give you any of the first six rounds and maybe I should have. I gave you all the last four rounds.' If I had just gotten one of those first six, it would have been a draw."

But it wasn't. There would be no IBF world title fight for Seán. What got to him was that he had beaten Hutchings before, and he knew that he was capable of beating him again. He remembered Mike Flaherty's question after the Errol Christie fight.

"I wonder if you haven't done enough, Seán?"

By now, Seán Mannion was 31 years old. He had never intended to stay boxing for so long. "I used to say when I turned professional that I would be retired by the time I was 30. But it's like drink or drugs or anything else you put in your body. When it's in you, it's very difficult to let go."

And so he decided that he would give the European market one last shot. If he succeeded, he could make some real money before laying down the gloves. If he failed, it wouldn't matter. One way or another, the gloves were coming off for good.

His second-ever European pro fight was set for Paris, against the French middleweight champion and top 10–ranked Pierre-Frank Winterstein.

"Of all the places I have ever visited, that was the place I liked least," said Seán. "I've never been anywhere where the people were so rude!"

The fight was being held in the Cirque d'Hiver on a Monday night in November 1987, and in the theater dressing rooms Seán noticed a poster for the fight, publicizing it as an eight-rounder.

"I signed up for ten rounds and I'm not fighting eight," he told Rick Mandris, who had traveled to Paris with him instead of Dundee.

Mandris went out to check that the fight would be the 10 rounds originally agreed, and returned reassured.

As a spectacle, the Cirque d'Hiver had hosted plenty of entertaining nights over its 135-year history. This wasn't one of them. Winterstein was good, but not great. Seán was definitely slower than he had once been. The Frenchman had the upper hand initially, but as the fight went on, Winterstein appeared to tire. It had been over three years since his last ten-rounder, and he had only ever fought two of them. By the sixth, Seán was getting the upper hand and had full control of the ring for rounds seven and eight.

After the eighth round, it was obvious that Pierre-Frank Winterstein wasn't coming out of his corner. Seán was delighted. Victory. A shot at a European title, perhaps. It was then that he realized that Winterstein wasn't coming out as the fight was over.

"What the hell's going on?" he asked the referee, Alfred Asaro. "This is a ten-round fight and we've only fought eight."

Asaro didn't speak English.

"C'est fini," he replied, and turned his back on the Ros Muc boxer.

Years later, Seán would claim that a man came into his dressing room after the fight to tell him that, between the sixth and seventh rounds, someone from the Winterstein corner managed to convince the timekeeper that it was an eight-round fight.

For Seán, it wasn't just the end of a European dream. He had also acquired a new record he was loath to accept. He had now lost two consecutive fights for the first time in his career. That was it for Seán. That was the message he needed. He flew back to Boston, he returned to work, and he forgot about boxing. He spent spells working with his brother Tommy's construction company, spells working with the company he first started out with in the States, Devereaux, spells working with Gerry Mannion. Spells in the Twelve Bens, spells in the Emerald Isle, spells in the Blarney Stone.

By the time he had seen out the Christmas of 1988, Mannion was sick of Boston and of the cold, cold winters of Massachusetts. He decided to take the same journey Mike Flaherty took so many years earlier, and headed west to California for a change of climate and a change of life. He moved in with a second cousin, Joe Walsh and his wife, in Mill Valley north of San Francisco and settled into a new rhythm on the West Coast.

Waiting for the 5:25 a.m. bus to work at the top of the road. In over the Golden Gate Bridge to a carpentry job in San Francisco. Down to Newman's Gym on Leavenworth Street for a bit of training, a bit of sparring, just in case he would someday change his mind about retiring. He'd meet Joe at the gym, they'd be home again in Mill Valley by 8:00, sitting on the porch drinking cans of beer. Then to bed. The bus again at 5:25 a.m. He began to enjoy his new life.

There were a few decent boxers in Newman's Gym. Seán would spar with the likes of Pat Lawlor, a San Francisco boxing legend, and his brother Dennis. One evening, Roberto Duran walked in looking for a sparring partner. Seán gave him four rounds.

"He was as fat as a cow," laughed Seán. By that time, Duran was 38, still fighting for world titles in a career that spanned an incredible five decades. Six years his junior, Seán had already unofficially retired.

Inevitably, though, the offer to get back in the ring came, and it only took the one offer to get the gloves on Mannion again. He was asked if he would take on David Vedder, a light heavyweight from nearby San Jose. He had never heard of Vedder. Seán, of course, accepted the offer.

"You know David Vedder is pretty good, Seán?" Pat Lawlor asked in the gym the following day. "I'm not sure if this is a fight you should take."

Lawlor was right. Vedder was pretty good. He won the U.S. light heavyweight title in his next fight after taking on Mannion, and fought for the world title in the following fight. Seán Mannion, on the other hand, was a month short of 33, didn't have a trainer, and had been out of the ring for two years.

"It was probably too late to pull out of the fight once it dawned on me what I had gotten myself into," he said, "but to tell you the truth, I wouldn't give anyone the satisfaction of withdrawing."

It was more than pride steering Seán into the ring in August 1989, however.

"I was going to retire," he told the *San Francisco Chronicle* at the time, "but two things changed my mind. I saw Duran at 38 coming back to win a title, and In-Chul Baek of Korea is now the WBA super middleweight champion. I beat him six years ago; stopped his winning streak at 26, all knockouts. In all my fights I've only taken two beatings, against McCallum and Errol Christie."

If Baek could win a world title six years after being pummeled by Seán in Atlantic City, why couldn't he do the same himself now? What Seán hadn't taken into account, however, was that In-Chul Baek was five years his junior, and didn't seem to have the same interest in Budweiser.

Mannion's reputation meant top billing and a large Irish crowd at San Francisco's Civic Auditorium. With no trainer, Peter Kerr came out to California from Boston to be in his corner. Seán was rusty, he was heavy, but he went 10 rounds in a fight that wasn't one-sided. His third consecutive loss, nevertheless.

Angelo Dundee phoned him the following day with the same advice he got from Pat Lawlor before the fight. "You shouldn't have taken that fight, Seán."

For once, Seán agreed. After a long conversation with Dundee, they decided that it was time for Seán to put away the gloves once and for all. "Sean Mannion has hung 'em up," announced the *San Francisco Chronicle*.

After a year in San Francisco, Seán headed back to Boston in February 1990 to see Steve Collins fight Mike McCallum for the WBA middleweight title over 12 tough rounds. After the fight, Seán and Paddy went back to the dressing rooms in the Hynes Convention Center to congratulate the man they hadn't met since Madison Square Garden in 1984.

"Hey Mike," asked Paddy, "you want to give Seán another fight?"

"I ain't ever fightin' no Irishman again," was McCallum's reply.

Seán had planned on returning to California, but wasn't long settling back into a Boston groove. Days on the building site, evenings by the bar, and a very occasional visit to the gym. That's when he received an unexpected phone call from Germany.

Jean-Marcel Artz had spent 30 years becoming one of Germany's biggest boxing promoters and by the early nineties, with a huge increase in the German fight market, Artz needed someone to give his better boxers a challenge.

Artz asked Seán if he would travel to Germany to take on a young fighter named Nelson Alves. Despite not having been in the ring for over a year, Seán said yes. He didn't have a trainer, he didn't have a manager, but it didn't matter. A deal was struck there and then over the phone.

A friend from Connemara, Pádraic Ó Cuinn, flew with him to Düsseldorf to work his corner. On their way from the airport, the two were taken aback by the number of people celebrating on the streets. They had flown into Germany on October 3, 1990, the day East and West Germany unified. Mannion turned to Ó Cuinn in the taxi, joking that the real reason they had been brought over was to work the jackhammer and take down the Berlin Wall.

Nelson Alves had never lost a fight, and he didn't lose to Seán Mannion either. Again, a grossly unfit Seán went the 10 rounds and again, he wasn't knocked down. Alves would have 18 undefeated fights before his promising career was cut short by an eye injury.

Seán returned to Boston, but Jean-Marcel Artz soon called again. Having given Alves a good challenge, Artz was looking for more of the same against a fighter called Henry Maske. Maske was at another level entirely compared to Alves, however. He had a gold medal from the 1988 Seoul Olympics. He had a gold from the following year's World Championships. As a pro boxer, he had won all five of his fights by the time he met Mannion, and would go on to win the light heavyweight world title, successfully defending it ten times. The Maske fight was held in Hamburg in November 1990, and although Seán gave a decent account of himself, he was beaten on points after eight rounds.

"It was pretty lonely at the time, traveling to Germany with no one with me," Seán said. "I remember at the press conference beforehand being introduced as an Irish American. I pulled my passport out of my pocket and told them, 'that's not an American passport, that's an Irish passport.' I got a huge round of applause!

"I put up a good fight against Maske, and considering that it was at the end of my career, there wasn't that much between us."

Other than a local Dorchester fight against Miguel Rosa shortly after the Maske bout, Seán Mannion stopped fighting. Once again, he put the gloves aside. He even quit his visits to the gym, other than the occasional trip to the sauna to shift a few pounds in sweat.

On the evening of February 20, 1992, that changed again. Seán was just after getting back to his house on St. Mark's Road in Dorchester after a day's work on the complex cross-Boston tunneling project, the "Big Dig," when the phone rang. Jean-Marcel Artz. Again.

"Hey Seán, are you training?"

"No, I'm kind of retired," answered Seán. "I haven't been near the gym in months."

"I need a guy badly. Do you know anyone."

"Jesus, I'm afraid not. I'm not mixing in the circles at all these days."

"Well, how about you?"

"Ah no," he said. "I'm overweight, I'm not fit, I'm not training."

"Look Seán, do me a favor, I'm really stuck. Please."

Seán thought about it.

"When would I have to go over?"

"Well, you would have to be on the plane tonight."

"What? Tonight? When is the fight?"

"Tomorrow."

"Jean-Marcel, I don't even have a pair of togs."

Jean-Marcel promised him some shorts if he flew from Boston to New York, and then on to an eight-hour flight to Berlin. Seán landed at Tegel Airport early on the morning of the fight and, after a few hours' sleep, was brought to the Legien Center for the weigh-in. He stood up on the scales to be confronted by 190 pounds, 15 pounds over the light heavyweight limit. Seán was taken off the scales quickly. The records state that he weighed 174 pounds that night, a pound lighter than his opponent.

"Really, I shouldn't have taken that fight," he said of his journey to Berlin, "but the man was stuck, and I didn't want to leave him stuck."

His opponent had only ever had four fights, all victories of course, but Dariusz Michalczewski would go on to become one of the greatest boxers ever in his division. By the time the Polish fighter retired in 2005, he had won the WBO, WBA, and IBF light heavyweight titles, along with the WBO cruiser-weight world title.

In the second round of the fight, Michalczewski delivered a haymaker to Mannion's supposedly granite jaw.

"I didn't move," said Seán. "I think that he was so surprised I was still standing that he dropped his arms and I managed to get in four punches without reply. 'Anyone I ever hit with that shot, they went down straight away,' he told me after the fight."

Seán didn't go down, but like every other opponent to come Michalczewski's way at that point, he didn't go the distance. Neither ring skill nor a rock-hard jaw could compensate for age and a lack of fitness.

"I got a sharp pain in my side after the third round," said Seán, "and the doctor didn't let me out for the fourth."

"After the fight, the Michalczewski camp were asking me who was better, himself or Henry Maske. 'I can't really answer that,' I told them, 'because I was in some sort of shape against Maske and I haven't been to the gym other than to visit the sauna for the past year.'

"They kept looking for an answer so in the end I told them that Maske was the better boxer but that Michalczewski was stronger."

By the time Seán got back from Berlin, he had once again retired from boxing. At least in his own head. He still refused to say anything publicly, just in case an opportunity arose. And, of course, it soon did.

Johnny Gagliardi had promoted over 100 boxing tournaments in Massachusetts since 1978. He had made little in the way of money, however, and by 1992 needed some sort of scheme to draw a crowd. In the end, he came up with a very simple plan. It was called Muhammad Ali. Gagliardi organized a boxing night in the name of the Muhammad Ali Charity Foundation, with Micky Ward at the top of the card.

"Meet Mohammed Ali In Person! at our cocktail hour 6 to 7 p.m., $60 Per Person includes Free Cocktail and Hors d'oeuvres," announced the poster.

But Gagliardi had bigger problems than merely misspelling Ali's name on his poster. There was no Muhammad Ali on the night, and when Gagliardi announced to the crowd that their hero was ill and unable to attend, they didn't hang around to pay $60 for multicolored cocktails. Only 200 people stayed on at the Vista International Hotel in Waltham that night.

Seán Mannion wasn't even supposed to be there. He had only received an invite when Micky Ward hurt his hand and Gagliardi needed a last-minute replacement. Seán accepted immediately. Thanks to Angelo Dundee, he had spoken on the phone to his lifelong hero, but had never actually met Muhammad Ali. He wouldn't meet him this time either.

There was astonishment in Boston at Seán Mannion's return to the ring. Little had been seen or heard of Seán in the city for a few years, given that most of his fights since losing to McCallum had either been in California or Germany. "Aging boxer keeps on swinging for elusive title" was how the *Boston Globe* described his latest fight in September 1992, recounting how his nephew, John, kept a watchful eye on his uncle Seán as he pummeled a heavy bag in the basement gym of the South Boston Courthouse.

"I don't want to see him get killed, that's why I'm here. I know age takes its toll in the ring," said John. "That's why I'm around. I want to be sure he's OK."

Almost wistfully, the *Globe* also quoted his former trainer.

"'If only I had gotten him when he was 20 instead of 30,' lamented legendary trainer Angelo Dundee, who trained him from 1985–1989. 'He'd have been a champion, no question about it.'"

As it turned out, Seán's nephew had no reason for concern. His uncle beat Mike O'Han by unanimous verdict. After the fight, Seán announced that he was to continue boxing, despite being a week away from turning 36. "But next time I'm going to be in good shape," he promised. "I want more than three weeks to get ready."

A fortnight before Christmas, he fought Miguel Rosa again, stopping him in the sixth. Seán's confidence was beginning to return. He had just won two consecutive fights for the first time in six years, and had a new manager in Mickey Dwyer, a pub owner from South Boston with strong links to Whitey Bulger and to organized crime.

"My goal is the light heavyweight championship of the world," Seán told the *Boston Globe* after the Rosa fight. "I lost 15 pounds in a month and I probably lost the other 4 pounds [last night]. I've been there before and I know what it takes."

But he'd never find out again what it took. He was beaten on points over 10 rounds in his next fight against Fabian Garcia in Boston's Westin Hotel. It was reported in the newspapers afterward that Garcia wasn't sure if he had done enough to win.

"He told me that he was surprised that he was given the decision," said Seán. "'I'm shocked,' he told me. 'I thought you would be ok as the homeboy.' 'I'm not the homeboy here,' I said back to him, 'I'm from Ireland.'"

Reporters sought Seán after the fight, looking for some color on the Irish boxer who was about to retire.

"Instead they found him standing in a lobby outside the dressing room, one hand wrapped around a bottle of Budweiser and the other arm draped around the neck of Fabian Garcia, with whom he was chatting amiably away," wrote George Kimball in the *Boston Herald*.

"The better man won tonight," said a cheerful Mannion, who was paid $2,500 for his night's work.

As for the anticipated retirement talk, there was none.

"I'll be back," insisted Mannion. "In fact, I'm fighting on a St. Patrick's Day show in Chelsea in a couple of weeks."

And he was. Seán Mannion beat Terence Walker in the Chelsea Armory, Boston, on another John Gagliardi card. By the time the 10 rounds had finished, Seán's nose was pouring blood after what was an easy victory.

Afterward, Seán threw his gym bag into the back of Mickey Dwyer's car and promptly forgot about it, going out instead to celebrate St. Patrick's Day.

Three weeks later, Seán bumped into his nephew, Colm, as he walked down Fields Corner after work.

"Let's go for a pint," said Seán.

They had just sat down in the Emerald Isle when Mickey Dwyer arrived from his own pub 150 yards up the street. Mickey was pretty sure that he'd find his man in the Emerald Isle, with Seán stopping in regularly after taking the train home from work.

"Seán, here," said Mickey, handing him his gym bag. "You left your gear in my car."

"Thanks, Mick." Seán had completely forgotten about the bag.

"By the way, any idea when we'll have my next fight?"

Mickey Dwyer took a deep breath.

"Listen Seán, you've had a good career. You've won your last fight. Why don't you call it quits now and you can go out on a high?"

Seán rubbed his chin. He looked down at the torn label on the Budweiser bottle in his hand. He looked back up at Mickey Dwyer.

"Alright," he said. "Alright then."

"That's it so."

And that was it. Seán Mannion had finally quit boxing on April 6, 1993.

Afterward, he headed home to St. Mark's Road, and readied himself for a night out. His nephews, Tommy's kids, were competing in a darts tournament in Nash's, and he had arranged with Colm to meet him there. They were just in the door when Tommy's son, Michael, came over to him.

"Sorry to hear about your trainer, Seán," he said.

Seán presumed he was referring to his earlier conversation with Mickey Dwyer. The story wasn't long getting around Dorchester, it seemed.

"My trainer?" he asked, laughing. "To be honest, Michael, I've only really had one trainer in my entire life and he's back home in Ireland. Mike Flaherty."

"Yeah, that's the guy I mean. Didn't you hear? He died today."

Seán was stunned. He knew Mike Flaherty had been ill. He had visited him in hospital a while back when he was home at his brother-in-law's funeral.

"I couldn't stay in the room with him for more than two minutes when I saw him in hospital," said Seán. "'I'll be back in a few minutes, Mike' is what I told him but I had to leave because I didn't want him to see me crying."

Mike Flaherty died on the day Seán Mannion decided to finally quit boxing. Twenty-five years after walking into the hall of that old school in Ros Muc.

"Life is funny," said Seán. "We started out together, and we finished up together."

EPILOGUE

January 27, 2013.

It's 12 degrees Fahrenheit outside. Soft, white snowflakes fall onto the pavement of Parkman Street, lit by the yellow glow of street lamps as they float like feathers to the ground.

Behind a parking lot by the road, there's a warehouse with a new sign in gold lettering above the door. "Dorchester Boxing Club." Inside, the familiar staccato noises of boxing fill the large open room. Somehow, it feels colder inside the gym than it does outside. There's no heating system in the building, and it's so cold you get a headache just from standing still.

A broken Coca-Cola machine is pushed up against the wall by the front door. Beside it, a large tractor wheel waits for boxers looking for strength training. At the back of the room, a metal cage used to lock up the boxing equipment completes the industrial look.

In total, there are seven boxers training in the Dorchester Boxing Club tonight. Some of them are hitting punch bags. A young guy works the skipping rope.

Standing in the ring, under a large mural of Marvin Hagler, is Seán Mannion. He wears boxing pads on his hands, a young man from Donegal attacking them as Mannion murmurs instruction. Michael McLaughlin is yet another Irishman who has traveled to Boston looking to fulfill his dream of professional boxing. Mannion, who has experienced almost every high and every low of the world McLaughlin seeks, advises him. Michael listens to the advice. Every word. They're preparing for a fight in the Dorchester Armory next month.

When the day finally arrives, Michael McLaughlin walks into the ring, the former U.S. light middleweight champion in his corner. He knocks down his opponent within 15 seconds. The fight doesn't get past the first round. He listened to every word.

~

Seán Mannion quit boxing at the age of 36. Six years later than he had originally planned.

"The first few years after I retired were my heaviest on the drink," he said. "I had spent my whole life focused entirely on boxing and in the end, when I finished up, I had nothing to show for it.

"That bothered me, I had this thing building up in me, how I failed to achieve what I set out to achieve, how I let down the people of Connemara and the people of Ireland. Drinking was a way of relieving that pain."

Without the focus of boxing, there was little to stop Seán from falling into a pit of introspection and self-loathing. One of the few distractions from his inner turmoil was his daughter, Theresa. Theresa was 10 when Seán quit boxing, born in 1983 at the pinnacle of his boxing career. His relationship with Theresa's mother was brief and fractious, but Seán has remained close to his daughter, one of the few beacons of hope in his life after he quit fighting.

With boxing behind him, Seán returned to working construction full time. When Boston's epic urban tunneling project, the Big Dig, began in the early nineties, Tony Cardinale secured Seán's membership in Local 88, the tunnel workers' union. Like many others from Connemara, he earned a good wage from digging. But there was something missing, and it wasn't turning up in the tunnel.

With an invitation to open a boxing gym in Galway in 2000, Seán returned home to Ireland and to Ros Muc. A TV reporter at the opening of the gym interviewed the ex-boxer, but Mannion had questions of his own.

"How's Maureen, Áine?"

Áine Lally was the reporter, and Maureen Mulkerrin was her aunt. Maureen and Seán had spent a few years seeing each other in Boston in the early eighties but broke up before Maureen left the United States for England.

"Will you give her my number and tell her to call me?" Seán asked.

Maureen called him. They met. They realized that they missed one another. That there was still something there. They were married within a year. Living in Ros Muc for the first time since 1976, Seán decided that he would give others the same opportunity he had been given and opened a boxing club on the same site where he had started out all those years ago. He was only ever going to give it one name. The Mike Flaherty Boxing Club, Ros Muc.

Along with training young kids in the area, Mannion began working with Irish pros such as Michael Sweeney and Declan Timmins. With help from Maureen, he quit drinking.

In 2009, he received an invitation to return to Madison Square Garden, 25 years after his fight with Mike McCallum. An all-star Irish boxing night, "Erin Go Brawl II," had been scheduled in the Garden for the night before St. Patrick's Day, featuring the likes of former WBC bantamweight champion Wayne McCullough, and the Emanuel Steward–trained Andy Lee.

There was also to be a special event acknowledging a boxer who never did get much acknowledgment for what he achieved in the sport. A man who fought for the world title at a time when that was a genuine achievement in itself. A man who came to the fore during the most competitive era in the history of middleweight boxing. A man who fought five world champions. A man who left eight opponents deciding never to return to the ring again. A man who was never knocked down in 57 professional fights.

A man who earned his place in Irish and in world boxing history.

But the acknowledgment never came. Not enough tickets were sold for the big night in Madison Square Garden, and "Erin Go Brawl II" was cancelled two weeks before St. Patrick's Day. There would be no event recognizing Seán Mannion's achievement.

The man Irish boxing forgot.

~

Today, the Dorchester Boxing Club sign on 82 Parkman Street has been taken down. The boxing ring has been relegated to a cramped room upstairs, where a few old-timers wait at a desk for customers that never arrive.

In the space of a couple of years, all has changed on Parkman Street. Boxing has been all but banished. Downstairs, the walls have been painted a moody black, covering over Marvin Hagler and his menacing stare. This is now Crossfit 617, a high-intensity gym that sells branded hoodies and posts workout videos on Instagram.

All has changed, too, for Seán Mannion. The return home to Ros Muc, the marriage to his old flame, the sobriety, the perfect ending, the happy ever after. It has all disappeared.

Today, he is back in Boston. He is back digging holes and pouring concrete. He is back on the drink. Sometimes. He is back with a former girlfriend. And he is happy. Most of the time.

Like many Irish emigrants, Seán Mannion is caught in a bind. His heart is in Ros Muc. His perfect life is in Ros Muc. His home is in Ros Muc. Except that it's not.

Seán has been living in Boston, on and off, since he was 17 years of age. All his friends, all his family lived there with him. His entire working life is Boston. His entire social life is Boston. Everything about Seán Mannion is Boston, except for that stubborn space in his heart called Ros Muc.

When Seán returned home to live in Ros Muc, he slowly realized that most all of his life had stayed behind on the other side of the Atlantic. In Ros Muc, he had no work. The boxing club fell apart. Idleness turned to drink. Drink turned against his marriage.

He might never admit it, to himself even, but Ros Muc is no longer home for Seán Mannion. Home now is Boston.

∼

Seán Mannion might be the forgotten man of Irish boxing, but he hasn't been forgotten in the United States. Attending a pro boxing night with him in the Boston Garden, it's difficult not to be impressed, surprised even, by the queue of people making their way ringside to meet him. Former world champions, former managers, former trainers, all looking for a few words with one of the big boys of 1980s boxing.

Beyond Connemara, Seán Mannion has never received in Ireland the recognition he gets on the other side of the Atlantic. Partly because he never fought as a pro in Ireland. But mostly because the overriding opinion of Seán Mannion among the Irish public was formed while watching the Mike McCallum fight, the only fight of his to be shown live on Irish TV. And the fight against Errol Christie, the fight broadcast on Raidió na Gaeltachta and on British TV. The two worst fights he ever had.

Apart from a few lines here and a paragraph there, little was reported in Ireland of Mannion's stateside boxing achievements. The first man to beat In-Chul Baek. The man who extinguished the boxing careers of young stars such as Jimmy Corkum, Nino Gonzalez, and Rocky Fratto. The man ranked number one in the United States by *Ring Magazine* in 1982. Ahead of Tommy Hearns, ahead of Tony Ayala, ahead of Mike McCallum even. The man who fought for the world title when only the WBA and the WBC existed. The man who fought for another world title and won, but didn't get the belt due to a dispute over money.

More than that, and in every way, the man who was never knocked down.

BIBLIOGRAPHY

Abramson, Mitch. "Dispute KO's Duddy from Garden Card." *New York Daily News*, February 12, 2009.

Ahern, John. "Mannion KO in 6th Shatters Corkum." *Boston Globe*, November 8, 1979.

Anderson, Dave. "'O Set Him Up for K.'" *New York Times*, October 21, 1984.

Anderson, John Ward. "1,500 Protest as Thatcher Speaks." *Washington Post*, February 21, 1985.

"Angelo Dundee (Obituary)." *Telegraph*, February 2, 2012.

Applebome, Peter. "Seeking to Lure the Crowds Again: But Hold the Borscht." *New York Times*, July 9, 2012.

Archdeacon, Tom. "Tiger Small: I'm No Angel but I'm Not Alone." *Miami News*, November 23, 1981.

——. "'The Underbelly of Boxing': Tony Torres Stumbles into a Nightmare." *Miami News*, November 21, 1981.

Arnot, Chris. "'Talking to Teenagers Was More Terrifying than Boxing.'" *Guardian*, May 12, 2010.

"The Art of Self-Defence." *Connacht Sentinel*, February 13, 1945.

Assael, Shaun, and Mike Mooneyham. *Sex, Lies, and Headlocks: The Real Story of Vince McMahon and World Wrestling Entertainment*. New York: Three Rivers Press, 2002.

"Ayala Is Guilty in Rape Trial." *New York Times*, April 14, 1983.

Baker, Mark Allen. *Title Town, USA: Boxing in Upstate New York*. Charleston, SC: History Press, 2010.

Beatty, Jack. *The Rascal King: The Life and Times of James Michael Curley, 1874–1958*. Boston: Da Capo Press, 1992.

Berkow, Ira. "Cus D'Amato's Gym." *New York Times*, November 7, 1985.

——. "Of the Times; From Movie 'Cuts' to Ring Cuts." *New York Times*, October 20, 1984.

Bernstein, Al. *Al Bernstein: 30 Years, 30 Undeniable Truths about Boxing, Sports, and TV.* New York: Diversion Publishing, 2012.

Binns, Katie. "Against the Odds?" BBC.com. May 12, 2006. http://www.bbc.co.uk/bradford/content/articles/2006/05/12/bradford_irish_katie_feature.shtml.

Black, Chris. "Chao from Dot. Ave." *Boston Globe*, September 12, 1993.

"'Black Market' in Big Fight Tickets." *Irish Times*, August 23, 1945.

Blair, William G. "Garden to Close the Felt Forum for Two Years." *New York Times*, January 27, 1989.

Borges, Ron. "For a Few Years, He was the Greatest Manager That Ever Lived." TheSweet-Science.com, July 8, 2009. www.thesweetscience.com/articles-of-2009/6986-for-a-few-years-he-was-the-greatest-manager-who-ever-lived.

——. "Going Another Round Like His Legendary Grandfather, 'Rip' Valenti, Boston Boxing Promoter Al Valenti Is Fighting to Keep the Family Business Alive." *Boston Globe*, December 16, 1990.

——. "Heavy-duty Promoters Duvas Are in Control of Top Division." *Boston Globe*, September 6, 1992.

——. "He's Out of Their Class: Norris Carries Too Much Weight for Chavez Camp's Liking." *Boston Globe*, March 14, 1993.

——. "McCallum Favorite Son." *Boston Globe*, February 2, 1990.

——. "Twenty-five Years Is a Long Time to Carry a Memory." ESPN.com, November 13, 2007. www.espn.com/sports/boxing/news/story?id=3107079.

——. "Vecchione Starred in Personal Fight Game; McNeeley's Manager Was True Friend of Local Boxing." *Boston Herald,* July 12, 2009.

"Boxer Is Jailed after Shooting Death." *Modesto Bee*, June 10, 1977.

"Boxing: Christie's Comeback." *Times* (London), August 29, 1986.

"Boxing: Joe Frazier 1944–2011: Rolling with the Punches: The Life of a Legend." *Guardian*, November 9, 2011.

Breathnach, Seán Bán. Interview with Máirtín Thornton. *Laochra Ceoil.* RTÉ Raidió na Gaeltachta, October 17, 1979.

Breheny, Martin. "Mannion Is on the Way Back." *Irish Press*, December 21, 1987.

——. "Raring to Go!" *Irish Press*, October 29, 1986.

Bulger, William M. *James Michael Curley: A Short Biography with Personal Reminiscences.* Carlisle, MA: Commonwealth Editions, 2009.

Burgess, Glenn. "Sugar Ray's Latest Victory Seen by Record Maine Crowd." *Lewiston Evening Journal*, November 4, 1978.

Caneollos, Peter S. "Curley's People." *Boston Globe,* January 3, 2010.

Cannon, Lou. "Actor, Governor, President, Icon." *Washington Post,* June 6, 2004.

"Cape Cod Coliseum to Be Converted into Warehouse." *Boston Globe*, May 17, 1984.

Carfado, Nick. "Curto Lost Chance." *Patriot Ledger,* July 22, 1983.

Carlson, Michael. "Obituary: Willie Pep." *Guardian*, December 2, 2006.

Carp, Steve. "'It Was a Brutal Fight.'" *Las Vegas Review-Journal*, November 13, 2007.

Carroll, Brendan. "Connemara Boxer Is 'Knock Out' Sensation in Boston." *Connacht Tribune*, November 16, 1979.

Carter, Leon H. "Tony Ayala: A Life Lived on the Ropes." *Newsday*, January 26, 1992.

Celizic, Mike. "And in This Corner . . . Lou Duva, Ring Master Success Crowns Love Affair with Boxing." The *Record*, June 17, 1990.

"Center Pro Bouts Set for Friday." *Bangor Daily News*, November 3, 1978.

Christie, Errol, and Tony McMahon. *No Place to Hide*. London: Aurum Press, 2011.

Clarity, James F. "Ros Muc Journal: On Europe's Edge, Irish Fear Being Left to Drift." *New York Times*, November 21, 1991.

Clusiau, Christina. "The Disappearance of the Borscht Belt Hotels." *Time*, June 23, 2011.

Corry, Eoghan. "I Let You All Down: Mannion." *Sunday Tribune*, October 21, 1984.

Cullen, Kevin. "Someone Else's Turn in Dorchester as Irish Ascendancy Wanes." *Irish Times*, March 26, 2008.

Curley, James Michael. *I'd Do It Again: A Record of All My Uproarious Years*. Englewood Cliffs, NJ: Prentice-Hall, 1957.

"Curry Knocks Off Finch to Win Crown." *Ocala Star-Banner*, May 5, 1982.

Dente, Jim. "Impressive Win for Mannion." *New Jersey Herald*, January 22, 1982.

"Doctor Advises Sugar Ray Not to Fight Again." *Sarasota Herald-Tribune*, February 15, 1984.

Doherty, Kieran. *Puritans, Pilgrims, and Merchants: Founders of the Northeastern Colonies*. Minneapolis: Oliver Press, 1999.

Donovan, Mark. "With a First-round Knockout, Tony Danza of 'Taxi' Proves He's More Than Just a Hack." *People*, May 14, 1979.

"Duran, Hearns Matched for June 15." *Washington Post*, March 21, 1984.

"An End to 15-Rounders." *New Straits Times*, October 24, 1987.

Epstein, Eve. "Judge Still on Bench, Despite Gross Misconduct." *San Francisco Chronicle*, April 4, 1991.

"Fáilte Mhór Do Ó Mainín." *Connacht Tribune*, November 16, 1984.

Fenton, Jim. "City of Champions Rang True in Brockton Ring; Rocky Marciano's Reign Inspired Generations of Brockton Boxers to Follow His Winning Ways." *Enterprise*, June 14, 2011.

Fernandez, Bernard. "A 'Matinee Idol' Turns 50: Czyz Reflects on His Charmed, Tough Life." *Ring*, June 25, 2012.

"Fighter Retiring." *New York Times*, November 20, 1982.

Fiske, Jack. "Cooney Fight Back on for Cow Palace." *San Francisco Chronicle*, May 6, 1986.

———. "Foreman Against Cooney: 'Senior Tour' Is Heating Up." *San Francisco Chronicle*, September 12, 1989.

———. "Gloves, Museum in S.F.: Something Old, Something New." *San Francisco Chronicle*, February 10, 1986.

———. "Is Olajide Merely a Pretty Face?" *San Francisco Chronicle*, January 31, 1987.

———. "'Little Ezzard' Meets an Old Friend." *San Francisco Chronicle*, February 14, 1987.

———. "Lopez Can Pack a House." *San Francisco Chronicle*, October 3, 1987.

———. "The Old Urge Won't Leave Sugar Ray." *San Francisco Chronicle*, April 26, 1986.

———. "Prince Gets Shot at Ranking." *San Francisco Chronicle*, January 6, 1987.

Fitzgerald, Ray. "The Makings of a Fighter . . . It Has the Making of a Movie." *Boston Globe*, November 8, 1977.

Foderaro, Lisa W. "Bankruptcy and Success Meet in Catskills Hotels." *New York Times*, August 14, 1990.

"Former Boxer Jailed in Galway." *Irish Independent*, May 28, 1954.

"Former Champion Boxer Jailed." *Irish Times*, February 20, 1950.

Frommer, Myrna Katz, and Harvey Frommer. *It Happened in the Catskills: An Oral History in the Words of Busboys, Bellhops, Guests, Proprietors, Comedians, Agents and Others Who Lived It*. Albany: State University of New York Press, 2009.

Fry, Darrell. "McCallum Fighting for Respect." *Tampa Bay Times*, November 21, 1996.

"Galway Lettermore Boxing Tourney." *Connacht Tribune*, November 16, 1984.

"Galway Ovation for Thornton." *Connacht Tribune*, February 17, 1945.

"Galway Sportstars Boxing." *Connacht Tribune*, January 11, 1985.

Giambra, Joey, Gina Giambra, and Joey Giambra Jr. *The Uncrowned Champion: Boxing and the Mafia in the Golden Era*. Bloomington, IN: AuthorHouse, 2009.

Goldenstein, Richard. "Angelo Dundee Dies at 90; Trained Ali and Leonard." *New York Times*, February 3, 2012.

———. "Johnny LoBianco, Referee in Controversial Duran Bout, Dead at 85." *New York Times*, July 21, 2001.

Goldstein, Alan. "McCallum, 'The Invisible Man,' Aims to Show Toney His KO Punch." *Baltimore Sun*, December 13, 1991.

Gray, Ed. "Aging Boxer Keeps on Swinging for Elusive Title." *Boston Herald*, September 27, 1992.

———. "Boxing Notebook: Rosenblatt Masters Another Art." *Boston Herald*, March 14, 1993.

———. "Mannion Holds On, Beats Ohan." *Boston Herald*, September 29, 1992.

Gregerson, John. "South Station: Derailed by 'Progress,' A Boston Landmark Reclaims Its Role in Urban Life." *Building Design & Construction*, November 1, 1990.

"Hagler Denies Problem with Alcohol, Drugs." *News and Courier*, July 5, 1987.

Halloran, Bob. *Irish Thunder: The Hard Life and Times of Micky Ward*. Guilford, CT: Lyons Press, 2007.

Hamill, Pete. "The Great White Hope." *New York Magazine*, June 23, 1969.

Harvin, Al. "McCallum Winner in Garden." *New York Times*, June 12, 1982.

Hayes, Charles. "Rocky Fratto Scores 27th Victory, Then Retires." *Geneva Times*, April 2, 1973.

Heaney, John. "Book by *Irish News* Journalist Tells Boxing Legend's Life Story." *Irish News*, October 8, 2008.

Hoffer, Richard. "Boxing: Tubbs Has a Big Title but Little to Show for It." *Los Angeles Times*, September 28, 1985.

Horovitz, Bruce. "'Designer Boxing': Old Sport Becomes a Yuppie Fad." *Los Angeles Times*, October 23, 1985.

Iamele, David. "Interview: Emanuel Steward." Wail! The CBZ Journal, April 2003. www.cyberboxingzone.com/boxing/w0403-di.html.

Interview with Angelo Dundee. *Off the Ball*. Newstalk Radio, 2010.

James, George. "In Person: Slugging It Out All These Years." *New York Times*, June 9, 2002.

Katz, Michael. "Duran's Next Foe Unranked." *New York Times*, July 7, 1981.

——. "Finding Profit in Roadwork." *New York Times*, October 5, 1983.

——. "Hagler Bout Judges Switched." *New York Times*, October 19, 1984.

——. "Hamsho and Flood: Rare Boxing Team." *New York Times*, October 18, 1984.

——. "Holmes–Coetzee Title Showdown Is Getting Closer." *New York Times*, February 22, 1984.

——. "Loser with Perfect Record." *New York Times*, October 17, 1984.

Keeler, Sean. "Rise & Fall of Boxing Champion Michael Nunn." *Des Moines Register*, July 6, 2008.

Kilgore, Ray. "Michael Nunn Still Second to None." SecondsOut.com, n.d. www.secondsout.com/usa-boxing-news/main-usa-news/michael-nunn-still-second-to-none.

——. "O'Grady Stresses the Importance of Life after Boxing." *Seconds Out*, June 18, 2006.

Killeen, Austin. "Danny Long: The Man in Blue." *IBRO Journal*, no. 94, June 2007.

——. "Mike McCallum: The Body Snatcher." IBROResearch.com, June 26, 2012. www.ibroresearch.com/2012/06/mike-mccallum-the-body-snatcher/.

Kimball, George. "Boxing Notes: Lake Up Creek for Actions." *Boston Herald*, June 26, 1994.

——. "Chief Can't Shake New Notoriety." *Boston Herald*, February 28, 1993.

——. *Four Kings: Leonard, Hagler, Hearns, Duran and the Last Great Era of Boxing*. Edinburgh: Mainstream Publishing, 2008.

——. "If Michelangelo Had Been a Boxing Manager." TheSweetScience.com, July 4, 2009. www.thesweetscience.com/articles-of-2009/6977-if-michelangelo-had-been-a-boxing-manager.

——. "Mannion in Unimpressive Win." *Boston Herald*, August 12, 1984.

——. "Marvin: I'm in Mannion's Corner." *Boston Herald*, October 17, 1984.

——. "My Manager Vinnie Vecchione's Work Finally Produces McNeeley Payday." *Boston Herald*, May 30, 1995.

———. "A Spy Saga at a Training Camp." *Boston Herald*, September 23,1984.

Kram, Mark. "Frazier–Ali: The Three Classics." *Philadelphia Daily News*, November 8, 2011.

Kriegel, Mark. "A Step Back: Families Continue to Heal 30 Years after Title Fight between Ray Mancini and Duk-koo Kim." *New York Times*, September 16, 2012.

Lee, Veronica. "Boxing: My Weapons Were My Fists—Now It's Guns and Knives." *Independent*, June 6, 2010.

Lehmann-Haupt, Christopher. "How a Mountain Paradise Became the Borscht Belt." *New York Times*, November 13, 1989.

Lehr, Dick. "A Lover of Boxing and a Fighter in Court, Boston Lawyer Tony Cardinale Has Earned a Reputation as the Toughest Defender . . . in the Mob's Corner." *Boston Globe*, September 23, 1997.

Lehr, Dick, and Gerard O'Neill. *Black Mass*. New York: Public Affairs, 2000.

Leo, Tom. "Fratto and Mihara Finally Meet." *Finger Lakes Times*, November 6, 1981.

———. "Fratto Loses 10 Rounder, Unanimously." *Finger Lakes Times*, October 8, 1982.

———. "Knocked Down 3 Times, Fratto Loses by TKO." *Finger Lakes Times*, April 6, 1983.

———. "Thursday TV Bout Offers Fratto Exposure." *Finger Lakes Times*, October 5, 1982.

Leonard, Roger. *In the Shadow of a Champ: Pathway to Recovery*. Bloomington, IN: Xlibris Corporation, 2012.

Leonard, Sugar Ray, with Michael Arkush. *The Big Fight: My Life In and Out of the Ring*. New York: Viking Penguin, 2011.

"Let's Do It—Mannion." *Irish Independent*, October 29, 1986.

Levinson, Scott. "Cocaine and Boxing: How Coke Shaped the Boxing Landscape." ProBoxing-fans.com, February 28, 2010. www.proboxing-fans.com/cocaine-and -boxing-how-coke-shaped-the-boxing-landscape_022810/.

Lewis, Ron. "Emmanuel Steward's Kronk Gym Is Consigned to Boxing History." *Times* (London), November 1, 2012.

"Life a Carousel to Rocky Fratto." *Evening News*, October 20, 1981.

Little, Darragh. "Seconds Out on the Champ." *Irish Medical Times*, October 2010.

Livingston, Bill. "Duran Can't KO Memory of 'No Mas.'" *Cleveland Plain Dealer*, December 18, 1992.

"Long Time Grossinger's Social Director Dies at 90." *Mid-Hudson News Network*, April 4, 2012.

Mac Amhlaigh, Donall. *An Irish Navvy: The Diary of an Exile*. Trans. Valentin Iremonger. Cork, Ireland: Collins Press, 2013.

Mac Aonghusa, Prionsias. *Gaillimh agus Aistí Eile*. Dublin: An Clóchomhar Tta, 1983.

———. "Ros Muc." In *Pobal na Gaeltachta: A Scéal agus a Dhán*, edited by Gearóid Ó Tuathaigh, Liam Lillis Ó Laoire, and Seán Ua Súilleabháin, 396–408. Indreabhán, Ireland: Cló Iar-Chonnacht, 2000.

———. *Ros Muc agus Cogadh na Saoirse*. Dublin: Conradh na Gaeilge, 1992.

Mac Con Iomaire, Tomás. "Pócaí Folamh Is Cloigeann Tinn." *Croch Suas É!*, edited by Mícheál Ó Conghaile. Indreabhán, Ireland: Cló Iar-Chonnacht, 1986.

Mac Dubhghaill, Uinsíonn. "The Joy of Homecoming is Short-lived." *Irish Times*, December 23, 1996.

MacDonald, Michael Patrick. *All Souls: A Family Story from Southie*. Boston: Beacon Press, 1999.

"Mannion Beaten on Points." *Irish Times*, October 20, 1984.

"Mannion Declared Winner in Fight." *Los Angeles Times*, September 27, 1985.

"Mannion Gets a Cead Mile Failte." *Connacht Tribune*, November 16, 1984.

"Mannion Gets Back in the Ring." *Irish Times*, June 26, 1998.

"Mannion Gets Danish Offer." *Irish Independent*, February 15, 1985.

"Mannion Now Star of U.S. Boxing Big-Time." *Connacht Tribune*, May 4, 1979.

"Mannion Punches Way into Rankings: Is on Verge of a World Title Chance." *Connacht Tribune*, February 5, 1982.

"Mannion Ruins Gonzalez' Hopes for a WBC Championship Fight." *Los Angeles Times*, January 22, 1982.

"Mannion Welcome." *Connacht Tribune*, November 16, 1984.

"Mannion Works Hard for 10-Round Win." *Ocala Star-Banner*, August 31, 1986.

Marantz, Steve. "Bumphus Gets His Shot Today." *Boston Globe*, January 22, 1984.

——. "Champion by Rights Won't Be There for Title Bout." *Boston Globe*, July 31, 1983.

——. "Curto Back? First Test Is Shuler." *Boston Globe*, July 10, 1983.

——. "Early Fallout Surrounding Ayala Case." *Boston Globe*, January 23, 1983.

——. "Hagler Asks for Men Officials." *Boston Globe*, October 17, 1984.

——. "He's Known the Ropes for 86 Years." *Boston Globe*, August 28, 1983.

——. "Justice: NY KO's Lewis." *Boston Globe*, July 3, 1983.

——. "Mannion Fighting for His Country." *Boston Globe*, October 17, 1984.

——. "Mannion May Get Shot at Leonard." *Boston Globe*, December 15, 1983.

——. "Mannion's Big Chance." *Boston Globe*, June 26, 1983.

——. "Of Hype, Fressers and the Greatest Fight Ever." *Boston Globe*, July 17, 1983.

——. "State to Investigate Mannion's TKO of Burgess." *Boston Globe*, May 15, 1985.

——. "Tale of South Boston's Long Shows What's Wrong with Sport." *Boston Globe*, June 7, 1981.

——. "They're Farces, Not Fights." *Boston Globe*, May 19, 1985.

——. "Troy Pumping Life into the Club Scene." *Boston Globe*, May 30, 1982.

——. "A Walk in Leonard's Designer Shoes . . ." *Boston Globe*, December 18, 1983.

Martin, Douglas. "Michael Flannery, an Advocate of a United Ireland, Dies at 92." *New York Times*, October 2, 1994.

Matthews, Wallace. "Matchmaker, Matchmaker . . . Brenner Turned the Garden into Mecca of Boxing." *New York Post*, January 9, 2000.

McGarry, Fearghal. *Eoin O'Duffy: A Self-Made Hero*. Oxford: Oxford University Press, 2005.

McIlvanney, Hugh. "Angelo Fought Ali's Corner." *Sunday Times*, February 5, 2012.

McNamara, Eileen. "One Last Trip Down the Aisle." *Boston Globe*, September 21, 1996.

"McSwain Loses to Mannion." *Miami Herald*, December 15, 1985.

Megliola, Lenny. "The Fight Crowd." *MetroWest Daily News*, September 29, 1992.

Mifflin, Lawrie, and Michael Katz. "Return of Duran Inspires No Fear." *New York Times*, July 8, 1982.

Milford, Barbara. "Medical School Training Begins in Boxing Ring: Baltimore Intern Hangs Up His Gloves." *Washington Post*, August 11, 1985.

"'Mister Boxing' Jean-Marcel Nartz geht in Rente." *Der Westen*, July 2, 2009.

Mitchell, Kevin. "Nigel Benn v Gerald McClellan—The Tragic Fight Continues to Haunt." *Guardian*, December 2, 2011.

Mladinich, Robert. "Boxing's Dirty Dancing Connection." TheSweetScience.com, May 15, 2008. www.thesweetscience.com/articles-of-2008/5903-boxings-dirty-dancing-connection.

———. "The Danny Long and the Short of It." TheSweetScience.com, March 31, 2006. www.thesweetscience.com/articles-of-2006/3588-the-danny-long-and-the-short-of-it.

———. "A Tough, Tough Guy Named Mustafa Hamsho." TheSweetScience.com, January 22, 2006. www.thesweetscience.com/articles-of-2006/3245-a-tough-tough-guy-named-mustafa-hamsho.

Murphy, Shelley. "Subpoenas Add Heat to Fed Probe of Whitey." *Boston Herald*, August 14, 1991.

Murray, Vince. "Notebook." *Ocala Star-Banner*, October 8, 1982.

———. "Title Bout Next Stop for Tony Ayala." *Ocala Star-Banner*, May 3, 1982.

Muscato, Ross A. "Back in the Day—Summering in Easton." *Easton Patch*, July 6, 2011.

Nack, William. "Let the World Know I'm O.K." *Sports Illustrated*, September 28, 1987.

———. "Sugar Sure Is Sweet." *Sports Illustrated*, November 26, 1979.

Nee, Patrick, Richard Farrell, and Michael Blythe. *A Criminal and an Irishman: The Inside Story of the Boston Mob–IRA Connection*. Hanover, NH: Steerforth Press, 2006.

Neuffer, Elizabeth. "Drug Agents Sweep City, Seeking 51 Linked to Reputed Crime Boss." *Boston Globe*, August 11, 1990.

Newman, Bruce. "We've Grown Accustomed To His Face: Lou Duva Has Become Boxing's Most Ubiquitous Personality." *Sports Illustrated*, April 10, 1989.

Ní Eadhra, Róisín. Interview with Jimmy Connolly. *Aisling Ghéar*. TG4. 2000.

———. Interview with Jimmy Farrell. *Aisling Ghéar*. TG4. 2000.

Ó Croidheáin, Caoimghin. *Language from Below: The Irish Language, Ideology and Power in the 20th Century*. Bern, Switzerland: Peter Lang, 2006.

Ó hÉithir, Breandán. Interview with Máirtín Thornton. *Féach*. RTÉ One. December 10, 1974.

O'Connor, Thomas H. *The Boston Irish: A Political History.* Boston: Back Bay Books, 1995.

"Olympic Team Ties with Finns." *Toronto Star,* August 27, 1986.

"Ortiz Charged in Shooting." *Sarasota Herald-Tribune,* June 10, 1977.

Pacheco, Ferdie. *Blood in My Coffee: The Life of the Fight Doctor.* New York: Sports Publishing, 2005.

"Pacquiao Trainer and Detroit Boxer's Common Ground: Hall of Fame Inductees Relate to Thrill of Victory, Agony of Defeat." *Jackson Citizen-Patriot,* June 13, 2012.

Palmer, Bill. "Mannion to Begin Comeback in Troy." *Schenectady Gazette,* March 7, 1985.

Parks, Brad. "A Fighting Chance for a Fresh Start—The Question Isn't Whether Tony Ayala Jr. Will Box Again—It's Whether He'll Rape Again." *Star-Ledger,* April 21, 1999.

Parrillo, Ray. "Carol Polis Recalls Her Days as the First Woman to Judge a Pro Boxing Match." *Philadelphia Inquirer,* July 15, 2011.

Poliquin, Bud. "Graziano Headed to Bare Knuckle Boxing HOF." *Post-Standard,* July 31, 2012.

Powers, John. "Jimmy Corkum: Brockton Welterweight Taking Heavyweight Courses at Stonehill." *Boston Globe,* August 19, 1979.

Prendergast, John. "The Thomas a Becket: A Popular Haunt for Boxers, Drinkers and the Odd Ghost." *Southwark News,* May 6, 2008.

Pugmire, Lance. "Lou Filippo, 1925–2009: Boxing Hall of Famer Had Roles in 'Rocky' Movies." *Los Angeles Times,* November 5, 2009.

Putnam, Pat. "For Leonard It Was Down, and Then Out." *Sports Illustrated,* May 21, 1984.

——. Hamsho Put on Some Kind of Show." *Sports Illustrated,* July 25, 1983.

Quinlin, Michael. *Irish Boston: A Lively Look at Boston's Colorful Irish Past.* Guilford, CT: Globe Pequot Press, 2004.

Rafael, Dan. "Gonzalez Revels in Surprise Upset of Michalczewski." *USA Today,* October 21, 2003.

"'Reborn' Duran to Meet Hagler for Title Tonight." *Evening News,* November 10, 1983.

Richman, Irwin. *Catskill Hotels.* Charleston, SC: Arcadia Publishing, 2003.

Roberts, Randy. *Jack Dempsey, the Manassa Mauler.* Chicago: University of Illinois Press, 2003.

Robinson, Tim. *Connemara: A One-Inch Map, with Introduction and Gazetteer.* Roundstone, Ireland: Folding Landscapes, 1990.

Rogers, Thomas. "Some Deft Work Outside the Ring." *New York Times,* March 21, 1984.

Sama, Dominic. "Zachary 'Zach' Clayton, 76, Ali-Foreman Bout's Referee." *Inquirer,* November 23, 1997.

Sammarco, Anthony Mitchell. *Dorchester*. Charleston, SC: Arcadia Publishing, 2005.

———. *South Boston*. Charleston, SC: Arcadia Publishing, 2006.

Santiago, Antonio. "Boxing Looks Back at Former Junior Middleweight Contender Clint Jackson." *Ringside Report*, July 25, 2006.

Schmemann, Serge. "Evolution in Europe; Germans' Day of Exultation and Marlene Dietrich Too." *New York Times*, October 4, 1990.

Schulberg, Budd. *Ringside: A Treasury of Boxing Reportage*. Chicago: Ivan R. Dee, 2006.

Schwartz, Larry. "Sugar Ray Was Ring Artist." ESPN.com, July 11, 2006. www.espn .com/classic/biography/s/Leonard_Sugar_Ray.html.

Scott, Gerald. "Mannion Pounds Out a Unanimous Decision Over Lee." *Los Angeles Times*, July 23, 1985.

Sen, Srikumar. "Back with a Two-fisted Bang." *Times* (London), October 30, 1986.

———. "Boxing: Hard Slog Has Little Reward for McKenzie." *Times* (London), September 22, 1986.

———. "Boxing: New-look Christie Stakes Future under Tibbs Wing." *Times* (London), October 24, 1986.

"Sensation in America." *Connacht Tribune*, January 25, 1980.

Shannon, William V. *The American Irish: A Political and Social Portrait*. New York: Macmillan, 1963.

Shea, John "Red." *Rat Bastards*. New York: HarperCollins, 2006.

Smith, Red. "Two Fists and Four Names." *New York Times*, July 8, 1981.

Smith, Timothy W. "After 16 Years in Prison, Ayala Starts Road Back." *New York Times*, April 21, 1999.

Smizik, Bob. "Hagler Cherishes His Biggest Win." *Pittsburgh Press*, November 11, 1983.

Solomons, Jack. *Jack Solomons Tells All*. London: Rich & Cowan, 1951.

Stapleton, Johnny. "Seán Mannion's World Title Bid to Be Recalled at Big NY Fight Night." *Connacht Tribune*, February 27, 2009.

Stevens, Peter F. *Hidden History of the Boston Irish: Little-Known Stories from Ireland's Next Parish Over*. Charleston, SC: History Press, 2008.

Stockton, Paysha. "Mickey's Goes Down for the Final Count." *Boston Globe*, October 16, 2005.

"Successful Boxing Tournament in Rosmuck." *Connacht Tribune*, May 23, 1969.

"Sugar Ray Is Still Too Sweet." *Telegraph*, November 4, 1978.

"Sugar Ray Too Much for Washed-up Muniz." *Nashua Telegraph*, December 11, 1978.

Sweeney, Emily. "Dot. Dot. Dot. Before There Was Boston, There Was Dorchester." *Boston Globe*, September 18, 2005.

"Thornton Threw in the Third Round." *Irish Independent*, August 25, 1945.

Toperoff, Sam. "Getting It Wrong, Getting It Right." In *Come Out Writing: A Boxing Anthology*, edited by Bill Hughes and Patrick King, 176–192. Edinburgh: Mainstream Publishing, 1999.

Toulmin, Vanessa. *A Fair Fight: An Illustrated Review of Boxing on British Fairgrounds*. Oldham, UK: World's Fair Limited, 1999.

"Trial of the Convent Rioters." *Jesuit or Catholic Sentinel*, December 13, 1834.

Valerio, Joe. "Referee Tony Perez Wallops Ali with a $20 Million Damage Suit." *People*, May 5, 1975.

"Verdict Goes to Sean Mannion." *Irish Press*, May 6, 1986.

Wakefield, Louise. "This Is the World Famous Thomas a Becket: The Old Kent Road's Most Famous Gin Palace, Revived and Rejuvenated." *London Society Journal*, no. 461, May 1, 2011.

Waters, Mike. "Hall Calls on 'Hitman' Hearns' Inclusion in International Boxing Hall of Fame Was Long Overdue." *Post-Standard*, June 6, 2012.

Watson, Iarfhlaith. "Teilifís na Gaeilge as a Public Sphere." *Irish Communications Review* 7, no. 1, 1998.

Watters, Andy. "Irish Ropes Hit Back at Lee Claims." *Irish News*, April 1, 2009.

Weatherford, Mike. "Politically Charged." *Las Vegas Review-Journal*, April 20, 2007.

Welshman, John. *Churchill's Children: The Evacuee Experience in Wartime Britain*. Oxford: Oxford University Press, 2010.

White, Jerry. *The Radio Eye: Cinema in the North Atlantic, 1958–1998*. Waterloo, Canada: Wilfrid Laurier University Press, 2009.

Wiley, Ralph. "Then All the Joy Turned to Sorrow." *Sports Illustrated*, November 22, 1982.

Willis, David K. "Piercing Moscow's Fortified Olympic Village." *Christian Science Monitor*, July 15, 1980.

Winkeljohn, Matt. "Former Olympic Boxer Jackson Held on Kidnapping Charge." *Atlanta Journal-Constitution*, August 24, 1988.

Wood, Daniel. "The Land of Goodbyes." *Globe and Mail*, July 14, 2007.

"Woodcock Confident of Winning." *Irish Times*, August 24, 1945.

Yakovlev, Pavel. "In This Corner: Anthony Cardinale Reflects on a Life as a Boxing Lawyer, New York City Boxing History, and the Muhammad Ali Boxing Reform Act." DoghouseBoxing.com, February 28, 2012. www.doghouseboxing.com/DHB/ Pavel022812.htm.

INDEX

ABOUT THE AUTHOR

Rónán Mac Con Iomaire is an award-winning author and broadcaster, and is Group Head, Irish Language, at RTÉ, Ireland's national broadcaster.

His first book, *Rocky Ros Muc*, became the fastest-selling Irish-language book of all time, and Rónán was honored with the New Writer of the Year award at the 2013 Oireachtas Literary Awards. The book was later adapted into a feature-length documentary film of the same name, and has won a number of awards at various film festivals in both the United States and Ireland.

Prior to being appointed RTÉ's first-ever Group Head of Irish Language, Rónán worked as Deputy Head of RTÉ Raidió na Gaeltachta, Ireland's national Irish-language radio station. Before that, he spent many years in print and broadcast journalism, working for RTÉ and Independent News & Media, among other media organizations.

Rónán has won a number of prizes for his journalism, including the Oireachtas Journalist of the Year award for breaking the story around a personal money-raising function organized for former Irish Taoiseach [prime minister], Bertie Ahern.

He is a keen runner and triathlete, and in 2010 founded TríSpórt, a triathlon club for the Connemara Gaeltacht area of the west of Ireland, where he lives with his wife, Máirín, and children, Marcas, Cóil, and Róisín.